UNWILLING IDLERS
The Urban Unemployed and Their Families in Late Victorian Canada

Unemployment has been, and remains today, a critical policy issue, yet many studies on the subject offer only cursory historical preambles. To better understand unemployment and its ramifications, it is first necessary to discover how the issue and the discourse surrounding it emerged within our own past.

Unwilling Idlers looks at the unemployed and their families in the late nineteenth and early twentieth centuries in six Canadian cities: Victoria, Vancouver, Winnipeg, Hamilton, Montreal, and Halifax. The authors provide a social profile of the men and women who identified themselves as unemployed, relate the phenomenon of unemployment to family characteristics and life cycles, and explore the importance of geographical location and seasonal occupation as defining characteristics of the unemployed. The authors assess the impact of unemployment on living standards and show how workers and their families tried to cope with the problem.

This is the first book to examine the unemployed in the period of Canada's 'industrial revolution.' Its interdisciplinary focus gives it broad appeal, and it will be useful to social and economic historians, labour and family historians, sociologists, and geographers.

PETER BASKERVILLE is a professor in the Department of History at the University of Victoria and author of *The Bank of Upper Canada*.

ERIC W. SAGER is a professor in the Department of History at the University of Victoria and author of *Seafaring Labour: The Merchant Marine of Atlantic Canada, 1820–1914*.

PETER BASKERVILLE and ERIC W. SAGER

Unwilling Idlers: The Urban Unemployed and Their Families in Late Victorian Canada

UNIVERSITY OF TORONTO PRESS
Toronto   Buffalo   London

© University of Toronto Press Incorporated 1998
Toronto   Buffalo   London

Printed in Canada

ISBN 0-8020-4320-8 (cloth)
ISBN 0-8020-8144-4 (paper)

Printed on acid-free paper

Canadian Cataloguing in Publication Data

Baskerville, Peter A. (Peter Allan), 1943–
   Unwilling idlers: the urban unemployed and their families in late Victorian
   Canada

   Includes index.
   ISBN 0-8020-4320-8 (bound)   ISBN 0-8020-8144-4 (pbk.)

   1. Unemployed – Canada – Social conditions.   2. Unemployed – Canada –
   History – 19th century.   I. Sager, Eric W., 1946– .   II. Title.

   HD5728.B38 1998   331.13'7971'09034   C97-932662-1

University of Toronto Press acknowledges the financial assistance to its publish-
ing program of the Canada Council for the Arts and the Ontario Arts Council.

To Fran
and
in memory of Dorothy Sager

Contents

Figures and Tables

xii   Figures and Tables

Acknowledgments

We did the analysis and wrote this book together, in that precious time between teaching and administrative work, over a period of eight years. It will be apparent, given the volume of evidence on which we base our conclusions, that we could not have completed the research ourselves. Most of the hard work of entering information from the censuses was undertaken by a diligent team of assistants at the University of Victoria: Bob Beck, Raymond Frogner, Darryl Green, Teresa Hartman, Rollie Holowaty, Jocelyn Partington, Kathleen Pickard, Christopher Roberts, Nancy D. Wilson, and George Young. We also thank Christine Godfrey for granting us access to her data on the Kootenays. For their valuable assistance with other sources we are grateful to William Burrill, Jamie Disbrow, Monica Perry, Keith Smith, and Tamara Vrooman. For technical assistance in the last stages of the work we thank Douglas K. Thompson and Marc Trottier, data entry supervisor and computing assistant, respectively, with the Canadian Families Project at the University of Victoria.

We are indebted to the Social Sciences and Humanities Research Council of Canada for two research grants and to the President's Committee on Research and Travel at the University of Victoria. We thank the always-helpful archivists at the British Columbia Archives and Records Service, the Provincial Archives of Ontario, and the National Archives of Canada. For their creative assistance with the structuring of databases we acknowledge with gratitude Richard Chadwick, Eugene Dean, and Li Ping Zhang of Computing Services at the University of Victoria. Roger Davidson of the Department of Mathematics and Statistics at the University of Victoria offered valuable advice on logistic regression. Gordon Darroch of York University and Larry McCann of the University of Victoria read parts of the manuscript, offered valuable suggestions, and saved us from serious errors. We presented parts of the book at conferences, and for their comments we are indebted to Bettina Bradbury, Chad Gaffield, and Brian Gratton. We have learned more than they realize from many undergraduate and graduate students at the University of Victoria. The final version benefits from the meticulous care of our copy editor, John Parry of Toronto.

Much of this book refuses to flow easily within the prevailing currents of social history in English Canada. We have attempted a work of social science history rather than an essay in cultural studies or discourse analysis. We turn to the geographer and the sociologist for our methods rather than to the literary critic or the semiotician. Prior to publication this book received six assessments by five readers. Among them one neoclassical economist and one labour historian, elsewhere unlikely allies, were united in denouncing our work, each insisting that we should have written a labour history based more extensively on trade union records, labour newspapers, and government reports. The Aid to Scholarly Publications Program turned down our application for a grant in aid of publication. We offer particular thanks to those who offered positive assessments, and we acknowledge that even the two assessors who thought the book should not appear helped us to improve the published version.

This book found its way into print because the University of Toronto Press has its own peer review process and accepted the positive recommendations of its outside readers. We are indebted to the Manuscript Review Committee of the Press, and we offer particular thanks to Gerald Hallowell, whose confidence in us and in our work held firm throughout. Flawed though our book may be, we believe that its publication is testimony to the integrity and independence of an important Canadian institution, the university press.

Though most of the work was completed before the Canadian Families Project began, we are pleased that this book led us into a new and wider collaboration, among friends who are helping us to think again about the intersection of family and labour history. This book, we hope, is but a small beginning.

This drawing reflects labour's view that assisted immigration was a major cause of unemployment. (Toronto *Globe*, 21 February 1891; National Library of Canada, NL 19386)

'The head of the household is a laborer. He has not had a stroke of work since the beginning of November.' (Toronto *Globe*, 21 February 1891; National Library of Canada, NL 19388)

Unemployed men in the Toronto House of Industry in 1890. (Archives of Ontario, C 3367, D-153, #1597)

W.J. Thomson's portrait of the unemployed poor seeking relief at a Toronto Poor House, 1890. (Archives of Ontario, C 3367, D-153, #1597)

UNWILLING IDLERS

1

Introduction

Unemployment is a global problem of post-industrial capitalism. It is also a condition with deep roots in the nations of western Europe and North America. In Canada we associate mass unemployment with the 1930s, for it was in that decade that the problem became 'the single greatest challenge to the legitimacy of capitalism as an economic system.'[1] The challenge long preceded the 1930s, however. Unemployment emerged as a social problem in the last half of the nineteenth century, when 'the unemployed' – a collective noun identifying a distinct group of urban poor – became a commonplace of Canadian political discourse. 'The unemployed,' soon followed by 'unemployment,' announced the discovery of a social problem and the belated recognition of a profound change in the nation's political economy.[2] Our title reflects that recognition: 'unwilling idlers' was a term used in both the labour and the bourgeois press to describe the condition of being without waged work. Very probably the unemployed found other ways of contributing to the family economy, but terms such as 'enforced idleness' and 'unwilling idlers' reflect workers' deepening awareness of wage dependence, of their sense that to be without wage was to be without work, an 'enforced' condition to be resisted.[3]

This book is about the discovery of unemployment, especially as it took place among urban workers and their families in the late Victorian era. We seek to achieve three general objectives: to provide a profile of the men and women who said that they were unemployed; to assess by various measures the impact that unemployment had on their lives and on those of their families; and to determine, where possible, how working-class men and women and their dependants coped with unemployment.

The Canadian working class discovered unemployment; workers and many of their leaders tried to explain it. The state responded by ignoring the discovery or denying its importance and commenced a long process of evasion that continued into the twentieth century. Canada's urban workers could not escape the problem, however, for the majority of working-class families had to contend, at one time or another, with the effects of joblessness among one or more of their members. Unemployment became part of class conflict in Canada. By the end of this era of discovery, the framework had been set for Canadians' understanding of unemployment in the first half of the twentieth century.

Among the shifting currents of debate in our discipline, we occupy a position that should be made clear at the outset. As writers of regional and local histories, we understand the limits of microhistorical analysis and seek to transcend those limits by examining not one community but six very different cities.[4] The result is a study of unemployment in several major nodes of industrialization in different regions of Canada: we concentrate on Halifax, Montreal, Hamilton, Winnipeg, Vancouver, and Victoria.[5] The unemployed also appeared in rural areas, of course. In no way should our focus on large urban places obscure the extent and the effects of both wage labour and unemployment far beyond Canada's industrializing cities. It is clear, however, that awareness of unemployment, and willingness to identify oneself as unemployed, took place more often in urban than in rural places. As the *Western Clarion* put it in 1905: 'It is difficult for those of us who have lived for years in the country districts or smaller towns, to conceive of the unspeakable miseries that must be the daily portion of the great sweltering mass of unemployed and starving wretches that are herded together within the confines of the great cities.'[6]

Whatever rural residents understood by the word 'unemployed,' very few in April 1891 thought that it applied to them.[7] We believe it to be no coincidence that where there were few unemployed there were also relatively few wage-paid workers, for, as we argue in this book, wage dependence and unemployment were deeply interconnected historical conditions.[8] If in the 1880s and 1890s one moved from rural areas dependent on agriculture into other resource hinterlands, small towns, or larger cities, one was more likely to encounter both wage labour and the unemployed.[9] Unemployment as a social problem was first defined and debated in those areas – Canada's towns and cities – where proletarianization was most developed. Indeed, in the six cities examined below, 80 per cent of the workforce in 1891, and 83 per cent in 1901, were wage earners. Thus we do not pretend to offer a national study but present instead urban benchmarks, where none has existed before, and in so doing we try to transcend the limits of microhistory.

Sensitivity to space and location may be a particular quality of Canadian historical scholarship; certainly it is part of any discussion of unemployment in this country. We wish to comment on the relative importance of location as a determinant of the basic characteristics of unemployment. How far did residence in one city rather than another affect one's chances of being unemployed, and how much did it influence one's ability to cope? We certainly make such comparisons among cities, but we also ask a broader question: to what extent did locality really matter? By examining the condition of the unemployed in six cities, we can go some distance towards separating the general from the particular, and we can test the hypothesis that unemployment was a condition present in an industrializing process occurring across space as well as over time. Our choice of cities was dictated not by the availability of potentially fruitful sources but by our wish to allow for difference in certain key variables, including region, size of city, stage of industrial development, ethnic mix, resource base, and settlement pattern.

To locate the discovery of unemployment in time, we need to say something about the much-debated process of industrialization as it emerged in Canada. The 'army of unemployed' first appeared at a particular stage in the development of capitalism in Canada. If there was an industrial 'revolution' here (and the term may be inappropriate for a process that was gradual and regionally specific), it was intermittent in the seven or eight decades after the middle of the nineteenth century. 'Industrialization' does not refer simply to a shift towards manufacturing: between 1870 and 1910 manufacturing's share of gross domestic product remained remarkably stable.[10] Much more important were certain related changes in the structure of industry: the steep rises in the ratio of capital to labour (especially in the 1880s and the early 1900s) and of capital to output; and the increasing size, spatial concentration, and ownership concentration of firms and factories.

The problem of unemployment appeared during the first stage of industrialization, the era of competitive capitalism that culminated in the National Policy tariffs of 1879 and the industrial growth that followed in the 1880s. The slower growth rates of the 1890s were accompanied by larger concentrations of jobless workers in the cities, especially in winter, and a growing awareness of 'the unemployed' on the part of municipal politicians, trade unions, and social reformers. Reactions to the problem of unemployment became entrenched in the 'wheat boom' decade of the early 1900s, which saw a sudden acceleration of growth in manufacturing, railway building, mining, and other resource-based primary industries. At the end of this decade, and especially in the years just before the First World War, unemployment produced a crisis of unprecedented proportions in many Canadian cities.

We share with many other scholars a concern about the narrow boundaries and appeal of some historical writing.[11] We respond by drawing on methods from disciplines other than history, by relating our findings to those of social scientists who write about labour markets and unemployment in the United States and elsewhere, and by striving to explain our findings in jargon-free prose, even where our methods may be unfamiliar and the results complex. To those who lament the passing of a grand narrative tradition that Canadians might share, we say that the struggle to understand and to control labour markets was, and remains, a nation-wide problem, transcending the barriers of region and 'limited identities.' The search for work, and the nature of one's connections to labour and commodity markets, were and are basic to one's identity; they are matters of 'public self-understanding.'[12] While it is unlikely that a history of unemployment a century ago can offer unambiguous lessons about unemployment today, we think that the evolution, meaning, and effects of unemployment in the past should be known to all who grapple with the problem currently.

As social historians, we do not forget the many ways in which culture intersects with the material conditions of life.[13] We attend closely to the voices and the language of Canadian workers a century ago, and we begin, in chapter 2, with a survey of responses to 'want of employment,' by workers and others, up to the 1880s. While language provides an imperfect reflection of social events and processes, discourse is none the less intertwined with the social and economic environment within which it is found. In chapter 2 we pay close attention to the changing vocabulary relating to the condition of being without a wage-paying job. We attempt to show that this changing vocabulary emerged when increased wage dependence and debilitating cyclical depressions sharpened workers' awareness of their vulnerability in capitalist labour markets. We sometimes hear that 'if a man wanted a job' in the late nineteenth century, 'the chances were excellent that he would find one.'[14] The changing social discourse that surrounded those 'out of work' in late Victorian Canada provides a first indication that this impression is misleading.

We have listened to the voices of workers and their leaders, but we seek also to locate the speakers in the material realities of their everyday life. We have tried to determine, in a systematic way, who the unemployed *were*. We have not written a merely cultural study of unemployment, in part because we see too often in cultural studies a tendency to draw general conclusions on the basis of instances, anecdotal evidence, or scattered quotations.[15] Locating and identifying the unemployed is difficult, however, because there are few government reports on the problem as it existed before the 1930s, and reports by trade unions reflect the experience of a minority of workers.[16] It is easy to see why earlier historians of unemployment focused on the Depression decade: both the plethora of sources for the 1930s and the impact of unemployment in that decade drew historians and popular writers to the subject. Impressive results followed, most notably in the work of James Struthers. Udo Sautter contributed a valuable article on early efforts to measure unemployment and a study of the Employment Service, the labour exchanges created following dominion legislation in 1918.[17] These pioneering works emphasized the emergence of state policies and the constraints that limited those policies. More recently Ruth Pierson and Ann Porter have revisited the debates on unemployment insurance, uncovering the pervasive influence of gender and specific notions of the 'family wage.'[18] Nevertheless, the nineteenth-century origins of unemployment as a social problem have remained obscure, not least because of the absence of comprehensive sources on the unemployed themselves.

Moving back in time from the 1930s, we have tried to locate the unemployed themselves, as individual men and women, as family members, as workers, as city dwellers. Was there something about them that distinguished them from those who were employed? Were they an identifiable subset of the population possessing characteristics that left them at a disadvantage in emerging capitalist labour markets? These questions put to the test assumptions that existed a century ago and survive into our own time. Both the early state evasions, and many of the public policy initiatives that eventually appeared in the twentieth century, assumed that the source of the problem lay within the supply side of labour markets, specifically with the people who were out of work.[19] 'The unemployed are, as a class, a selection of the unfit,' wrote the English investigator of poverty Charles Booth, and many Canadians would have agreed.[20] In 1916 the Ontario Commission on Unemployment argued: 'Personal causes of unemployment have received, heretofore, a disproportionate amount of attention.' It then qualified this statement and reintroduced personal deficiencies into the core of the problem and its solution: 'Not that they [personal causes] are less involved in the solution sought for, but with an improved economic adjustment, and a more efficient industrial organization, personal deficiencies may be found to have less room for growth and greater opportunity for repair.'[21]

By the First World War secular language sometimes veiled the Protestant roots of social reform, but the emphasis on individual responsibility survived, and with it the association of work with manhood and the duty of the male breadwinner to provide for his family. Weaken self-reliance, many believed, and one would undermine self-respect. Extended activity on the part of the State would result in the loss of virility, initiative, and perseverance in the class that most needed these qualities. A 'plan of relief' for the unemployed must therefore 'place great emphasis on the necessity for considering personal factors. ... The home should be kept together and the mother enabled to give proper care to her children without suffering the loss of her own health through the strain of too heavy a load.'[22]

Conceived in this way, the problem required remedial action directed at the unemployed themselves. There followed a long series of initiatives aimed at 'improving poor people' (to use Michael Katz's apt phrase), including moral reform, employment offices, relief work, schooling, retraining, and workfare.[23] Whether as a recipient of relief or as the target of reform, the unemployed person, invariably male, was set apart as a distinct 'other.' He was not 'the right sort' of workman but the 'wrong sort' – 'unadaptable,' 'too fond of his beer,' and 'too fond of taking a holiday.'[24] He was a man whose personal condition or personal deficiency, though sometimes no fault of his own, nevertheless had left him temporarily outside the norm of breadwinning head of household.

The assumption that the unemployed are a distinct 'other' resurfaces in periods when unemployment is most acute. In the 1980s and 1990s unemployment, for instance, acknowledges few boundaries: young and old, men and women, skilled and unskilled, Maritimers and central Canadians, are all at risk. Yet public perceptions ignore that reality. The National Anti-Poverty Organization cites as one of nine common myths or stereotypes about people on welfare the notion that rising unemployment in Canada is caused by the inadequacies of workers.[25] But what if the notion of the unemployed as other had always been at best myopic, at worst self-serving? It is worth testing that possibility, since it may be that the premise underlying much of our past policy and current public perceptions is untenable. In this way an intensive analysis of the social composition and characteristics of the unemployed at the dawn of the twentieth century may be of value to a society in its attempts to cope with widespread unemployment at the close of that century.

Who were the unemployed? The question takes us to the core of assumptions behind policy, and it takes us also to the core of recent historical theorizing of unemployment. Perhaps most influential has been Alexander Keyssar's *Out of Work: The First Century of Unemployment in Massachusetts*, published in 1986. Examining primarily the social dimensions of unemployment, and using a wide range of sources drawn from government reports, charitable agencies, and labour organizations, Keyssar demonstrates that being unemployed was central to working-class experience in Massachusetts in the late nineteenth and early twentieth centuries. Perhaps the most valuable finding in his rich and wide-ranging analysis is the contention that the only social variable that affected in any appreciable way one's chances of being without work was whether or not one was a member of the working class. Within the wage-earning class, Keyssar argues, no single characteristic, nor any combination of measurable personal-social qualities, determined one's chances of being unemployed. Other scholars, employing data from other regions of the United States, have subjected Keyssar's hypothesis to more sophisticated statistical tests. These analyses have confirmed, with only minor qualifications, the strength of his central finding.[26]

In chapter 3 we test Keyssar's hypothesis in the context of Canadian cities in 1891 and 1901. We rely on information generated by government, but our evidence is very different from that found in the reports of most government commissions. Pressured by the Trades and Labor Congress of Canada, in 1891 the dominion government briefly recognized the existence of the 'unemployed.' For the first time it instructed census enumerators to ask a question about the unemployed: were you 'unemployed in the week preceding the census?' The government quickly lost interest, and answers to the question were neither tabulated nor published.[27] A decade later, during a resurgence in trade union organizing, Ottawa returned to the issue, this time in an unprecedented effort to gather information about the labour force, and wage earners in particular. The 1901 census contains fourteen discrete pieces of information about labour-force activity with data much more extensive than in either the British or U.S. census at the turn of the century.[28] Among the details gathered were responses to a question, addressed to wage earners, asking the number of months worked during the year in a factory, at home, and in 'other occupation than trade in factory or home.' We have taken randomized, 10 per cent samples of households for six Canadian cities from the 1891 and 1901 nominal census returns. These data are the basis for our profiles of the unemployed in chapter 3, as well as for the discussion of standards of living in chapters 6 and 7.[29]

In using the routinely generated information in census enumerators' schedules, we have kept in mind the fact that these documents record the oral responses of workers, in answer to questions read by an enumerator from a text created by official manipulators of knowledge. Like other historical documents, censuses were and are constructed with particular purposes in mind. Yet, as with so much in history, the intentions of those in power were often qualified and used for different purposes by those who lacked formal power. The censuses of 1891 and 1901 allowed workers and their families to reveal themselves in ways the state neither anticipated nor desired. Since we use the censuses quite extensively throughout this book, we provide a detailed analysis of their strengths and weaknesses in Appendix A.[30]

The Canadian censuses, especially that of 1901, are free of certain limitations that characterize other sources used in North American histories of unemployment. Our data are not restricted by region, by firm, by an unacceptably high level of aggregation, or by unspecified sampling procedures.[31] The Canadian census permits us to go beyond the common unit of analysis in many studies of unemployment for our period: the individual, generally male, head of household. Valuable as such studies are, the limitations resulting from this focus are serious. Keyssar, for instance, does as much as he can with the family context of unemployment, but his data are often at a level of aggregation that does not allow individuals to be seen in the context of family. Often he must rely on the testimony of individuals about the family context.[32] All sources have limits, but our censuses allow us to link individuals with other members of their family, with other members of their dwelling place, and with the labour markets whose imprint is recorded in the fourteen variables relating to labour-force participation.

Making connections between individuals, families, and labour-force activity, and doing so for thousands of people in six cities, requires certain statistical techniques and the presentation of results in tabular or graphic form. Our methods are necessary, given our purposes, but we are also trying to demonstrate the value of social science methods that we believe are too little known among social historians in English Canada. Distinctions between 'qualitative' and 'quantitative' are often self-limiting; the historian who carries an incomplete tool-box into the archives, for fear that the social scientist's methods result in abstracted empiricism, may find only a part of what the sources contain.[33] Historians who do not use quantitative methods sometimes suspect that by summarizing human behaviour in statistical aggregations one loses sight of diversity and trivializes the complexity of human behaviour. This suspicion may reflect little more than a failure to understand methods that are designed to display diversity and complexity. As Daniel Scott Smith has noted, 'Individual practice varies considerably, and meaning does not emerge until averages are calculated.'[34] The average is not the same as a universal, but unless we know what was most frequent or most common we cannot identify the deviant or the uncommon. The methods that allow us to estimate means also allow estimates of standard deviation, and hence an appreciation of the diversity of action and experience.[35] No source can stand alone, of course. The census recorded workers' answers in a structured context. We take care to use many other sources, and, especially in chapters 2 and 8 those that recorded workers' voices and views in other contexts.

Following our profile of the unemployed, we look in chapter 4 at the nature of the era's labour markets and workplaces, the context in which workers were laid off and sought jobs. We show that late-nineteenth-century labour markets were different from those of today. They were less well integrated and relatively localized. At the same time the structure of those markets was undergoing significant change. Seasonality, while still an important determinant of job availability, was no longer the only major influence on employment opportunities. New technologies, new workplaces, and new occupation structures increasingly set the context within which job seekers sought to survive.

In chapter 5 we shift from labour markets and workplaces to homes and neighbourhoods. Where did the unemployed live? For historians, spatial variation and residential patterns are often residuals, the dimensions of experience that might matter if more were known, or merely the spatial stage on which larger influences, such as those of class and gender, played themselves out. Historical geographers insist that place is more than mere backdrop and ask key questions about the spatial context of working-class experience and consciousness. They also offer tools for understanding and comparing the social and economic characteristics of those who lived in different residential spaces.[36] We use these tools to determine the degree to which the unemployed were segregated spatially from the employed. The degree of segregation in turn relates to our hypothesis about the unemployed as 'other.' Segregation and concentration have implications for the extent to which the unemployed were able to react in a cohesive or collective way to unemployment.

Focusing on the residential segregation of the unemployed, however, raises questions of a broader nature that cannot be ignored. The unemployed were, after all, a subset of the working class. Those geographers who have been interested in patterns of residential segregation have constructed measures of class by aggregating occupational designations. This procedure has a long lineage, not only in historical geography, but also in social history.[37] Those who use it are aware of its potential flaws and generally surround their analysis with caveats to that effect. The sources used in this book allow us to escape the ambiguity inherent in relying on occupational designation alone as a surrogate for class. Both the 1891 and the 1901 censuses allow the researcher to separate the wage-earning working class from owners of the means of production, be they employers or self-employed. Using this far clearer measure of class we determine the degree to which social classes in late-nineteenth-century Canadian cities lived apart from each other, and we connect our findings to a broader literature on the spatial positioning of urban classes in this era.[38] In doing so, we take into account the degree to which residential neighbourhoods were distinguished by other social characteristics, such as ethnic origin. We conclude this chapter with some general speculations as to what positioning in urban space might have meant for the development of class consciousness among wage earners and for those who were unemployed.

While in chapter 5 we look at where the unemployed lived, in chapters 6 and 7 we place the unemployed in the context of their families by asking with whom the unemployed lived and how they coped, respectively.[39] In doing so we seek to provide a new perspective on the meaning of unemployment for the working class at the turn of the twentieth century. The economic dimensions of family life in this era have been examined from a number of directions. Historians sensitive to the interaction of class and gender have taken us into the complex inner dynamics of family and pointed to the changing meanings of family as a prescriptive term and cultural construct.[40] Those interested in the standards of living of workers and their families have contributed several important studies, especially covering the period following 1901. A prize-winning book by Bettina Bradbury has added immeasurably to our understanding of the workings of the family economy in late-nineteenth-century Montreal.[41] Several shorter studies have provided indices for income and expenditures for other regions.[42] As yet, however, neither the Canadian nor the international literature on family economies in the period of early industrialization has provided satisfactory measures of the extent to which unemployment affected family income, and by extension the quality of life experienced by working-class families.[43] In chapter 6 we offer a measure of the impact of unemployment on total family earnings. In chapter 7 we construct measures of costs of living for families in each of the six cities in our study and explore the relationships between place of residence, family income, unemployment, and cost of living.[44] We also comment on strategies employed by working-class families to cope with unemployment in an era that antedated state-sponsored welfare support.

In chapter 8 we examine organized responses to unemployment in the late nineteenth and early twentieth centuries. Gradually trade union leaders and pro-labour newspapers entered into a dialogue with reformers and politicians on the subject of the unemployed and labour markets. Early exchanges took place during the hearings of the Royal Commission on the Relations of Capital and Labor in the 1880s.[45] By the early 1900s, and especially in the years just before the First World War, the dominion and a few provincial governments felt compelled to respond, even if indirectly. At this point Canada's economic development intersected with a liberal political culture to produce a specifically Canadian pattern of reductionism and evasion. By 1914 unemployment was unmistakably a national problem. The remarkable lack of attention by the Canadian state requires explanation. The province of Ontario appointed a commission to investigate the problem; British Columbia struck a royal commission to examine general labour issues in 1912; and some dominion politicians discussed employment exchanges. Yet the dominion Department of Labour persisted in its preoccupation with prices and with strikes and lockouts. The problem of unemployment, chronic and pervasive though it was in working-class experience, was either neglected or subsumed by other issues. The official reactions of the first decades of the twentieth century ensured that unemployment would remain a recurring theme in labour's dialogue with the state.

Identifying the unemployed and observing their responses requires that we focus on the urban places where they lived. More needs to be said about our choice of cities. Of the six cities that we have selected for intensive study, each reflects characteristics of the regions within which it was situated. Of equal significance, the functional characteristics exhibited by each city resulted in part from pressures inherent in an evolving continental urban system.[46] At its broadest level, differentiation within this system has most often been attributed to the relative advantages of location, in terms of both proximity to markets and to raw

14   Unwilling Idlers

TABLE 1.1
Six Canadian cities: rank by population, 1891 and 1901

| City | 1891 | | 1901 | |
	Rank*	Population	Rank*	Population
Montreal	1	219,616	1	267,730
Hamilton	4	48,959	5	52,634
Winnipeg	9	25,639	6	42,340
Halifax	7	38,437	7	40,832
Vancouver	12	13,709	11	26,133
Victoria	11	16,841	12	20,816

Source: *Census of Canada*, 1901, 1, Table 5, 22.
*The rank is in relation to all Canadian cities in each year.

materials or staples that could be processed. According to this perspective, heartland cities such as Hamilton and Montreal enjoyed specific
advantages. Hamilton was strategically situated at the head of Lake
Ontario, with easy access to a flourishing agricultural and developing
industrial hinterland. Montreal, in the 'Laurentian school' interpretation
of Donald Creighton and others, was nicely positioned on the important
commercial artery, the St Lawrence River, which had given the earlier
settlement access to the western fur trade routes as well as to the North
Atlantic. Both the staple approach and the Laurentian view tend to
assign our other cities to peripheries: Halifax, Winnipeg, Victoria, and
Vancouver lacked the locational advantages of the heartland cities.

Canada's economists and regional historians have challenged many
key findings and assumptions of these older approaches. Yet given the
importance of these schools in our historiography, and the continuing
influence of heartland–hinterland models, we examine (Table 1.1) two
heartland cities and four very different cities in regions distant from
central Canada.

Victoria, perched on the southern edge of Vancouver Island, was
founded as a fur trade depot in 1843 and had long been British Columbia's central administrative and economic centre. We chose the city for
other reasons as well. In 1880, among forty-five Canadian towns and
cities with a population in excess of 5,000, Victoria ranked a respectable
fourteenth in per-capita value of industrial output. By 1890 it stood fifth
out of the twenty Canadian towns and cities with a population over
10,000. During the 1890s, however, no Canadian city in that population

TABLE 1.2
Six Canadian cities: industrial output, 1891 and 1901

City	1891		1901*	
	Total	Per capita	Total	Per capita
Montreal	65,331,707	297.48	65,021,838	242.86
Hamilton	14,037,721	286.72	17,122,346	325.31
Halifax	7,198,143	187.27	9,066,118	222.03
Winnipeg	5,094,146	198.69	8,616,248	203.50
Vancouver	3,751,122	273.62	6,937,722	265.48
Victoria	4,597,681	294.38	2,722,593	130.80

*See text for a discussion of the change in enumeration practice.
Source: *Census of Canada*, 1901, 3, Table 20.

bracket declined in manufacturing production to the degree that Victoria did. By 1901 it had dropped from the top 25 per cent to the bottom 20 per cent in per-capita value of manufacturing output. Nor is this erosion simply a statistical illusion created by the change in industrial enumeration implemented in the 1901 census (beginning in 1901, all firms employing fewer than five people were not counted). Victoria experienced significant erosion at all levels of capitalization.[47] Of the cities under review, it most dramatically reflects the condition of deindustrialization (see Table 1.2) and thus provides an excellent micro-environment within which to examine the impact of rapid deindustrialization on the configuration of the workforce and on the character and extent of unemployment.

It may seem strange to choose two cities in one province having a relatively small population. We selected Vancouver, as well as Victoria, for reasons other than the fact that both authors of this book happen to reside in British Columbia. Vancouver, the most recently established city in our sample, was one of the fastest growing of all Canadian cities founded in the 1880s. By 1901, it had surpassed Victoria's population (see Table 1.1). Located at the western terminal of the Canadian Pacific Railway (CPR), Vancouver has often been pointed to as a centre of working-class radicalism, a 'mecca of the unemployed,' a city, in short, that exhibited all the characteristics of a frontier resource-based town.[48] In fact, Vancouver's economy, like Victoria's, was much more diversified than the term *resource-based* might indicate. As Table 1.2 shows, it generated one of the highest per-capita industrial outputs of our six cities.[49] Nevertheless, it can be examined to determine the extent to which unemployment may reflect conditions peculiar to seasonal, resource-based enterprise.

Some scholars argue that staple production is the key to understanding Vancouver's development in this era.[50] In 1901, its workforce was more highly concentrated in the primary resource sector than was that of any of our other cities. And in 1891 the city possessed the highest percentage of general labourers, reflecting its recent origins and the rapid influx of workers from eastern Canada following completion of the CPR. Given that context, one will want to know the degree to which the social profile of its unemployed resembled that of the unemployed in the older eastern cities where industrialization began earlier. Vancouver and Victoria offer another relevant contrast to the eastern cities: their ethnic mix was much greater. Two-fifths of Vancouver's residents and close to half of Victoria's had been born outside Canada. Large Asian contingents resided in both cities, and one will want to know the effect of their presence on local unemployment patterns.

Winnipeg offers a different context in which to examine the relationships among ethnicity, class, social space, and unemployment. Like Vancouver, Winnipeg has a rich history of labour organization and ethnic and class conflict.[51] First settled in the 1860s, Winnipeg by the 1890s had earned its reputation as the gateway to the west. Its eastern location on the prairie's edge made it an ideal transshipment point for east–west trade. The arrival of the CPR in 1881 suddenly expanded the east–west flow of people and goods and weakened the earlier north–south lines of transport and communication. The entrepôt function led to the emergence of a middle class of wholesale and retail merchants, augmented by a significant group of real estate speculators. Railway repair shops, metal trades, and the building trades were major employers. More important than manufacturing industry, however, were the clerical, sales, and services sectors, which employed two-fifths of the workforce by 1901 – the highest proportion among our six cities.

Winnipeg enjoyed a relatively buoyant economy in the late nineteenth century: its industrial production remained fairly constant during the troubled 1890s, and its population increased markedly in that decade (see Tables 1.1 and 1.2). Many immigrants sought work there: by 1901 almost two-fifths of the population had been born outside Canada; one-half came from the British Isles, and many of the rest arrived from Austria-Hungary, Russia, Germany, and Iceland. By 1901 over one-third of Winnipeg's residents were of non-British origin, a relatively high proportion compared to many other Canadian cities at the time.[52] Although Winnipeg's population was predominantly Protestant, ethnic differentiation was further accentuated by the presence of a sizeable Jewish group, many members of which were recent immigrants. Municipal politics and the local press were, as early as 1891, much embroiled in ethnic conflict.[53]

In a perceptive commentary on Winnipeg in 1901, Daniel Hiebert has pointed out that during certain times of the year Winnipeg's labour force was swelled by a high proportion of unskilled workers who were sought by railway companies, farmers, and lumbering operations. During summer and winter those employers drew the unskilled away from the city, whose population contracted considerably.[54] Our data files, however, do not indicate a large, floating population of unskilled labourers. In both 1891 and 1901 such men form almost exactly the same proportion of the total workforce as the average for all six cities. Presumably the unskilled had already left Winnipeg by the time the census was taken in April. One can therefore feel confident that the population analysed in this book reflects more those permanently settled in Winnipeg than the seasonal transients.

Founded by the British in 1749 as a military and naval outpost, Halifax had evolved into a city on the verge of industrialization by the mid-nineteenth century. During the 1880s and 1890s, Nova Scotia's capital benefited from the National Policy tariffs and experienced marked industrial growth. The completion of the Intercolonial Railway in 1876, with Halifax as its Atlantic terminus, seemed to promise a prosperous future for Nova Scotia's premier city. For most Haligonians, however, it was a dream never to be realized. This might seem a puzzling statement, given that the data in Tables 1.1 and 1.2 point to a reasonably healthy economic situation: its rank by population remained stable, and its per-capita industrial output increased at a faster rate than any of the other cities in our sample. Yet, as Larry McCann has pointed out in a seminal analysis of Halifax's economy in this period, the city's manufacturing structure exhibited severe weaknesses, which would curb future growth.[55] Halifax's landward hinterland set limits to the city's industrial potential, for it did not provide a rich staple to process and the city could not easily dominate the lines of transportation and communication to the province's large number of dispersed communities, many of which were served by coastal schooners. A legacy from the region's mercantile past, when many ports competed for control of an international trade in lumber, fish, and ships, the scattered outports continued to vie for economic control in the emerging industrial era.[56] As a result, Halifax's industrialists had difficulty capturing markets either in central Canada or in their own region. Industrial firms depended on local markets and often survived not by cutting the costs of material inputs (which were higher than in any of our other cities) but by reducing wages; labour costs as a result were lower than in any other city in our analysis.[57]

Given the context within which Haligonian workers lived, immigrants did not flock to this Atlantic port, a point noted by a local newspaper in the early twentieth century and confirmed by the census of 1901: only 12 per cent of the city's residents were immigrants, the lowest proportion of our half-dozen cities.[58] Halifax was thus a hinterland city whose economic and social profiles differed markedly from those of Winnipeg, Vancouver, and Victoria. It remains to be seen how those differences affected the lives of the unemployed in this eastern metropolis.

Situated at the head of Lake Ontario, Hamilton celebrated its seventy-fifth year of existence in 1891. In the period of our study Hamilton was the most ethnically homogeneous of the cities considered here. In 1901 only 13 per cent of its population had been born outside Canada, and almost all of the 6,800 immigrants came from the British Isles.[59] Up to the 1850s it had competed with its larger urban rival, Toronto, for control of a common commercial hinterland. Following the 1870s the city's entrepreneurs began to concentrate on manufacturing. Steel mills, machine works, nail factories, and assorted stove, furnace, and tinsmith enterprises took advantage of Hamilton's central trading location and its proximity to raw materials. By 1891, the city was commonly known as the 'Birmingham of Canada.' As well, cotton mills and men's and women's clothing production expanded. Indeed, by 1891 four of the six biggest industrial-sector employers were in general clothing enterprises.[60]

This particular mix of industrial activity shaped the composition of Hamilton's workforce. In 1891 and again in 1901, the city boasted the highest proportion of its workforce in manufacturing of all six centres. Of equal significance, the city also housed the highest percentage of women workers in 1891 and was only marginally behind Montreal in that area in 1901. Though far behind Montreal in total industrial output, it had by 1901 significantly outpaced all rivals in per-capita output (Table 1.2) and therefore we rank it as the most heavily industrialized. It even competed for industrial supremacy with Toronto. In the period covered by this book, Hamilton's labour force was more heavily concentrated in the industrial sector than was that of Toronto, which ultimately surpassed its rival in per-capita industrial output.[61] Hamilton thus provides an excellent example of a heartland city that had become a dominant industrial centre. The composition of its workforce and the relative homogeneity of its population also set it apart from the other cities considered in this study.

By 1850, some two hundred years after its founding, Montreal was poised to dominate the emerging urban industrial system in Canada. Situated at the centre of a fast-developing railway and water system that linked the eastern coast with Ontario and the American midwest, Montreal's business community began to extend its enterprise from mercantile affairs to industrial pursuits. The opening of hydraulic mill sites along the Lachine Canal in 1846, followed by establishment of the Grand Trunk Railway shops in the mid-1850s, set the foundations for the city's economic transformation. Further development of hydraulic power in the late 1860s and early 1870s, followed by the electrification of mass transit in the 1890s, also facilitated continued industrial growth. During the last half of the century, large-scale factory production, characterized by foundries, machine shops, cotton mills, and sash, door, and rubber manufactories, emerged along the Lachine Canal and adjacent suburban areas. The old downtown core contained a larger number of smaller factories producing boots and shoes, clothing, and jewellery. While these enterprises benefited from the interconnections facilitated by clustering or by agglomeration, larger firms that integrated a number of processes within one enterprise could more easily stand alone and thus take advantage of locational opportunities at the city's periphery.[62] By 1901 no Canadian centre could match Montreal's total industrial output (though several, including Hamilton, exceeded its per-capita output), and none came close to its number of residents.

That population was swelled by foreign and domestic immigration. By 1861, Irish Catholics represented one quarter of Montreal's people. The 1880s and 1890s saw the arrival of large numbers of rural French Canadians and significant numbers of Protestants from England and Jews from eastern Europe. Yet by 1901, Montreal was far from a city peopled by immigrants: only 13 per cent of residents reported a foreign birthplace in that year.[63] A majority of the residents, however, acknowledged French as their mother tongue. Many analysts have noted the high degree of class as well as ethnic segregation evident at that time. In the same vein, it has been claimed that Montreal's entrepreneurs offered unusually low wages and exploited male and female job-seekers from rural areas.[64] Our data, as described below, suggest that both views stand in need of qualification.[65]

A more accurate general perspective acknowledges difference in the context of wider patterns. In Montreal, as in other cities, a complex interaction between class and ethnicity conditioned residential segregation. While its employers often took advantage of local conditions to pay less than a living wage, Montreal no longer appears unique in the extent of its poverty.[66] It may be that the size of its population and of its industrial output led to a form of exceptionalism, reinforced by the pioneering social investigations of Herbert Ames in the 1890s, which assumed that Montreal stood alone at the forefront of change.[67]

Recent comparative analyses have already tended to put less emphasis on Montreal's uniqueness. The city was neither a benchmark of Canada's industrialization nor a harbinger of its urban future. It was nevertheless the nation's largest metropolis, exhibiting key differences from other Canadian cities in its history, its economic structure, and its social and ethno-religious profiles. In this context we may begin to see how Montreal's unemployed differed from or resembled the unemployed in other urban places.

This book has its own context in the late twentieth century, when unemployment remains our major social problem. Official rates have stabilized at 9 to 10 per cent; real rates of unemployment and underemployment are much higher. Transnational capitalism and 'globalization' are accompanied by entirely new forms of labour-displacing technology. Income inequalities in North America are widening, and the postwar social welfare system is threatened with erosion or destruction. It is time to rethink paid work, unpaid work, labour markets, family economies, and unemployment. We hope that our study of the unemployed during the transition from a commercial to an industrial economy will provide a useful framework for those who seek to understand unemployment in the transition from an industrial to a post-industrial era.

2

The Discovery of a Social Problem

The search for work is as ancient as poverty itself. 'Unemployment,' however, is a recent concept: it refers to the enforced idleness of those who want remunerative work but cannot find it. During the gradual and uneven development of industrial capitalism in North America in the nineteenth century, this 'want of work' became a social problem distinct from poverty and idleness. The discovery of the problem can be traced from the appearance and evolution of the word 'unemployed,' to the later arrival, in the 1880s and 1890s, of the word 'unemployment.' Beyond the changes in language lay social events that cannot be read as literary text. Veiled by language though the material conditions of nineteenth-century capitalism may be, the discursive changes signify profound shifts in the social relationships of work, family, and class. The vocabulary surrounding 'the unemployed' itself became contested terrain and part of the class relations in which unemployment was embedded. In this chapter, we observe the growing awareness of unemployment as a condition of capitalist labour markets; in the chapters that follow we consider the unemployed themselves.

The word 'unemployed' appears rarely in the early nineteenth century. It was a participle, referring to something that was idle, or not being used. Just as land might be unemployed, so could farmers be 'idle' or 'unemployed' at certain times of the year. The word did not always imply suffering, because work had its seasonal rhythms, and pre-industrial society assumed that institutions existed to care for the destitute. The condition of being 'unemployed' applied to no one group, and as yet there was no distinct subset of the working class known as 'the unemployed.' To describe the condition of joblessness there were many terms other than 'unemployed,' and they usually referred to the seasonal slowing of economic activity, particularly in winter: 'idleness,' 'want of work,' 'without means of living,' and 'out of employment.'

Colonial towns in British North America witnessed the plight of poor families every winter, as farming, fishing, seafaring, and shipbuilding shed their summer and autumn labour and workers gathered in the towns in search of casual work or relief. Municipal relief, poorhouses, and charity grew in response and often served the purpose of employers by maintaining a local labour supply for employment in spring. Judith Fingard quotes a Halifax writer in 1816: 'In a climate like ours a very considerable number of labouring men in town, must be without employment, the greater part of the winter; otherwise the community must be very deficient in the quantity of labour required in the summer.'[1] Charity bore the imprint of class interest, and distinctions between deserving and undeserving poor guided delivery of relief. To the givers of charity the 'idle' were not always blameless, even if being 'without work' was usually the consequence of seasonal conditions that could not be controlled. There were always those professional beggars and paupers whose threat was as much moral as economic and for whom vagrancy laws served as a disciplinary tool.[2] Relief must bear with it the moral lesson of the need to work: 'The truest charity is to find employment that will give food; and not food without employment.'[3] Fear mingled with sympathy, and the epithet 'idleness' bore more than a hint of laziness or 'loafing.' Nevertheless, both workers and their masters saw those 'without work' as the victims primarily of seasonal fluctuations and a northern winter.

The system of private charity and public relief confronted new threats in British North America in the 1830s and 1840s, as immigration increased the labour supply and as the concentrations of wage labour in shipping, shipbuilding, and canal building expanded. The loss of work was connected still to season, of course, but also now to labour supply. While it was possible in the 1830s for contractors and politicians to believe that there was a shortage of canal-building labour,[4] by the 1840s the more common problem was labour surplus. The immigration peaks of the mid-1840s swelled the numbers of job-seekers in both Lower and Upper Canada and brought widespread demands for limits on immigration.[5]

The canal workers were not the first to confront the capitalist labour markets in the colonies, but they confronted more directly than others the nexus of labour surplus, waged work, and state repression. When canal construction reopened in 1842, workers from the United States moved towards the Welland, meeting new immigrants also seeking work. 'Privations and suffering will every day be augmented that these poor men remain unemployed,' said a justice of the peace in 1843, referring to the dire poverty of canal builders.[6] In the winter of 1844 a 'vast accumulation of unemployed labourers' remained 'throughout the entire line of the Welland Canal.'[7]

Under these circumstances both the perception and the reality of unemployment began to change and congeal. First, it became increasingly possible for the employed to view the unemployed as a distinct 'other,' a group of 'strange labourers' composed of 'the redundant and transient population of not only British America, but the United States.' Primarily of Irish background, early canallers were quickly labelled trouble makers and 'evil' doers despite the desperate circumstances of their work and family life, a situation well known both to their employers and to those who lived in communities close to the construction sites.[8] The new stereotype of the unemployed as a distinct subset of the working class would prove both durable and for those in positions of economic and political power, extremely useful.

Second, by the early 1840s being 'without work' was no longer merely a condition of winter; many thousands lacked work in summer as well. Navvies were free to sell their labour where they could but found few employers who wanted all of it. And the navvies of 1842 often lacked the alternatives available to their predecessors, who had moved back to farms or lumber camps in winter. Being unemployed around the canals was no longer merely a seasonal condition; it was a condition of wage dependence. The canal builders experienced directly the connection between labour surplus and the employers' ability to adjust both wage levels and hours of work. In these conditions a new vocabulary appeared: 'lost time,' 'lost days,' and 'broken time' signified the power of the employer to limit work not only seasonally but also on a monthly or daily basis.[9] The labour surplus of the 1840s severed the bonds between master and labourer and transformed class relations in canal construction.[10]

The canal builders were not alone in confronting capitalist labour markets. In November 1857 between two and three thousand 'unemployed persons' gathered outside the city hall in Quebec City and presented a petition to the mayor. Most of the petitioners were ship carpenters, who said that 'they did not want alms, but work at any price.' The absence of work in shipbuilding was not due to the onset of winter, for shipbuilding regularly occurred in winter. The unemployed ship carpenters knew that

their plight was 'the effect of "the crisis" upon the ship building interest.'[11] Theirs was not a class-based protest against shipbuilding capital,
however. Instead, like the canal builders, they demanded 'work or bread'
and sought relief 'either from the Government, the corporation, or the cit-
izens.' The shipwrights prompted a sympathetic response, perhaps
because of their importance to the city's economy, and the newspapers
reflected no fear about the pauperizing effects of relief. The Quebec *Mercury* argued that the colonial government should 'grant a sum of £50,000
for the relief of the labouring population during the present winter.' Fore-
shadowing municipal responses to unemployment in the last quarter of
the century, the city invested in new drains to provide work, and a committee of leading merchants and politicians was struck to find ways of
providing additional employment.[12]

Scarcity of employment was both a rural and an urban problem at mid-
century. Urban employers recruited wage labour from the farms, and
the same labour returned to farming in spring and summer. Yet there
was more than seasonal unemployment here, for the problem originated
in the failure of both rural and urban demand to absorb all the labour on
offer. A resident of a rural Quebec parish explained the problem in 1868:
'The main problem with our townships is the lack of work. It is evident
that a young household that settles on new soil, most often without any
resources, cannot live right away from the products of the land. The
man must then find ways to earn something, and clearly it is not the few
saw mills we have here and there that can provide sufficient employment for these new settlers.'[13] The problem was rooted not so much in
the barrenness or scarcity of available land as it was in the determination of so many landless Canadians to become self-sufficient farmers.
The quest for independence and prosperity drove many rural workers
into wage labour, in order to supplement the farm's meagre output and
ensure its survival.

In an economy where workers moved so frequently between rural
work and urban labour markets, 'lack of work' presented itself as a seasonal problem in the distribution of workers. The birth of a structural
problem – that of 'surplus labour' – was concealed by its seasonal
appearance. It was all too easy for politicians, newspapers, and colonization societies to focus on the symptoms of the problem: 'Pourquoi y a-
t-il tant de milliers de personnes qui se trouvent presque tous les hivers
sans emploi dans nos villes? Nous avons déjà eu plusieurs fois l'occa-
sion de le dire, c'est parce qu'on fuit les travaux des champs pour venir

s'accumuler dans les villes, où la classe pauvre ne rencontre que décep-
tion et désappointement. Elle y est venue chercher le travail, elle n'y a
trouvé que la misère.'[14]

It is under these conditions in 1857 that the noun 'le chomage' makes
an early appearance, though clearly associated with 'un hiver de six
mois.' The reduction of 'le chomage' to a problem of distribution of
labour led to an obvious solution: government should lower or remove
those tariffs that increased the costs of agricultural development, and so
help people to remain on the land: 'Quand la population agricole est
ainsi traitée et d'une manière aussi ruineuse, il n'est pas étonnant qu'elle
laisse de dégout la culture de la terre qui la charge de tant d'impots.'[15]
Such analysis was not inconsistent with that of government emigration
agents, who insisted that there was plenty of work available in agriculture. The problem was an inefficient distribution of immigrant 'agricul-
turalists': 'In many parts of the Province the farmers complained of
great inconvenience and loss for want of this description of labour.'[16]
Such were the reactions of a rural society to the arrival of labour surplus
in capitalist markets. In these reactions we see the precursors of a common solution to unemployment in late Victorian Canada – the idea that
more labour should return to the land and its natural abundance.

In the third quarter of the nineteenth century, labour shortages took pre-
cedence over unemployment in the discussion of labour markets. In
Lower Canada (Quebec) rural colonization became a nationalist project
– that of securing stable and attractive work for families that might otherwise emigrate. In Upper Canada (Ontario) the movement towards
farm ownership in the 1860s increased the number of farmers concerned
about the rising cost of casual labour. Labour shortages, however seasonal and localized, dominated discussions of labour and immigration.
Immigration societies appeared, and Ontario, after surveying availability of land in 1870, confidently declared that over fifteen thousand new
agricultural labourers were required.[17] The first government employment offices were created in order to help meet the farmers' demand for
seasonal labour; in turn they helped to define 'want of work' as a problem in the movement of labour to locations where it was needed.

The emerging problem of surplus labour was therefore camouflaged
by the particular conditions of industrial development in a northern,
resource-dependent economy. The uneven development of industrial
capitalism also inhibited the development of a broader consensus by
labour and a united reaction by workers to labour markets. Unskilled

labour demanded 'work or bread' from municipal authorities in winter, but such protests had only intermittent support from the emerging organizations of craft workers. The craft workers of the first industrial revolution had their own ideas about how to control labour markets in order to maintain stable employment for their members. Coopers, printers, moulders, machinists, and others sought to control admission to their crafts. They knew that 'employers like to see an overplus of men about' and that the 'overplus' threatened their right to 'steady work' and a 'fair and uniform remuneration, throughout the year.'[18] Artisans were well aware of the effects of machinery on employment, but instead of trying to repel or destroy the new technology they more often sought to control its application and integrate it with their craft skills and traditions. Coopers pledged to 'allow no one to teach a new hand [in order] to control the supply of help.'[19] Moulders' shop committees dictated the 'set,' – the number of pieces that a member was allowed to produce in one day. In 1845 the Toronto Typographical Society reacted to the new cylindrical presses at George Brown's *Globe* by condemning the use of unskilled 'boys'; the effect was to 'throw numbers of men out of employment and ultimately reduce the wages of the whole.'[20] Printers also tried to limit the hiring of the feared 'country mice,' – the non-union, small-town workers who migrated to the larger urban centres in search of work.[21]

Craft unions struggled to control labour markets and to maintain 'steady work,' but they did so within the framework and the language of craft traditions. They did not yet share the navvies' experience of chronic labour surplus; the craft discourse was slow to absorb a rhetoric of labour surplus and unemployment. The Nine Hours movement of 1872, that oft-used window into craft politics of the period, was in no small part about control of labour markets, yet only occasionally did it present itself as a solution to unemployment. There was a connection between shorter hours and surplus labour, of course; the links had often been noted by advocates of shorter workdays in Britain, and certain Canadian labour leaders saw the connection: reduced hours might require that employers hire more workers to maintain the same level of production.[22] Nine hours therefore would help to eliminate the cruel irony that many toiled for sixty hours and more a week, while others had no work at all. John Hewitt stated the case: 'For surely had not the mechanic of today, who by superior skill and the introduction of labor-saving machinery could represent the productive energies in ten hours which a man who lived fifty years ago could not do at the same business in fifteen or twenty hours, a right to make a demand for a more equal distribution of labor among the human family, which had become a crying want.'[23]

Nevertheless, the 'more equal distribution' of employment was not a primary justification for fewer hours in 1872. At times it was possible to foresee the continued presence of 'a large non-producing mass' even after workdays were shortened. Here is John Hewitt again: 'They had found that if machinery reduced labour 50 per cent, the reduction only tended to swell the ranks of non-producing humanity. If working men had their rights they could supply the world with food, clothes, &c., and still keep up a large non-producing mass, on eight hours of labour per day.'[24] The defenders of nine hours focused more often on other benefits: the more equal distribution of knowledge, wealth, and power that was owed to labour; the opportunity for the male breadwinner to spend more time with his family; and the need for skilled workers to spend more time educating themselves for both citizenship and productive work.

There is some evidence also that the Nine Hours pioneers were concerned to avoid a possible contradiction in their arguments. They insisted that workers would be as productive in nine hours as in ten; fewer hours would not therefore produce a cost either to employers or to the Canadian economy. It would be quite inconsistent then to argue that shorter hours would reduce output, thereby requiring employers to hire more workers in order to make up the difference. A correspondent writing to the *Ontario Workman* about the Scottish experience of nine hours understood that Canadian workers could not have it both ways: 'I have no faith in the theory that a man will produce as much in 9 hours as he will in 10, but believe thoroughly that in proportion to the reduction of hours is the increase in the number of hands employed.'[25] In 1872 Canadian craft workers said less about increasing the number of hands employed, and much more about winning a 'fair share' of what their labour produced and of the benefits of technological change.

The decade that followed was a watershed in the history of unemployment in Canada. It could be argued that the real discovery of unemployment took place in the 1870s and early 1880s, even if a more concentrated assault on the problem came in the 1890s. A series of interrelated changes in the 1870s prompted a more sustained articulation of the problem of labour surplus. The economic slow-down of that decade meant that cyclical unemployment overlapped with and exacerbated seasonal lay-offs. Unemployment was a by-product of manufacturing industry, as even some employers admitted, in the context of arguments for and against tariff protection: 'Fifty percent of the manufacturing population of the country are out of work,' declared an industrialist in 1876.[26] For perhaps the first time we see skilled artisans sharing the platforms with unskilled labour in the winter demonstrations for 'work or bread.' The Conservative party, and John A. Macdonald in particular, made a calculated appeal for working-class votes and linked their national policy to the promise of more secure employment for Canadian workers. Many labour leaders were soon disappointed by the national policy, and the rhetoric of the 'producer ideology' and pan-class mutual interest dissolved into the class-based appeal of the Knights of Labor.

The *Ontario Workman*, the Toronto labour paper founded at the height of the Nine Hours struggle in 1872, reflected growing awareness of unemployment as the trade depression deepened in 1874. Before the effects of the depression were fully apparent, articles on 'Emigration' and 'Convict Labor' concentrated on specific labour-market threats to craft skill, rather than on a structural problem of labour surplus. The use of prisoners as contract labour 'enables a certain portion of the community to enter into unfair competition with the rest.'[27] Government assistance to immigration was criticized as an injustice to immigrants themselves, who were being misled by the propaganda of immigration agents, 'making the most exaggerated and untruthful statements in relation to the matter of wages and cost of living' in Canada.[28] In April 1873 an editorial in the *Ontario Workman* could argue even that government should adopt a 'liberal policy' on immigration, since 'Our country can absorb large numbers of skilled workmen and mechanics.'[29]

Such apparent complacency did not long survive the onset of depression. By January 1874 the paper knew that 'among our own laborers *and artizans* there is a growing scarcity of employment.'[30] The experience of the unemployed in New York offered a warning: there were 182,000 men seeking work in that state, and 'the majority applying for relief are teachers, clerks, skilled mechanics, with here and there a laborer.' The distress of 'the unemployed' was caused 'by the wicked and criminal recklessness of the stock gamblers.'[31] Unemployment, in this analysis, was part of a wider conspiracy among capitalists, who used any available method to undermine craft skills and wage levels. A writer in the *Ontario Workman* quoted the English positivist E.S. Beesly on the logic of employer self-interest: 'Let every man in trade be employed, and the labor market is in its most advantageous condition to command good wages. "Employers," says Professor Beesly, "aim at keeping a certain number of men unemployed that the rest may be at their mercy. Hence they prefer having a few men to work overtime more than a large number to work at reduced time. They will even sacrifice their immediate interests to this object."'[32] Before the depression, craft workers had experienced 'lost time occasioned by bad weather.' Now they were learning about 'the many other causes that operate in throwing out of employment the workman in a majority of trades.'[33] The *Ontario Workman* also told its readers that the depression threatened them both at work and at home, for 'nearly all' of the unemployed had 'families dependent upon them.'[34]

The Canadian Labor Union and pro-labour newspapers took up the issue of stable employment as the depression struck and quickly linked job creation to protection for Canadian industry.[35] 'Large numbers of workingmen were already unable in many cases to support their families.'[36] Now trade unionists began to link the problem to wider questions of political economy and 'economic law': 'They considered it a gross violation of economic law to import large numbers of skilled workers into this country when the market for skilled artisans was already overstocked.'[37] The analysis was still that of the craft unionists, however: they understood the 'overstocked' labour market as being the result of unfair competition against 'legitimate labour.' There were simply too many goods and too many people: 'The present depression of trade is caused from over-production and over-importation of goods and labor.'[38] Some craft workers advocated the abolition of 'all immigration offices and agencies.'[39] Others insisted that the only solution was to reduce the supply of goods and to stimulate domestic production through a strong protective tariff.

By 1876 John A. Macdonald had enunciated his national policy program, and the Workingmen's Liberal Conservative Union of Canada (WLCU) set out to win the workingman's vote with proposals for keeping industrial jobs and industrial workers in Canada. The WLCU took up some of the labour-market demands of the Canadian Labor Union and erected a full platform of job-protection proposals: expanded public works, reservation of land grants for bona fide settlers, the end of government assistance to immigration, the abolition of prison labour, the prohibition of Oriental immigration, protection for Canadian industry, and free trade in raw materials. Many of these reforms had been suggested before, and many became political staples in labour politics in the

decades that followed; this was perhaps the first time that all such proposals appeared in one political program in Canada. All were designed
to convince working-class voters that the Tory–labour political alliance
would protect jobs for white male breadwinners.

The WLCU–national policy platform was the opening exchange in a
long dialogue between workers and the state over labour markets and
labour surplus. The effect of the national policy promises cannot be
underestimated: since they did not solve the problem of unemployment,
they could do little more than raise workers' expectations and encourage them in their assumption that solutions to unemployment were a
matter of state power and appropriate policies.[40] Protection for Canadian industry was a cunning political promise: it insisted on the common mutual interest of capital and labour, and by treating 'the
employment of our working classes' as the key object of policy, it could
appeal to the artisanate by appearing to answer a growing fear – that
industrial progress meant the replacement of craft skill by machinery,
followed by irregular employment, reduced wages, or the necessity of
emigration to the United States in search of work. The national policy
raised false expectations, not least because it was never intended to be a
policy of full employment or an unemployment relief policy. Its job-
creating effects were supposed to maintain Canadian labour supply by
stemming the flow of emigration to the United States.[41]

In the depression of the 1870s 'the unemployed' became a collective
noun in Canadian political discourse. It referred not simply to the condition of being idle, but to a specific group of workers who were 'out of
employment' or 'out of work.' Furthermore, though winter and seasonal
lay-offs were the immediate cause of joblessness, these workers knew
that solutions existed even in winter. They had heard the promises of
the national policy. They saw unemployment not as a structural problem but as a political one.

In April 1877, three hundred unemployed men gathered in the market
square in Ottawa. There was nothing new in such a gathering, in Ottawa
or other Canadian cities. These men were 'the usual number of unemployed workingmen' who gathered 'in the hope of catching a stray
hour's work.' 'Some of them succeeded; others were less fortunate.' The
events that followed were unusual, however, and suggest the extent to
which the unemployed believed that the state held the solution to their
plight. The 'less fortunate' talked things over and decided to apply to
the mayor for work or assistance. Soon there were three hundred men

assembled outside city hall, several of them telling their stories to a newspaper reporter. The first had had no work since the previous autumn; the next had had none for four months; another had been out of work since November; a German immigrant 'had been living on soup since Christmas'; another man had worked for two weeks since September. Many stressed the desperate condition of their families: 'I don't know what will become of me and my family. ...'; 'my family and myself have been starving ever since ...'; 'I am a man with a big family of twelve'; 'my family have suffered great privation.'[42]

The mayor promised that the city council would consider spending more money on a drainage system, but the crowd was not satisfied. The suggestion that the national government held the answer appears to have come from the crowd: 'Voice – Wouldn't it be possible for the Dominion government to give us any assistance.' The men moved to the Parliament Buildings nearby and sent a message asking to see Prime Minister Alexander Mackenzie. When they received no response, some went into the buildings to the door of the Railway Committee room, where Mackenzie was in a meeting. A second message was sent, and again no reply was received. One of the men suggested that they wait and 'starve them out.' Another said that he would 'open the door and then boys give three rousing cheers for Sir John A. Macdonald. As soon as the door opened three deafening cheers were given.'

That evening an even larger crowd (the newspaper estimated a thousand people) gathered in the market square. The mayor promised to spend between two and three thousand dollars on public works. The meeting heard that the prime minister would see a deputation of the unemployed. After a brief meeting the next morning Mackenzie addressed the unemployed from the steps of the Parliament buildings. His speech did little more than reiterate the Liberal position on relief of poverty. In response to the idea that government should provide 'work or bread,' he answered: 'The Government was as powerless as any one present to contribute in that direction.' Nevertheless, it had spent a great deal on public works; he attributed the present problem to the fact that these projects had now ceased. 'The present distress was a matter to be dealt with by the local Legislature and local charities.' Finally, Mackenzie reverted to the equation of empty land and endless opportunity – the answer that became a constant refrain in the response to unemployment in Canada. 'He pointed to the great advantages offered the agriculturalist in the Northwest Territories, where a man could get 100 acres of good land for nothing, and while working on it look forward to future affluence.'[43] For the first time a mass meeting of the Canada's 'unemployed laboring classes' had confronted the national state directly.

The speakers at such gatherings of the unemployed were aware that 'the wealth of the earth was unequally distributed,' and they knew that their plight was part of such inequity. They did not yet see unemployment as a structural condition, however. It was primarily seasonal, and their best hope was that 'in a few weeks the mills would commence work, and give employment to 5,000 men.'[44] Unemployment was a personal and familial 'privation' to which government could apply 'relief.' 'There's stacks of money locked up in the city and county.' 'The Corporation can get money for other purposes when they want it, why can't they get it to give the starving people work?'[45] The language and the solutions were not unlike those of the unemployed canal builders thirty-five years before: government must get rid of unscrupulous contractors; it must 'make provision for such employment as will meet our immediate necessities, and put us into the spring, when improvement in times may enable us to secure work elsewhere.'[46] The power of the Tory national policy was that it appeared to speak directly to such appeals for stable employment. The national policy would 'bring back from the United States ... men who despite their skill, energy and constructive ability, have not been employed here and have gone to a foreign country ... This country will have a new era of prosperity, will rise from its present slough of despond.'[47]

As early as 1880 disillusionment with the new Tory government's national policy became apparent, and the Liberal-Conservative Workingmen's Associations were on the defensive. Another meeting of 'the unemployed laborers' of Ottawa in March 1880 demanded to know why there were still so many unemployed. 'We are here to listen to the city members to explain why pledges made some 18 months ago are not carried out ... We do not exactly understand the why and the wherefore of the non-fulfilment of those pledges, and as modest, humble men we now ask those men who knew all about it in 1878, to rise and explain.'[48] They heard the answer that prosperity was returning and that 'less men are out of employment.' And they heard a repeat of Alexander Mackenzie's advice that they go west in search of work: 'Labor would have to follow the capital, which was now being expended in building railways in Manitoba.' Soon it was Macdonald's turn to confront the unemployed: on 23 February 1880 three hundred unemployed marched to the

Parliament buildings and demanded to see the prime minister. They were met by a 'posse of the Dominion police ... not as a guard of honour, but as a guard of defense.'[49] Much less eager to speak to an assembly of workers than he had been two years before, Macdonald did no more than receive a petition.

The unemployed meetings of 1880 display an anger and a potential for violence not apparent in 1877 and 1878, and the speakers did more than demand jobs on public works. Some denounced the national policy as a fraud, while others dismissed the palliatives on offer. 'They tell us to go to the Pacific Railway and get work, but that is out of the question as the distance is too great. They might as well put a loaf of bread in an iron case and then tell you to take it.' Workers who saw labour as the source of wealth rejected the idea that some of them were now 'surplus population.' 'It was very unfair to ask men to leave the city who had assisted so much in building it up. It was nonsense to ask residents of the city to go away west and live with Indians and half-breeds, and to work upon the railway in British Columbia, competing with Chinese cheap labour.'[50] Labour mobility was no solution to unemployment: even where, as in Ottawa, the population had declined steeply in recent years, and thousands had left to seek jobs elsewhere, the 'want of work' remained chronic. The unemployed also exposed a contradiction in a national policy that promised to reserve labour markets for Canadians, while at the same time encouraging massive immigration. 'There is something inconsistent in the action of the Government in assisting the immigration of mechanics and labourers.'[51] 'Protection in Canada and the United States was never intended to benefit Labor. Our tariff, like theirs, was framed solely in the interests of capitalists. ...'[52]

The unemployed of 1880 knew that their plight was not simply the result of seasonal lay-offs. The problem was rooted in labour markets and government influence on them. They brought a new symbol into the political arena: the black flag of the unemployed. The black flag was a 'fitting symbol' because it signified death – both the possible starvation and death faced by the unemployed and their families and their own vow of 'death to the government.' They knew that the flag was provocative and that with such a symbol 'they would be clubbed by the Police and shot down like dogs.'[53]

The unemployed also knew that their dilemma was not a moral one. Their moral and physical fitness was often questioned, however. 'If there was a particle of manliness in them they will hide their poverty as

they would a rent in their nether garments, and make work for themselves or perish, as they must in any case under their present state, for
pauperism kills both body and soul.'[54] The assault on the manliness of
the breadwinner had its effect: 'A mechanic out of employment, who
does not want to be seen asking for bread, sends his wife for something
to eat.'[55] Another response was to assert one's responsibility to family
and one's fitness for the manly dignity of breadwinner. 'I am a man of
no habits ... put that down, as some might think that I drink liquor.'[56]
The unemployed had to defend themselves, and in doing so they forged
ever more firmly the links between masculinity and stable, sober participation in the labour force.

The ability to provide for one's family was a sign of manly virtue.
'Why do you not act as a man ... ?' charged a wife whose husband did
not provide.[57] The affront was deeply felt, and it is surely no risky psy-
chohistorical speculation to suggest a connection between the fear of
joblessness and the frequent reiteration of manly duties that we find in
articles about companionate marriage in labour newspapers of the 1870s
and 1880s. Christmas, a relatively recent ritualization of family time,
emphasized the failure of many breadwinners in their paternal duty.
'Many a poor man's child sobbed out its bitter disappointment last
Christmas morning because Santa Claus had unaccountably overlooked
its stocking in the lavish distribution of Christmas gifts.'[58] Manly virtue
must be redeemed by the collective power of male breadwinners. 'There
is no quality of blood or birth higher than that of manliness – there is no
title higher than that of Man ... As working men grow in power and
unity of purpose, a more just and equal distribution of wealth will inevitably follow; and then manliness will assert its godlike supremacy.'[59]
One writer, in an article on 'the present competitive system of society'
entitled 'The Modern Hell,' went so far as to suggest that unemployment was threatening not only the status of the male breadwinner, but
marriage itself. Why are young men 'less inclined to marry'? 'They do
not receive a rate of wages that will allow them to maintain a wife and
family,' or they 'are constantly in fear of losing their jobs.'[60]

Craft workers enunciated the doctrine of manliness, and they did so
in part because by the 1870s and 1880s many of them had joined the
ranks of the unemployed, along with the unskilled, casual labourers.
There is no systematic survey of the unemployed of the 1870s, but it is
clear that those who found shelter in Houses of Industry, and those who
joined the 'work or bread' demonstrations, were not merely unskilled
casual labourers or farm labourers suffering winter lay-offs. In the

crowds of those without jobs in Ottawa early in 1880 Debi Wells has identified printers, carpenters, carters, a blacksmith, a plasterer, a stone-cutter, and probably as many skilled workers as there were unskilled. In the late 1870s the number of people receiving relief or assistance from charities increased. Both men and women applied to Houses of Industry for relief, but it seems that men often sent their female kin to apply for relief on behalf of the family. The occupations of the destitute cannot be traced exactly, but of the men admitted to the Toronto House of Industry between 1879 and 1882, according to James Pitsula, some 42 per cent were 'labourers'; the second largest group were workers in the building trades, and skilled crafts in general accounted for 39 per cent of the men admitted. The Toronto institution's records suggest that unemployment was the single most important cause of destitution (more significant than sickness or strikes), and possession of a skilled craft was no guarantee against unemployment.[61] Contemporary impressions are consistent with this conclusion: 'hundreds of blacksmiths, machinists and other mechanics ... are today – through no fault of theirs – part and parcel of the great army of tramps.'[62]

The pattern continued in the 1890s. In February 1894, the president of the British Columbia Benevolent Society, a charitable organization based in Victoria, noted that 'the number of ... unemployed men [seeking assistance] have embraced in their ranks painters, plasterers, clerks, labourers and one druggist.' In the same month, when the street commissioner of Toronto offered 'tickets entitling the holder to two days' work at street cleaning,' he confronted some fifteen hundred applicants. He issued tickets to bricklayers, carpenters, clerks, tailors, iron workers, and 'representatives of many other trades.'[63]

Casual labourers, long accustomed to winter lay-offs, now met a new breed of unemployed – urban artisans being introduced to the harsh reality of cyclical unemployment in the recurring depressions of industrial capitalism. Even the most secure craft workers were vulnerable: on 7 December 1876 the Grand Trunk Railway announced that train service would be reduced by 20 per cent because of 'a continued stagnation of business.' Within a few days sixty-six of the company's 375 locomotive engineers, and seventy-one of 365 firemen, received lay-off notices. The sudden and 'intolerable' unemployment of so many of the railway's elite workers was a major factor in the strike of 1876–7.[64] The gap between craft workers and unskilled labourers was not often or easily bridged, of course. More often the mass of poor unemployed who congregated in city squares in winter served as political ammunition for the craft elite in their own political battles and as evidence in support of their own solutions. Yet the fear and the reality that members of their own craft might descend into destitution and into the ranks of the casual unskilled helped to dissolve the rhetoric of pan-class mutual interest and put the 'want of work' and its many synonyms into the political discourse of the 1880s.

By the 1880s the consciousness of unemployment was well developed. It is nowhere better revealed than in the testimony to the dominion Royal Commission on the Relations of Capital and Labor in the late 1880s. The commissioners often asked about 'constancy of employment' over the year. Unfortunately they changed the wording of their questions on this point, and they often forgot to ask the question.[65] The dialogue was a gendered one, in which duration of employment was assumed to matter much more for male workers than for women; questions addressed to women relate much more to the length of the working day, rather than to employment over the year. Sometimes 'muffled' and always refracted through the lens of gender, workers' voices can still be heard.[66] Often men themselves turned the discussion towards constancy of employment and workers' solutions. The word 'unemployment' does not appear, but its contemporary surrogates are frequent enough: lost time, idle time, slack season, idle season, out of work, partial employment, surplus labour.

Of those interviewed in Halifax, Montreal, and Hamilton, 165 said something about constancy of employment in their workplace or industry. About 16 per cent said that work was available full-time for twelve months. Eighteen per cent spoke of a 'slack season' or 'slack time' when work might be available but hours of work were cut. Another 24 per cent said that they lost time over the year but did not specify the number of weeks or months 'lost.' Almost 27 per cent said that three or more months in the year were 'lost' in their primary occupation or industry.[67] Experiences varied, even within the same occupation, and many made clear that work duration could not be predicted from one year to the next. The experience of 'lost time' was unpredictable; awareness of the problem was ubiquitous.

Workers contested the employers' view that labour markets were like any other markets. William McDonald, the Montreal tobacco manufacturer, explained why he cut hours and wages in winter: 'Because of the superbundance of labour at that time, and in the spring it has to be raised. It is a remarkable commodity ... I have to follow the course of the labour market ... I have to have sufficient business ability to run my factory, which, I need hardly explain, is run solely on business principles ... It is a matter of supply and demand.'[68] The opinion, as much as the lay-offs themselves, offered workers a lesson and a debating point. McDonald justified lay-offs by referring to 'business principles' and laws of 'supply and demand.' In doing so he detached work from seasonality and let the genie out of the bottle: unemployment was a matter of principles, of laws, of political economy.

The word 'season' in the mouths of workers now had a deep ambiguity. Sometimes it referred to the changes in season and climate that affected so much in Canada, from the fluctuations of output in staple trades to the costs of fuel for winter survival. It could also mean the work season – 'busy season' or 'idle season.' The correlation between work season and climatic season was no longer exact. Halifax printers could be idle in summer.[69] For Montreal plasterers, spring might be the 'slack time.'[70] In the cotton factory, lost time had more to do with broken machinery, repairs, or consumer markets than with seasons. Fishermen lost time not only because of seasonal fluctuations but because of the competition of trawls and overfishing.[71] Hamilton cigar makers sometimes took unwanted 'holidays' in summer.[72]

'Short time' could occur even in summer during the economic boom of the early 1900s, as BC sawmill workers discovered in June 1904: 'Many of the mills and camps are running upon short time, or short-handed as a result of the depression in the lumber business. Many men who under other conditions would be at work in the camps and at the mills still remain in town idle.'[73] The connection between work rhythms and climate was being broken:

Q. If you only work six months in the year is it because the climate will not let you work, or is it because there is not work to do?
A. No work to do.[74]

Busy and idle seasons were connected instead to competition in markets for products, as a Hamilton stove moulder noted:

Q. Could employers extend the work over a greater portion of the year ... ?
A. They used to do so several years ago, but of late years, and especially in the stove business, they calculate that there have been a great many changes in the patterns, from the new designs being introduced, and the difficulty is to know exactly what they are going to sell.[75]

The word 'season' could now refer to a market condition: 'When it is the right season for one class of goods, it is not the season for another.'[76]

Among trade unionists 'season' retained its ambiguity well into the twentieth century. When the Ontario Bureau of Labor sent its survey questionnaire to trade unions in the early 1900s, they asked how many days workers were idle in the year, and they asked trade unions to state 'the general cause of idleness.' The answers of bricklayers and others in the building trades usually mentioned winter or the weather. Others had clearly detached idleness from climate or 'season': 'slackness of trade' (tailors); 'too much night work' (machinists); 'want of orders' (carpet weavers); 'falling off in business' (locomotive firemen).[77] Occasionally the responses put 'idleness' in the context of class relations: 'cause of idleness, the unjust laws which make it legal for the capitalists to rob the producer of his purchasing power.'[78]

The royal commission of the 1880s witnessed the emerging awareness of class interests underlying the problem of unemployment. A Montreal moulder told it: 'When they [moulders] do not find work at anything else, they walk the streets and wait till work recommences, and when the bosses see that they are hard up for work, they try to reduce wages and put them as low as possible. There are today stoves which I made three or four years ago, for which I had three or four dollars per stove, and today the price is from one dollar and seventy-five cents to two dollars per stove.'[79] Workers also saw that employers had ways to create a labour surplus. As one moulder explained, employers were 'manufacturing' the surplus of moulders in Montreal: 'Those employers who have been complaining so much about the lack of good men are those who have been manufacturing inferior moulders in Montreal, and they have done this for many years.'[80]

Employers wanted immigrants, and workers knew why: they had heard the unapologetic explanations of employers who played off one part of the labour surplus against another:

Q. Have you had working men employed by you from abroad?
A. Yes.
Q. Have you had any difficulty with them?
A. Not more so than with the Americans in our employ. The Americans wanted a lesson, and we got Scotchmen and Frenchmen here, and when they saw that we could do without them, they came to terms.[81]

The threat of surplus labour to trade unions was obvious: 'The capitalists now have the most powerful weapon that can be conceived of to beat down the most efficient trade union. Its name is SURPLUS LABOR.'[82] Idleness was no longer a condition of climate or weather, but part of class relations.

The new consciousness of unemployment did not lead to a consensus about solutions. The testimony before the royal commission of the 1880s suggests a tendency to reduce unemployment to 'competition' from other workers or a surfeit of people, rather than a shortage of jobs. There was widespread awareness of the 'labour-saving' (or labour-displacing) effects of machinery.[83] There was awareness that unemployment, by diminishing overall consumer demand, had wider economic costs.[84] There was agreement that the state had a responsibility to deal with the causes and effects of unemployment. A more coherent analysis of the problem was emerging, however, and in chapter 8 we explore the solutions offered by labour's 'brainworkers' and their ongoing dialogue with the state.

The argument of this chapter is that a new awareness of unemployment, and a new vocabulary, emerged when wage dependence and cyclical depressions generalized workers' vulnerability to the new capitalist labour markets. Craft workers might not always act together with unskilled labour, but they could no longer see unemployment as the condition of navvies, sailors, immigrants, or a subclass of casual labour. In the vocabulary of work and wage echoed the consciousness of family. For workers who thought of themselves as family breadwinners, unemployment could not be a solitary condition.

On 11 February 1891 the unemployed marched past the corner of Spadina Avenue and King Street in Toronto. A reporter estimated the marchers to number one thousand. 'There are many others hungry, but they could not trample shame under their feet and walk with us.'[85] 'Very many were married men, and hunger at home was a common topic.'[86] 'Work or Bread' was the motto of the family man: work was for him, bread for his children. 'For six weeks I have not done a stroke, and I have a wife and five children at home.'[87] 'I am almost ashamed to tell you. I have had to appeal to the charities – a thing I never did before in my life. But for them we should have had no fuel for the stove and no bread for the children's mouths.'[88] The mayor told the crowd that no more public works could be financed, and the crowd replied by shouting political defiance and family need. '"What about sewers?" yelled one man. "What about the National policy?" shouted another ... One of the unemployed yelled that on one sewer where married men were supposed to have the preference, Inspector Smith had more than half of single men at work.'[89] 'Necessity knows no law,' shouted one man, and his need was that of a 'dependent family.'

When the black flag of the unemployed reappeared in city streets in 1891 and 1892, the vocabulary of class relations was very different from that of the 1840s and 1850s. Beginning as a synonym for idleness, by the late nineteenth century 'unemployed' had become a collective noun, with much of its stigma removed, at least among the working class. 'The ragged, hungry horde of unemployed' were 'unwilling idlers,' unemployed not only because of seasonal conditions but because of 'the very congested conditions of the labour market.'[90] 'Want of work' was no longer a natural phenomenon occasioned by war, famine, plague, weather, or season. In the 1890s another new noun appeared – unemployment, a word detached from both moral stigma and seasonal plight. As used by the Toronto printers, it referred to a condition of markets and of technology and so denied that being without a job was the result of personal inadequacy. 'Unemployment is serious among our men ... 30% of our people are unemployed ... this is due to the introduction of machinery.'[91]

Moving even further in identifying a structural problem, working-class newspapers now deployed 'surplus labour,' 'reserve army,' and 'the army of the unemployed.' These words identified a problem rooted not in moral failings or seasonality but in the class relationships of industrial capitalism. Even Liberal papers such as the *Globe* now acknowledged 'the vast army of the unemployed,' and admitted that beside those who 'would prefer to be idle' were the 'respectable men' who had to endure 'enforced idleness,' – extended periods without waged work – 'through no fault of their own.'[92] 'I am not alone in my trouble,' an unemployed father of six told a Toronto *Globe* reporter in February 1891. 'There are two hundred members of the union to which I belong in the same position as myself.'[93] The Canadian working class had discovered unemployment and had begun to force this new reality of class relations into Canadian political discourse.

3

A Profile of the Urban Unemployed

Who were the unemployed? Perhaps they were a distinct minority of the population, carrying all the marks of the disadvantaged poor, a 'ragged horde' who suffered seasonal lay-offs and moved into the cities to seek refuge in winter. It may be, however, that the unemployed were from many groups and many backgrounds, sharing among themselves little other than the want of work and not so easily distinguished from their more fortunate contemporaries. To understand unemployment itself we must see the unemployed more clearly; to understand responses to the unemployed and the language of response we need to see those to whom the responses were applied. Much in the reaction may have been accurate; much may have been refracted through prisms of class interest and moral assumptions. Contemporary descriptions and solutions cannot be taken at face value. In this chapter we seek to go beyond such description and provide a clearer picture of the social composition of workers without work.

Alexander Keyssar's answer for Massachusetts is clear and cogent: unemployment in the 'age of uncertainty' was widely shared among many different groups. 'There was something both random and egalitarian about the distribution of the unemployed,' he writes (and his conclusion is sometimes referred to as a 'lottery' hypothesis because of his initial emphasis on the random nature of unemployment). Some groups fared better than others, but 'few members of the working class could realistically regard unemployment as somebody else's problem: the ranks of the unemployed always included men and women of all ages and nationalities.'[1] Class, rather than any personal characteristics, separated the secure from the insecure.

Does Keyssar's conclusion apply to Canada? To answer the question we must spend some time setting the context and describing our sources and methods. All of what follows, however, leads to one conclusion, which we think it helpful to state at the outset. The unemployed cannot be neatly categorized or separated from others in the working class. The unemployed resembled their neighbours: they were women and men, native-born and immigrants, young and old, and they came from the full spectrum of occupations. They were not a marginalized 'other,' and the contemporary language that draws attention to difference and personal disability distorts the social reality. To this extent Alexander Keyssar's conclusion applies to Canada.

Our methods, however, different from Keyssar's, take us beyond his conclusion. The contemporary observer was unable to see what the historian's methods can display: the unemployed were not a discrete subset of the population, in the sense that only people with a specific short list of characteristics comprised the unemployed. Yet unemployment was not random. Workers were subject to differing degrees of risk – some were more likely to find themselves out of work than others – and we can now say, more precisely than before, what characteristics and conditions were associated with increased risk. This conclusion leads (in chapter 4) to a further discussion of inequities and differences within the urban working class: waged work was much more stable for some workers than for others; stability of work may be as important as income differentials in creating distinctions and hierarchy within the working class.

We begin with the Canadian census of 1891, when enumerators asked those who claimed to be in the labour force whether or not they were 'unemployed' in the week prior to the taking of the census. The responses are limited to a specific moment in time – the spring of 1891. This means that we cannot identify all who were unemployed at some time in 1891; we can see only those who claimed to be such in April, when the economy was reviving after the long winter slowdown, when urban construction was under way again, and when many workers were leaving town in the hope of finding work in logging, mining, fishing, or railway construction. Limited as our answer must be, it is an essential beginning: the 1891 census was the only attempt ever made in the nineteenth century to identify and to count all the unemployed in Canada. It allows us to hear responses from across the country, rather than in a single location. Our analysis is based on a random sample of 10 per cent of all households in six cities, and the resulting file contains all the information that enumerators collected about individuals in those households. Since our focus is on the unemployed, we also created another file with all persons who stated that they were unemployed, together with all other members of their households.[2] Following our analysis of the 1891 census for six cities, we test Keyssar's hypothesis using the 1901 census.

The censuses of 1891 and 1901 must be seen in their Canadian context. Censuses are the constructs of human beings: they are not value-neutral data. It is essential to be aware of potential biases and nuances of meaning embedded in the source. The Canadian state constructed these censuses at a time of economic change and increasing concern over class relations. In order to reflect and understand the nature of these changes, the dominion government attempted to define the labour force more precisely than ever before. Its definitions were very different from those of the late twentieth century.[3] Historians' definitions of the workforce in the late nineteenth century have been based on whether or not an individual had an occupation. The absence of a stated occupation in the census is often taken to mean that an adult person is unemployed, except in the case of housewives and persons under the age of fifteen.[4] This definition makes sense before 1891, when censuses provided no information other than 'occupation' from which the historian might make inferences about labour-force participation. In 1891, however, the census provided two other pieces of information about labour-force activity: it asked whether individuals were unemployed in the week prior to enumeration and whether they were 'employers' or 'wage earners.'

At the same time governments elsewhere were attempting to define workforce characteristics more precisely. Indeed, by the late nineteenth century census construction was very much an international affair.[5] Canada's census takers paid close attention to the procedures implemented and the questions asked by their British and American counterparts. The queries concerning employee and employer were adopted from similar questions used for the first time in 1891 by British census officials. The unemployment question more closely parallelled American initiatives. The instructions to Canadian enumerators stated that the unemployment question 'indicates the condition of the labour market,' suggesting that census designers were groping towards a flexible definition of the labour force in which market participation was the key. The emphasis on market participation closely resembled the concept of 'gainful employment' used by American census takers in this period.[6]

It would be a mistake, however, to conclude that Canadian census offi-cials followed, with little thought, British and American precedents. In 1891, for example, Britain stopped asking questions about employment. Nor in 1891 and 1901 did the United States ask workers to define them-selves as employees or employers.[7] Clearly the Canadian census was more than a simple mirror image of American and British procedures. It also reflected local conditions and responded to local pressures.

Though the published censuses certainly reflected the ideas and goals of those in power, workers also had their say. In England labour unrest and the pressure from organized labour led to the creation of a Bureau of Labour Statistics and a Department of Labour. In Canada similar groups exerted similar pressure. Strike activity in the 1880s more than doubled that of the 1870s, and three-quarters of all strikes took place in urban centres. As we saw above, testimony given to the Royal Commis-sion on the Relations of Capital and Labor reveals a preoccupation with 'lost time.' The Trades and Labor Congress (TLC) underlined that con-cern when, in 1890, it forwarded to Ottawa a long list of possible ques-tions for the upcoming census; a query dealing with the unemployed headed the list.[8] As a result of this pressure, the government included the question about unemployment, and, though it never tabulated answers to it, and thereby exercised its control over public discourse on the issue, people did respond to questions about their employment sta-tus, and historians may use those answers.

The TLC also lobbied for creation of a labour bureau to gather and publish statistics about labour markets, wages, immigration, unemploy-ment, and related matters. The government responded in 1890 with a bill to provide for collection of labour statistics by a branch within the Department of Agriculture, which also oversaw census enumeration. In introducing the bill in the House of Commons, C.A. Chapleau linked the labour bureau to the census – 'The preparation of the census will coin-cide with the organization of this bureau' – and implied that many of the labour statistics would come from the census: 'It has often been stated as one of the grievances of the labouring classes that the different statistics obtained by governments and published by them were not such as would put their claims, their wants, their just demands before the public and before Parliament.'[9]

The connection between statistics and industrial relations continued throughout the 1890s. At the end of the decade the TLC was again demanding that the dominion government publish labour statistics on a regular basis.[10] The Conciliation Act of 1900 and the census of 1901 occurred in the context of renewed state concern over labour–management relations and labour markets. Strike activity continued to increase through the 1890s. More revealing, however, just over half of all strikes in that decade took place between 1898 and 1900. Several of these were large strikes in the mining sector, but manufacturing accounted for 69 per cent of all strikes and included 47 per cent of all striking workers.[11]

In a largely agrarian country, where most politicians were elected from rural areas, urbanization and industrialization were still relatively new phenomena, to be understood and controlled. The Conciliation Act created both a conciliation process and a Department of Labour 'to gather statistical information and other information affecting labour.' There was an explicit link between statistical information and voluntary conciliation as a means of settling disputes between capital and labour. William Mulock, who moved the Conciliation Bill, informed the House of Commons that, 'with more information, all parties to such controversies will be better able to understand each other's views and conditions, and [will be] more amenable to conciliatory arguments and more ready to adopt peaceful arguments for the settlement of controversies.'[12]

The principle of conciliation, predicated on the collection of relevant social and economic data, was part of the emergence of trained experts from the growing social science disciplines in Canada and elsewhere in the late nineteenth and twentieth centuries. Throughout this period, as recent works by Barrie Ferguson, Ken Cruikshank, and Marlene Shore have shown, these experts moved between academic and government positions, influenced much legislation concerning labour issues, chaired fact-finding and arbitration commissions, and in general helped set the context for (and perhaps influenced even more directly) the questions put to workers by the census enumerators in 1901.[13]

The collection of data on urban workers also advertised Canada's 'coming of age.' Industrial expositions had long been favoured sites for such proclamations. Similarly, a properly devised census could be an 'inventory' of industrial progress.[14] 'The more of that kind of work we do, consolidating our Dominion into one country and giving information of a national character, the more we are doing to make Canada a nation in the eyes of the world.' The census also had a direct role in economic development. According to the minister of agriculture, it would 'furnish information to people who want to invest money or to settle in this country.' 'To those who engage in the active life of this country,' the census would give essential information 'as to openings and the possibilities of development in their lines of business.'[15] Accordingly, the state constructed a census in 1901 that asked fourteen questions about employment, wage earners, and the labour force as a whole.

Censuses do not provide value-neutral data. An understanding of context and provenance is essential if we are to use the data sensitively and allow for the effect of bias. We know that nineteenth-century censuses, in Canada and elsewhere, undercounted the poor, transient, women, and ethnic minorities.[16] While these biases may limit the usefulness of answers to all questions asked by the enumerators, underrepresentation in these categories, which undoubtedly included significant numbers of unemployed, affects particularly the calculation of an unemployment rate for this period.

In fact the unemployment rate as calculated from the 1891 census was just under 5 per cent for urban wage earners. For people accustomed to the double-digit unemployment rates of the 1980s and 1990s, that figure seems almost to suggest a golden age. Yet it cannot be taken at face value. First, as suggested above, it masks a much more severe reality. The late nineteenth century was often noted as the era of the tramp, a period when a vast army, an 'irrepressible stampede' of young, single men, tramped the countryside in search of work. It is difficult to be precise about their numbers, which certainly fluctuated from year to year. During the 1890s, an annual average of 1,355 'casuals' spent at least one night at the Toronto House of Industry, and in 1891 the figure reached 1,701, the highest for the decade.[17] These men flocked to cities in search of work or relief in winter, leaving in early spring to seek work in rural areas. In census years, the timing of their exodus from urban centres overlapped with the enumeration, increasing the likelihood that they would be missed. Even those who stayed in the city lacked a quasi-permanent residence, and so for many the chances of being counted were slim.[18]

Occupation and employment information in the census were affected by the sexist bias inherent in that document. Census estimates of labour-force participation therefore reflect the segmentation of roles by sex: women working in the home are accorded little role in the larger labour market, despite the essential nature of their work. There is strong evidence to suggest that even when women were clearly engaged in a directly market-oriented function, the enumerator ignored it. As Edward Higgs has noted for Britain at a similar period, census taking was 'part of the process by which gender divisions were defined,' and therefore the results cannot be used uncritically for studying the place of women in the workforce.[19] These observations must condition any conclusions concerning rates of unemployment and, in particular, the employment and non-employment of women in late-nineteenth-century Canada. When they are relevant in the ensuing analysis, we make more specific comments on these biases and offer some estimate of their impact on the conclusions offered.

These inherent biases do not, however, render the census useless. Understanding them allows us to be more precise about what the census does measure. In 1891, the question about unemployment was addressed to those who had a wage-paid or salaried occupation and to a small number who reported no occupation but still wanted to be counted as unemployed. The definition of 'unemployed' therefore assumed that participation in the waged or salaried labour force was normal. Accordingly, we have a very large sample of the urban unemployed, but not all of those who were without paid work and were seeking it. Our sample underrepresents women, the very poor, and transients. Nevertheless, it does provide the most complete accounting of the self-declared unemployed for this generation of Canadians.

Beyond problems with the enumeration process, however, there are difficulties inherent in the very idea of an unemployment rate. First, rates calculated from the 1891 and 1901 censuses cannot be directly compared to those later in the twentieth century, since both the numerator and denominator are different from those used in later times. Second, as Alexander Keyssar has pointed out, a static indicator such as unemployment rate understates joblessness for wage earners and their families. Using data that gives length of time out of work over the course of a year, Keyssar has constructed an index with which to estimate unemployment frequency – the proportion of the labour force experiencing unemployment at some time during the year. He suggests that the frequency of unemployment was three times greater than the rate of unemployment in the late nineteenth and early twentieth centuries.[20] Even with our lower-bound estimates of unemployment, such a ratio suggests that over 15 per cent of urban Canada's workforce would experience some unemployment in 1891.

What then does this census survey reveal about the unemployed in late Victorian urban Canada? Only those outside the working class could see unemployment as a problem of others: the statement applies as much to Canada as to Massachusetts. Canadian enumerators asked whether individuals were employers and whether or not they were wage earners. It *was* possible, but very unlikely, for an employer to be unemployed: of 5,928 unemployed people in our six cities, only 64 (1.1 per cent) were employers.[21] Unemployment was a condition of wage earners (84.9 per cent of the unemployed) and of the much smaller number for whom enumerators entered no information in the 'employer' and 'wage earner' columns (most of whom were probably self-employed).

To say that unemployment was a condition of the working class is to state little more than the obvious. The overwhelming majority of the labour force in the six cities were wage earners, after all. More important, were identifiable subsets of the working class at risk of job loss? Were there any workers who could legitimately see joblessness as a condition of others?

Most of the unemployed were men. In our six cities, 22.4 per cent of the labour force were female; only 1.9 per cent of those women declared themselves unemployed. These results certainly reflect the fact that women, on leaving a wage-paying job, were presumed to be outside the labour force and hence not eligible to be unemployed. When asked whether or not they were unemployed, men were much more likely than women to answer affirmatively. Women were more likely to be assigned no occupation at all, even when they were not housewives. We go some distance towards countering the bias in the source if we look at the pool of non-measured labour. Any definition of this category will be arbitrary. Certainly the domestic labour of housewives was usually unmeasured, despite its importance.

We wish to highlight here those who lacked either a stated occupation or the non-waged position of housewife. The resulting non-measured labour pool was substantial, and it was dominated by women (Figure 3.1). Furthermore, a high proportion of women, especially those who were young and those who were older, were in the unmeasured labour pool – they had no stated occupations, and they were not housewives. A different census enumeration might well have included these women among the unemployed.

Even if we rely only on the gender-biased enumeration of 1891, it is clear that many women did say that they were unemployed – 616 in our six cities. As in Massachusetts and in England, unemployment was a condition of both men and women.[22] Certainly the woman who spoke to the demonstration of the unemployed in Toronto on 6 March 1894 knew the extent of the problem among women: 'Thousands of women were now out of employment. Even in the homes of the well-to-do, servants were discharged, and laundresses found it hard to get work. Hosts of women were walking about the streets, striving in vain to get some work to do, and suffering the pangs of hunger.'[23] There was also an

FIGURE 3.1
Non-measured labour pool, six cities, 1891

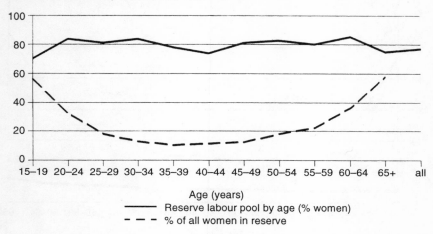

Age (years)
——— Reserve labour pool by age (% women)
− − − % of all women in reserve

awareness, in the working-class press, that unemployment could force women 'over the precipice into the sinkhole of perdition in which the jewel of womanhood is lost never to be regained.'[24]

Were the unemployed mainly young people waiting to enter the labour force and older workers being pushed out of it? Phrased this way, the question can be answered only with a resounding negative. As in Massachusetts, 'the reserve army of labor ... contained recruits of all ages.'[25] There was a relationship between age and being unemployed, but it was weak. Slightly more than half of all the unemployed were in their twenties or thirties. For some people unemployment was a lifelong risk. Nevertheless, the risk did vary somewhat with age, as Keyssar found in Massachusetts. Figure 3.2 shows (in the lower line) the unemployed as a percentage of the workforce in each age category.[26] It would appear that the relationship was weak until one reached the age of fifty, after which one's chances of being unemployed increased significantly.[27] Such a conclusion does not fit well with recent literature dealing with unemployment in the early twentieth century. That material suggests that unemployment should take the form of a U-shaped curve: higher among the young as well as among the old.[28]

Why do we not see such a curve? First, perhaps the census missed many of those at one extreme of the unemployment continuum – the tramps. In 1893 an American social scientist conducted a census of this group and found that 75 per cent were under the age of forty, 60 per

FIGURE 3.2
Unemployed and potential unemployed by age, six cities, 1891

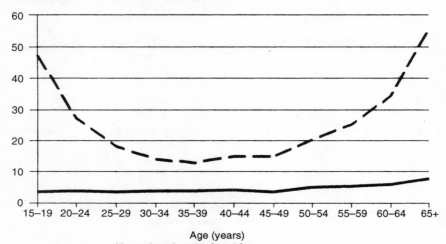

Age (years)
—————— Unemployed as % of workforce
– – – Unemployed + potential unemployed as % of potential workforce

cent under thirty-five, and only one out of twenty under twenty.[29]
If tramps in Canada shared this age profile, a large proportion
would have been in their twenties and, had they been well counted,
would have contributed to a U-shaped curve. Second, and, we think,
more important, the census question 'were you unemployed in the
previous week?' may have produced different responses a century
ago than it would today. Instructions to enumerators emphasized that
the question was meant to indicate 'the condition of the labour
market.'[30] It is clear, however, that those without a stated occupation
were not expected to reply. By excluding people without occupations one risks understating unemployment and non-waged economic
activity. If one includes the non-measured labour pool together with
those said to be unemployed, a dramatic U-shaped curve appears. The
top line in Figure 3.2 shows the sum of unemployed persons and those
without occupations as a percentage of the total potential workforce.
From this aggregation we exclude housewives, on the grounds that they
were already fully occupied.

   Participation in the measured workforce varied with age. Many teenagers were either unemployed or had not yet entered the workforce.
Unemployment and withdrawal from the labour force coincided: the

TABLE 3.1
Birthplaces of the unemployed and the not unemployed, six cities, 1891

Birthplace	% of unemployed	% of not unemployed
Canada	61.7	65.0
United Kingdom, including Ireland	25.4	23.3
Continental Europe	4.4	3.8
Asia	2.6	2.4
Other	5.9	5.5

Source: 1891 census. The percentage of unemployed is from the file of all unemployed in our six cities; the percentage of not unemployed is from the 10 per cent random sample of those cities.

probability of being unemployed, and the chances of being outside the measured workforce, increased sharply after the age of fifty – a point that we examine more closely below.[31]

The unemployed were men and women, and young and old, who came from many backgrounds. Despite the importance of ethnicity in Canada in the late nineteenth century, and the many ways in which employers were known to discriminate against people of specific backgrounds and races, birthplace made little difference to the chances of being unemployed. The profile of the unemployed closely resembled that of the labour force as a whole (Table 3.1).[32] Even when we leave birthplaces disaggregated, the result is the same.[33] One qualification is necessary, however. The fact that those born in Asia were less likely to be unemployed than those born elsewhere undoubtedly reflects the difficulty of interviewing the many Chinese residents in Victoria and Vancouver in 1891. The Chinese were overwhelmingly male, single boarders living in crowded lodgings fronting on a myriad of back alleys in small, ghettoized areas. For a high proportion of these men, the enumerator did not record an occupation and thus excluded them from the workforce. For many, too, the term 'Chinaman' was written in lieu of a name, suggesting that the individual was absent and that those who were present had only the vaguest knowledge of the man's present occupation and employment situation. Some scepticism is therefore warranted vis-à-vis Asians reported in Table 3.1.

Despite this qualification, it is clear that no background offered significant protection from unemployment, and, as in Massachusetts, the experience of the native-born was remarkably like that of immigrant workers.[34] Religion (which, in its effects, overlaps with birthplace in any case) prompts a similar conclusion: while Catholics were slightly more likely than others to be unemployed, the unemployed were to be found among all religions.

The unemployed who carried their black flags through the streets of Canadian cities often spoke about the needs of their families. Concern for their kin reflected a specific reality: the unemployed included both the married and the unmarried, in almost the same proportions as we find among those who were not unemployed. In fact, the single were slightly underrepresented among the unemployed: they were 49.9 per cent of the unemployed and 53.6 per cent of the not unemployed. The unemployed were heads of households (42 per cent of the unemployed), sons of heads (17 per cent), daughters of heads (4.8 per cent), lodgers (25.3 per cent), and members of secondary or subhead's families in a dwelling place (4.0 per cent). Again the unemployed refuse to be stereotyped or even neatly categorized: they looked very much like their urban neighbours.[35]

There were unemployed people in all the cities in our sample, but, though unemployment 'rates' certainly varied from city to city, we learn much more about the unemployed by discovering where they lived within cities – a subject to which we return in chapter 5. Unemployment was not primarily a regional problem: to know *only* the city in which an individual resided gives one no assistance at all in predicting whether he or she was unemployed or not unemployed. Cross-tabulating city with unemployed/not unemployed yields a chi-square significant at .01, but the contingency coefficient is only .04, suggesting that the two-way relationship is weak. If one wanted to escape unemployment in 1891, chances were little improved if one moved from one city to another. It was more helpful to change class status and become a manager or an employer – an option closed to all but a small minority.

As in Massachusetts, in Canada the unemployed were drawn from a wide range of industries and occupations. To this extent, once again, Keyssar's main conclusion applies: unemployment had a 'random and egalitarian' quality, and the unemployed were very like the labour force from which they were drawn. The largest group of urban workers was in the broad category of production or fabrication (including those in small workshops and those in large factories); the largest group of unemployed came from this category (Table 3.2).

TABLE 3.2
Occupation categories of the unemployed and the urban labour force, six cities, 1891

Occupation group	% of labour force	% of unemployed	UQ*
Professionals	6.5	2.4	.4
Government/managerial/supervisory	1.9	0.3	.2
Clerical	8.0	4.4	.6
Sales	12.6	5.2	.4
Service (excluding housewives)	15.5	5.3	.3
Primary industry	1.9	3.6	1.9
Craft and industrial production	37.2	39.5	1.1
Transportation	6.6	9.2	1.4
General labour	9.1	24.3	2.7
No occupation	0.6	5.7	9.5

*The standard labour quotient, discussed below on p. 53.

It is at this point that the model of a lottery begins to break down. There were groups within the working class whose risk of being unemployed was much higher than that of others in the same class. A useful way to show different risk levels is through a variation of the standard labour quotient, which we call UQ, where

$$UQ = \frac{U_1 / U}{O_1 / O}$$

U_1 is the number of unemployed in occupation 1, and U is the total number of unemployed; O_1 is the total number of people having occupation 1, and O is the total population (in this case, the total workforce in our six cities). The resulting quotient is a crude measure of probability: a quotient of 2 simply says that people in that category were twice as likely to be unemployed as one would expect, given the proportion of such occupations in the workforce as a whole. The quotients in Table 3.2 rank the occupation categories by degree of risk and identify specific groups enjoying relative immunity from unemployment. Particularly vulnerable, apart from those with no stated occupation, were general labourers, transportation workers, and those in primary industries. Production workers were also more vulnerable than we would expect, given their proportion in the labour force.

Table 3.2 is, however, but a first step in the analysis of occupations. To measure the risk, or the probability, of being unemployed requires more than simple bivariate comparisons – birthplace and unemployed, for instance. In real life any one experience is rarely, if ever, the result of association with simply one other condition. One's occupation may go a long way towards predicting the probability of one's being unemployed; but many other factors – gender, age, or region – may intervene.

From the plethora of instances that illustrate the methodological problem, we choose one: an unemployed man named John Anderson, who lived in Winnipeg in 1891. Anderson told the enumerator, Mr C.E. Field, that he was unemployed in the week prior to the taking of the census. Anderson also stated that he was a 'general laborer.'[36] The two-way association of occupation with the unemployed and the 'not unemployed' shows that unemployed people were overrepresented among labourers, and Table 3.2 also shows this overrepresentation. Readers might be tempted to conclude that Anderson's occupation was the cause or condition of his unemployment.

Such a conclusion would be a dangerous oversimplification. Most general labourers in Winnipeg were *not* unemployed. A range of other conditions must be considered. Anderson was not Anglo-Saxon, despite his name; he was an immigrant from Iceland, and he was a Lutheran. Both his parents had occupations, and neither was unemployed (his father was a labourer and his mother, a washerwoman). John Anderson was eighteen years old. Two of his siblings had occupations; neither was unemployed. In this instance, as in the wider population, being unemployed was probably related to a set of overlapping conditions: being young, being an immigrant, living in Winnipeg, residing in a particular neighbourhood in Winnipeg, and living in a family containing other employed wage-earners.

Though bivariate analysis suggests that being unemployed cannot be predicted from any single condition, certain conditions may, in the presence of others, increase significantly the chances of being jobless. Our shortlist of conditions associated with unemployment can never be definitive, since inevitably there are influences that neither the census nor any other document may record. We cannot fit the data perfectly into a model that predicts all unemployment; we can only seek 'a relatively parsimonious explanation in which the number of variables is small in comparison to the number of cases.'[37]

We are interested in knowing the significance of John Anderson's occupation, but it is seen most clearly when the influence of other variables is controlled. Does occupation make a difference, when other factors are held constant? Perhaps the unemployment 'rate' was relatively high among young immigrant males in certain types of family in Winnipeg, regardless of their occupation. Anderson's occupation attains significance to the extent that it yields a higher unemployment rate than other occupations among his subset of the population. Our target is the occupation, not the individual. We cannot know whether a fortuitous accident put Anderson among the jobless that week nor how he felt about being unemployed. Rather than theorize about the unknowable, we seek to isolate significant associations among variables for a large number of Canadian workers in several cities.

The most common procedure in social science for analysing a context of overlapping influences is multiple regression. This technique is normally applied to information that is 'interval' in character, such as dollars or bushels of wheat. Most of our data consist of nominal rather than 'interval' variables – city, religion, and household type, for instance. Furthermore, we have a single dependent variable (unemployment), which, in the 1891 census, has only two values – unemployed or not unemployed. The distribution of values in this dependent variable is extreme – the number of persons said to be unemployed is very small compared to those who were not unemployed. Fortunately, a well-known procedure in multi-way analysis can help solve to this kind of problem. Logistic regression has been used very effectively by a number of historians interested in family history, population history, and economic history.[38] Logistic regression estimates the probability that an event will occur and then converts the probabilities into odds, or an odds *ratio*. The odds that an event will occur – such as a person finding themselves unemployed – are simply the ratio of the probability that it will take place to the probability that it will not. If the probability of being unemployed is the same as the probability of getting heads when you toss a coin, the odds are 0.5 divided by 0.5, or 1. If the probability of being unemployed is the same as the probability of drawing a diamond from a deck of cards, then the odds are 0.25/0.75, or 0.33 – significantly less than one. With our database, the procedure gives us something very useful: a measure of the change in the odds of being unemployed, given a change in other conditions – from being employee to being employer, for instance, or from having a professional occupation to having a labouring occupation.

Table 3.3 presents many of the key statistics generated by logistic regression using SPSS-X – the Wald statistic, or 'Wald' in the tables; the estimated odds ratio, or exp (B); and significance (sig.). The program first presents the odds expressed in logarithmic form (called a 'logit'):

56   Unwilling Idlers

TABLE 3.3
Logistic regression with unemployed / not unemployed as dependent variable, by city, 1891

Variables	Wald*	Sig.*	Exp (B)*
Age	14.94	.0001	1.01
Employer/not employer	24.42	.0000	.13
City	17.40	.0038	
Victoria	.07	.7917	.92
Winnipeg	.68	.4094	.80
Halifax	.10	.7576	1.07
Hamilton	6.58	.0103	1.71
Montreal	3.44	.0636	1.43
Reference category: Vancouver			
Sex	11.76	.0006	2.11
Household type	10.60	.0141	
Simple	.80	.3706	.88
Multiple	.96	.3266	.87
Extended	9.52	.0020	.65
Reference category: households with no marriage			
Religion	12.97	.0435	
Catholic	2.46	.1171	1.32
Anglican	.69	.4053	1.17
Presbyterian	.70	.4029	.83
Other Protestant	.32	.5707	.86
Confucian	2.33	.1266	3.50
Other	.02	.8984	.95
Reference category: Methodist			
Marital status	1.45	.4831	
Single	.32	.5745	1.16
Married	1.20	.2741	1.33
Reference category: widow/widower			
Occupation	152.97	.0000	
Clerical	.95	.3287	1.37
Sales	.24	.6249	1.16
Service	3.68	.0552	1.82
Primary	24.66	.0000	5.50
Industrial/crafts	17.93	.0000	2.96
Transport	28.55	.0000	4.44
General labour	55.11	.0000	7.12
Reference category: managerial/professional			

TABLE 3.3 (concluded)

Variables	Wald*	Sig.*	Exp (B)*
Relationship to head	4.76	.3123	
Head	.24	.6216	.92
Son	1.35	.2455	1.27
Daughter	1.56	.2110	1.46
Lodger	1.65	.1983	1.25
Reference category: all others			
Birthplace	4.32	.3637	
Canada	.00	.9916	1.00
Britain	.00	.9493	1.01
Europe	.83	.3633	1.31
Asia	2.27	.1318	.38
Reference category: all other places			
Constant	119.50	.0000	

*Terms defined on pp. 55 and 57.

this coefficient can be interpreted as the change in the log odds associated with a one-unit change in the independent variable. Since it is easier to think in terms of odds than of log odds, we present (in the last column) the exp (B), and this number may be interpreted as the factor by which the odds change when the independent variable increases by one unit (or, with a categorical variable, in the case of a shift from another category into this category). Where the exp (B) is well below one, there is reason to believe that we are observing a significant immunity to unemployment. The Wald statistic is a chi-square and serves as a test of the null hypothesis that the B coefficient is zero (or, in other words, as a test of the hypothesis that there is no association between changes in the odds of unemployment and change in the independent variable). The column 'sig.' presents the significance level of the Wald statistic, and if we are to be very cautious we would expect a significance level of .05 or less before rejecting the null hypothesis.

We chose to enter into the equation all the variables that might have had some effect on the odds of being unemployed. We included only people between the ages of fifteen and sixty-five who stated an occupation, as well as those without an occupation who declared themselves unemployed. The only interval variable included was age. The second variable in Table 3.3 is a dichotomous variable indicating whether an individual was or was not an employer (most of the latter were wage earners). The next variable was city. Only five cities appear here, because the procedure requires that with a categorical variable one of the categories must be used as a reference category. The only statement one can make about changes in odds of being unemployed within the category 'city' is about the change by comparison to another city – in this case, Vancouver, which serves as the reference category here. The statistics for Victoria therefore indicate the effect of residence in that city compared to residence in Vancouver, and it is easy enough to compare the relative effects of different cities by comparing the odds ratio in exp (B). Among the other variables are household type (simple, multiple, and extended, where the reference category is a household with no married couple present); religion (the reference category is Methodist); marital status (the reference category is widow/widower); occupation category (the reference category is a single group comprising professional employees, managers, inspectors, and government employees); relationship to head of household (the reference category is others in the household); and birthplace (the reference category is all other birthplaces).

The results in Table 3.3 help isolate those factors that affect the odds of being unemployed. Taken together, these factors have significant predictive power, though some may be more important than others.[39] Logistic regression provides a means of measuring the relative importance of the variables in the model: the program discards, one after another, variables that make the smallest explanatory contribution, until it arrives at a set of variables, all of which should be retained, for the loss of any one would significantly weaken the model's explanatory power.[40] The variables removed by this procedure were, in the order of their removal, marital status, birthplace, and relation to head of household.

Given general stereotypes about the characteristics of the unemployed, removal of these three variables might seem surprising. A general assumption is, for example, that single people are more likely to be unemployed than those who are married and that household heads were less likely to be unemployed than other, younger family members.[41] Yet one must exercise some caution in interpreting these results. The weak influence of marital status and the 'relation to head' variable, for instance, may reflect in part a bias in the census rather than a larger reality. Tramps were, as we have noted, numerous, male, young, and often missed by census takers. Moreover, many young people who resided at home and who lacked an occupation were considered by enumerators to be outside the workforce, even though they may well have been actively seeking work.

The removal of birthplace is less likely to be the result of bias in the census, and Table 3.3 offers critical evidence in support of a conclusion stated above: despite a culture in which ethnic stereotyping was commonplace, labour markets paid little heed to background, and the native born were as vulnerable as immigrants, even when we control for other factors. To say anything about the odds that a person was unemployed in 1891, one needs to know other characteristics of that person: sex, city, age, occupation, household type, and even religion. This is the most parsimonious list of factors (together with the employer/not employer variable) from which to estimate the probability of being unemployed.

The positive coefficient for the sex variable in Table 3.3 indicates that the odds of being unemployed were higher for men than for women. Given what we said above about the enumeration of women in 1891, this result is no surprise. The Wald statistic for age (used here as an interval variable) confirms an association between age and unemployment. Table 3.3 tells us that a change of one year in age is associated with a multiplicative change of 1.01 in the odds of being unemployed. The relationship seems flat, but its significance stems from the increasing risk of unemployment for those over the age of fifty.[42]

Unemployment existed in all cities, and the problem cannot be reduced to a regional phenomonen. Location did make a difference, but the effect is largely related to only two cities: if one moved from Vancouver to Hamilton or to Montreal, the odds of unemployment increased (Table 3.3).

Religion – not birthplace – remained in the model, and this result demands explanation. Social historians have traditionally had difficulty in disassociating the effects of religion and birthplace on social behaviour. Most often the two are combined within ethnicity. Darroch and Soltow, however, have found religion alone to be a useful predictor of land and real estate wealth in late-nineteenth-century Ontario.[43] Can a similar case be made for the effect of religion on unemployment? In Table 3.3 the Wald statistic for religion, when all variables are present, is 12.97 with sig. .04 – but notice the exp (B) for each religion. The Confucians stand out, having higher odds of being unemployed, but the number of cases in this category is small, and it seems unlikely that they alone could account for the significant association between religion and unemployment. As with the variables age and sex, we know that a rela-

TABLE 3.4

Distribution of religious affiliations among a subset of the unemployed and a subset of all workers, six cities, 1891

Religions	Montreal			Winnipeg		
	% of all unemployed	% of all	UQ	% of all unemployed	% of all	UQ
Catholic	87.2	80.1	1.1	19.4	8.4	2.3
Church of England	5.8	9.8	.6	16.1	30.3	.5
Presbyterian	4.1	4.5	.9	17.2	21.1	.8
Methodists	1.1	2.7	.4	25.8	12.4	2.1
Other Protestants	1.5	1.8	.8	19.4	25.1	.8
Others	0.3	1.1	.3	2.2	2.8	.8

tionship exists; but what form did the relationship take? How exactly was religion related to unemployment?

The simplest way to answer these questions is to control for those factors that did affect unemployment rates and then observe the effect of religion. More precisely, this means taking a specific subset of our urban populations: male adults aged twenty to forty-nine, who lived in the same city and in types of households having similar unemployment rates, who were not employers, and who worked in blue-collar occupations. If religion made no difference to one's employment prospects, then unemployment rates would not differ significantly by religion among these workers.

A problem arises, however, when one is disaggregating a sample to observe a subset of this size: the small number of responses in any table that one constructs makes it very difficult to draw conclusions.[44] However, we have a file containing *all* unemployed persons in our six urban centres. Thus we can select the subset of unemployed workers according to the criteria mentioned above, and observe the distribution of religions among them. The next step is to select a comparable subset from all workers and observe their religions. If religion made no difference, then the proportion of religions would be the same in both groups. To reveal any difference we use the unemployment quotient UQ, calculated in the same way as for occupations in Table 3.2. If Catholics were overrepresented among the unemployed, their quotient will be greater than one.

In only two cities did religion appear to affect one's chances of being unemployed. Table 3.4 presents the distribution of religions among the unemployed, and among all workers, for those two cities: Montreal and Winnipeg. The quotients for Montreal relate directly to divisions between French Canadians and others. The probability of being unemployed was lower for Protestants than for Catholics, but most Protestants were not French Canadian. When looking only at non–French Canadians, we find that the probability of being unemployed differs significantly only for the Methodists, who seem to have been disadvantaged in labour markets. This means not that religion was unimportant but that in Montreal religion was fully part of ethnic identity in its effect on one's chances in labour markets. The interaction of religion with francophone identity in Montreal has, in fact, influenced critically the overall results for religion in Table 3.3. When French-Canadian Catholics are treated as a group separate from all other Catholics, the significance of religion falls, and most of the remaining significance is the result of the newly created variable French-Canadian Catholic.

Most but not all – because in one other city, Winnipeg, the relationship between religion and unemployment remains important, after we control for other variables. Catholics had a high probability of being unemployed. So too did Methodists, while other Protestants were much less vulnerable. Many Methodist workers must have been outside the networks of congregation and community within which stable jobs were offered and accepted; such networks were more likely to contain Anglicans. The results indicate that the relationship between religion and unemployment varied by city. Each city had its own economic structure and, with that, its own labour markets and occupational structure. Affecting all these factors, each city had its own culture and its own specific associations among religion, ethnicity, and employment opportunities.

One of the purposes of this book is to situate unemployment within families and households. Table 3.3 provides a first indication of the role of such relationships. The variable household type refers to four categories of households: those with no marriage; those with one marriage (simple); those with two or more marriages (multiple); and extended households, or those with one marriage and other relatives or lodgers, or other non-kin. The coefficients in Table 3.3 indicate that the odds of being unemployed are lower for those in simple, multiple, and extended households, compared to those in households where there was 'no marriage' (households with no marriage include people who were widowed, single, or married with no co-resident spouse). The coefficient for extended households stands out. For whatever reasons, such households contained married couples who enjoyed relative immunity to unemployment, and these couples were joined in the same premises by relatives, lodgers, or other non-kin who also had low unemployment rates. A question follows, to be answered more completely in chapters 4 and 5. Did family serve as a safe haven, sheltering the unemployed from the effects of joblessness? The evidence here indicates little safety in numbers: larger extended households were not sheltering disproportionate numbers of unemployed.

Apart from social class, nothing affected the odds of being unemployed so much as did one's occupation. Table 3.3 points to the important differences among eight occupation categories. The reference category is a single group comprising professional employees, managers, inspectors, and government employees. Compared to this group, all others had higher odds of being unemployed, but there is a difference among the odds ratios for those groups. For workers in the primary sector (logging, fishing, mining), in general labour, in transport, and in industrial production the odds of being unemployed were higher than for workers in clerical, sales, and service jobs.

Logistic regression offers powerful support for our conclusion about occupation: all other variables likely to affect one's chances of unemployment must be considered together with occupation. Why, for instance, did French-Canadian Catholics have relatively high rates? The answer is that occupation intervenes between ethnicity and unemployment: French Canadians were more likely to hold jobs in precisely those occupations where unemployment was highest.[45] This observation parallels Keyssar's point about immigrants: 'The gap between immigrant and native unemployment levels was largely the result of the types of jobs that immigrants held.'[46] Within production, transport, and labouring, unemployment 'rates' were very similar for French Canadians and for non-French Canadians (Table 3.5). To the extent that ethno-religious discrimination was present and contributed to unemployment, its impact was felt at the point of entry to the workforce rather than after entry.

A similar situation exists in the relationship between city and occupation: it was not location that affected the odds of being unemployed so much as the distribution of occupations in each city. We explore the point further in chapter 5, but here we note the high risk of specific occupations and the striking symmetry of risks across cities. Again we control for the effect of other variables by selecting a specific subset of the labour force: male adults, aged twenty through forty-nine, living in

TABLE 3.5
Percentage of French Canadians and non–French
Canadians in Montreal who were unemployed, 1891

Occupation	French Canadian	Not French Canadian
All occupations	5.3	3.7
Transport and industry	5.6	5.2
General labour	14.7	14.1

TABLE 3.6
The unemployed by occupation category (UQ), by city, 1891

Occupation category	Vancouver	Victoria	Winnipeg	Hamilton	Montreal	Halifax
Professional	.9	.2	.4	.3	.3	.3
Managerial/government	.0	1.8	.0	.0	.2	.3
Clerical	.3	.6	.5	.5	.5	.5
Sales	.3	.2	.2	.3	.5	.5
Service	.3	.9	.3	.4	.4	.4
Primary	2.5	1.7	1.3	1.0	1.1	1.8
Industrial production	.9	1.3	1.7	1.4	1.0	1.1
Transport	1.5	.7	.9	.6	1.5	.6
General labour	1.6	1.6	2.2	1.8	2.5	2.2

similar households and in the same city. Where the unemployed are overrepresented in an occupation category, the quotient in Table 3.6 is greater than 1. In all cities those in primary occupations, and those in general labouring, had a high probability of being unemployed. Those reporting 'white collar' occupations enjoyed the greatest job security. In predicting likelihood of unemployment, occupation is much more useful than city.

Regression analysis allows a more conclusive confirmation of the relative importance of city and occupation. In Table 3.3 we presented the effects of movement within categories on the odds of being unemployed: the effect, for instance, of moving from a managerial/professional job into labouring. We can also show the relative importance of occupation compared to city and all other variables. To assess the contribution of each variable, the procedure compares a saturated model (with all variables included) to models excluding one variable after

TABLE 3.7
Likelihood-ratio (LR) assessment of the relative importance of several variables as contributors to unemployment, six cities, 1891

Variable	−2 log LR	d.f.*	Sig.
Occupation category	191.8	7	.0000
Employer/not employer	48.9	1	.0000
City	27.5	5	.0000
Age	14.8	1	.0001
Sex	13.1	1	.0003
Household type	12.3	3	.0066
Relationship to head	4.6	4	.3271
Birthplace	3.7	4	.4480
Marital status	1.4	2	.5082

*Degrees of freedom.

another. A good model is one that yields a high likelihood of the observed results; as each variable is removed, the change in likelihood is estimated. Table 3.7 shows these changes through a statistic called the likelihood ratio (LR): the higher the LR, the greater the contribution of that variable.[47] The chances of being unemployed were affected far more by one's occupation than by any other factor that we can measure with census evidence (Table 3.7).

On the basis of our discussion of evidence drawn from the 1891 census it seems clear that occupation affected the chances of joblessness more than any other measurable factor. To this extent, then, the lottery model must be discarded. Yet what if 1891 was for some reason an anomalous year? We need other measures of the extent and characteristics of unemployment in early industrializing Canada. For several reasons the 1901 census allows a more rigorous test of the hypothesis that unemployment was a 'random and egalitarian' condition affecting the Canadian working class. By 1901 the role of the dominion in class relations was expanding. The state was prepared to incur much greater costs in gathering information about the population as a whole, and about the labour force in particular. The census taking prompted much discussion in our six cities, and residents (particularly women) were warned that responding to the enumerator could take a lot of time:

Have your counted up your freckles?
Have you figured up your sins?

For you know you'll have to tell 'em
When the census man begins ... [48]

The census was more comprehensive than ever before, and for our purposes three changes are central. First, the census takers in 1901 asked
not simply whether an individual was unemployed at a specific
moment in time; they asked instead how many months an individual
had worked in the year, and in doing so they were necessarily asking
about duration of unwaged time. Second, they asked how much an individual had earned during the year, from both primary and secondary
occupations. This information makes it possible for us to study the effect
of joblessness on individual and family incomes. Third, and equally
important, census takers collected information on 'months employed'
and 'earnings' for only a specific subset of the workforce: all employees
or 'wage-earners' (a term that appears above columns 22 to 27 in the
census). Thus members of a working class, in the new official definition,
were required to answer questions about months worked and annual
earnings. Employers, the self-employed, and people of 'independent
means' were usually excused from such probing. The document refuses
to allow confident comparisons in income and working time between
workers and others. Capitalists are assumed to be fully employed, or
outside the conditions of the labour market. Unemployment or underemployment was a characteristic of wage earners: what the 1891 census
revealed empirically the 1901 census assumed by definition.

These changes necessitate a change in our question about the extent of
unemployment. In using the 1891 census we asked what proportion of
the workforce as a whole was unemployed in the spring of 1891; now
we must inquire about the proportion of *employees* experiencing unemployment at some time during the year.[49] The response rate for employees is certainly adequate to justify cautious answers, despite underenumeration and gender bias. As in 1891, married women who stated
no paid occupation were deemed outside the labour force, and so the
columns on 'months employed' are usually blank for these women.
Usually, but not always – because enumerators did record 'months
employed' for thirteen of the 6,313 housewives in our six cities, and one
can only wonder at the exchanges that prompted such entries. Nevertheless, women in work and women seeking work were certainly under-
enumerated, and so also were an uncertain number of transient workers
and urban poor who might also be counted among the underemployed
had enumerators found them.

Between 17.8 and 21 per cent of employees (those aged between fifteen and sixty-five having stated occupations, excluding housewives) were unemployed at some time during the year.[50] The proportion might have been even higher if workers had been able to report the number of days that they had worked in the year rather than the number of months. If one had worked for the Nova Scotia Cotton Manufacturing Company in 1890, for instance, one might have worked for ten months in the year; but during summer one worked only three days in the week.[51] This 'short time' was certainly underemployment from the workers' perspective, but it was unlikely to be captured by the census enumerators in 1901. These figures also underestimate the proportion of all adults who wanted to be either employees or self-employed but could find no remunerative work. We cannot do much with the 10 per cent of the workforce who were 'working on their own account,' because most of them did not state how many months they worked. But of those who did provide information, almost 22 per cent declared that they were without work at some point during the year. Housewives – by census definitions not part of the workforce – certainly lacked direct payment for labour in the home, and they were about 22 per cent of the adult population.[52]

And what are we to make of those adults who had neither a stated occupation nor an employment status in the census? Some proportion were likely to be genuine 'unknowns' – people for whom the enumerators did not find information. But it is likely that most were simply outside the paid labour force and were waiting to enter it; or they were people without a single, clearly defined occupation of the kind that enumerators were seeking. Very probably many were doing unpaid work in their households; nevertheless, some portion of these adults should be included in any estimate of real underemployment, since most lacked paid work, yet were of an age to be employed.[53] If we deduct those who had an employment status (such as 'living on own means'), and assume that 80 per cent of the rest were potential employees, then we might add as many as 3,400 underemployed. The proportion of actual and potential employees who were without paid work at some time during the year is then between 35 and 39 per cent.

Who were the unemployed, according to the 1901 census? Erring on the side of caution, we focus on the severely underemployed – those whose months worked totalled less than nine. These we compare with those who claimed to be in work for nine or more months in the year. By reducing employment duration to a dichotomy in this way, at least in the initial stage of analysis, we can proceed by the same method as we applied to the 1891 census, and compare results from the two censuses. By focusing on the severely underemployed we also answer, in so far as we can, the objections that work duration is a poor surrogate for employed time and that months without work may not be the same as unemployment. It was possible, or so the objection runs, that people whose work duration was less than twelve months were employed in some non-market economic activity for the rest of the year, and so were not really unemployed. By concentrating on those who lacked paid employment for four months or more, we capture those who, by their own testimony, lacked a foothold in the labour market for a significant part of the year and so lacked the kind of employment increasingly necessary to survival in the urban environment.

It is true, of course, that some of those who lacked waged work for more than four months were in that condition because of illness. Illness, however, was far from the primary cause of unemployment. A Toronto carpenter told a local reporter that he worked 'about 200 days in the year on an average ... Very few mechanics put in more time from New Year's Day to 31st Dec., leaving sickness out of the question.'[54] James Pitsula analysed 2,051 applications to the Toronto House of Industry from the early 1880s and found that 'thirty-nine per cent of male householders on relief were unemployed for no other reason than because the market could not absorb their labour.' Illness and old age were the sole causes of poverty among less than 20 per cent of applicants.[55] Few other sources permit estimates of the contribution of illness to unemployment. One possible source is the membership records of the Independent Order of Odd Fellows in Ontario in these decades. These statistics report the number of members who were ill during the year, as well as the time lost to illness.

Two main conclusions can be derived from Table 3.8. First, there was a relationship between age and illness, and older men were more likely to be ill and to suffer prolonged illness than younger men. Second, whatever an individual's age, illness was unlikely to account for four months or more of joblessness. Even for men in their fifties the average duration of illness was less than two months. If we assume that the Odd Fellows attracted similar subsets of national populations, sickness rates in Canada were probably much lower than they were in Britain at the same time.[56] By focusing on those who claimed to work less than nine months in the year, and by examining only those aged fifteen to sixty-five in the major part of our analysis, we err on the side of caution: the vast majority of these workers were able to work.

TABLE 3.8
Illness by age, Independent Order of Odd Fellows, Ontario, 1901

Age (years)	No. of people	Ill members		Average weeks of illness	
		No.	%	For all members	For members who were ill
21–29	6,296	444	7.1	0.33	4.7
30–39	8,905	904	10.2	0.51	5.0
40–49	6,127	770	12.6	0.73	5.8
50–59	3,076	543	17.6	1.3	7.4
60–69	1,025	304	29.7	2.6	8.9
70–75	175	83	47.4	5.4	11.3

Source: Calculated from Independent Order of Odd Fellows, Ontario, Annual Report (Aug. 1902), 88–9.

As in 1891, the underemployed included men and women, married and single, immigrants and native born, and people of all ages, religions, and birthplaces. The majority were in industrial production or transportation, and once again those in primary industry, labouring, and industrial production were overrepresented. Two-way analysis suggests that occupation category was more important than city, but the relationship between city and employment duration was strong. And the data contain a surprise: the smallest proportion of underemployed was in Montreal, where 7.2 per cent of employees had labour-market jobs for less than nine months (in other cities the proportion ranged from 11.1 per cent in Halifax to a high of 19.5 per cent in Vancouver). Whatever the relationship between industrialization and unemployment, it was not simple or linear, because in 1901 a leading industrial city offered twelve-month employment to a relatively large proportion of its workers.[57]

As in 1891, there were no simple predictors of underemployment. The stereotyping of the unemployed by some contemporaries is belied by the data, which again reveal that the unemployed were not a discrete, homogeneous group. The odds of being unemployed varied, as they did in 1891, and here we need mention only a few conclusions. The short list of variables significantly associated with underemployment is slightly different than the list that appeared for 1891 (see Tables 3.9 and 3.10).[58] City, age, occupation, religion and household type remain in the model, but sex disappears. Other variables, not significant in 1891 – birthplace and relationship to head – now appear in the list, together with average monthly earnings (not available in 1891).

TABLE 3.9
Logistic regression with two categories of employment duration as dependent variable (less than nine months; nine months or more), by city, 1901

Variables	Wald	Sig.	Exp (B)
Age	11.37	.0007	1.01
City	126.74	.0000	
Victoria	.00	.9659	.99
Winnipeg	.31	.5770	.93
Halifax	5.48	.0192	.62
Hamilton	.89	.7661	.96
Montreal	65.99	.0000	.36
Reference category: Vancouver			
Sex	1.42	.2337	.84
Household type	7.23	.0649	
Simple	2.32	.1276	.86
Multiple	1.25	.2630	1.17
Extended	.97	.3243	.90
Reference category: households with no marriage			
Marital state	1.99	.3705	
Single	.90	.3422	.83
Married	1.92	.1655	.77
Reference category: widow/widower			
Relationship to head	28.82	.0000	
Head	2.20	.1379	1.26
Wife	8.38	.0038	2.95
Son	19.03	.0000	1.97
Daughter	3.30	.0693	1.39
Lodger	4.43	.0353	1.32
Reference category: all others			
Birthplace*	33.17	.0000	
Canada	1.38	.2400	.84
Britain	.30	.5857	.92
Europe	5.40	.0201	1.57
Asia	11.03	.0009	2.28
Reference category: all other places			

(continued)

TABLE 3.9 (*concluded*)

Variables	Wald	Sig.	Exp (B)
Religion	38.20	.0000	
Catholic	19.23	.0000	1.83
Anglican	11.40	.0007	1.60
Presbyterian	2.58	.1081	1.27
Other Protestant	4.59	.0321	1.43
Confucian	.04	.8445	.95
Other	16.18	.0001	2.17
Reference category: Methodist			
Occupation	283.84	.0000	
Manager/supervisor	8.08	.0045	.21
Clerical	1.70	.1924	.73
Sales	1.72	.1894	.69
Services	4.30	.0382	1.61
Primary	24.17	.0000	4.06
Industrial/crafts	32.27	.0000	3.17
Transport	2.30	.1295	1.46
Labouring	63.32	.0000	5.74
Reference category: professionals			
Average monthly earnings	34.40	.0000	1.01
Constant	77.91	.0000	

*The 1901 census also asked people to state the year of their immigration to Canada. This variable cannot be entered into the above equation because of its collinearity with birthplace. Omitting birthplace and including a variable for immigrants (with three alternatives: non-immigrant; immigrated in 1898 or later; immigrated before 1898) yield results quite similar to the above for all other variables, and the following for immigrant.

Variables	Wald	Sig.	Exp(B)
Immigrants or not*	8.66	.0132	
Arrived 1898 or since	5.46	.0195	1.41
Arrived before 1898	5.95	.0148	1.22
Reference category: born Canada			

Why was the sex variable not significant in 1901? The proportion of adult women who were housewives – married women with no stated occupation – was smaller in 1901 than in 1891. The labour-force participation rate of women in our six cities had increased, from about 26 per cent in 1891 to 30 per cent in 1901.[59] Since more women were included in

TABLE 3.10
Variables in the model, 1891 and 1901

1891	1901
Variables in the model	
Employer/not employer	Occupation category
Occupation category	City
Sex	Relationship to head
Age	Birthplace
City	Religion
Religion	Monthly earnings
Household type	Age
	Immigrant or not
	Household type
Variables removed from the model (in order of removal)	
Marital status	Marital status
Birthplace	Sex
Relationship to head	

the labour force in 1901 than in 1891, for that reason alone women were more likely to be among the unemployed. Furthermore, in 1901 women had greater tendency to appear among the underemployed, simply because the question 'how many months did you work?' was more likely to yield an answer that put them into the labour force, at least for part of the year (thus the increase in women's labour-force participation may result from the change in enumeration practice as well as from an actual increase in waged work by women). Consider, for instance, Jane Pollock, a Scottish immigrant who lived in the Ste Marie district of Montreal in 1901. Jane worked for six months as a nurse, earning a mere $150. Her husband, James, was a machinist who earned $680 in the year.[60] Most of Jane's working time would have been in the household. In 1891 such a 'part-time' wage worker might have been given no occupation at all in the census.

In these circumstances the differences between men and women become less significant. The two-way cross-tabulation still indicates that a larger proportion of men experienced severe underemployment. But when we control for other variables, the difference between the sexes all but evaporates. The result for 1901 compensates somewhat for the gender bias inherent in the taking of the 1891 census. In doing so, it confirms our qualified acceptance of the lottery paradigm. Unemployment affected both women and men; whom it struck depended on no single condition but on the interaction of a set of specific conditions within changing capitalist labour markets.

The relationship between age and unemployment in 1901 exhibited a pattern similar to that in 1891.[61] Our new measure of unemployment produced a stronger U-shaped curve even before we factored in the potential employees. The estimated odds ratio – the exp (B) statistic in Table 3.9 – indicates that age exerted pressure on the odds of being unemployed identical to the finding for 1891. The increased risk of job-lessness after age fifty raises interesting questions.[62] The trend to higher unemployment with advancing age seems to conform to a central tenet of modernization theory: as the economy shifted from agriculture to industry the aged were increasingly shunted 'to the industrial scrap-heap as useless and of no economic value.' Industrial employers found older workers less productive and therefore expendable. Some scholars have disputed this conclusion and pointed to emerging cultural biases as the operative discriminating force. Still others have suggested that, when measured by labour-force participation, older workers were never severely discriminated against.[63] Our data suggest that by 1901 the aged were at high risk of being unemployed in all six cities, compared to only three in 1891, and the data are consistent with much contemporary opinion.[64] Moreover, those elderly who were unemployed tended to stay without work for longer periods than the younger unemployed: 10.2 per cent of men fifty-five and over were jobless for six months or longer; only 6 per cent of men aged fifteen to twenty-nine suffered a similar fate. These differences cannot be attributed to the retirement of older workers. Census takers in 1901 asked whether people were retired, and the 9 per cent of men fifty-five and over who responded in the affirmative have been excluded from the above calculations.

The relationship between age and employment should not, however, be reduced to a zero-sum game; i.e., whether one is employed or unem-ployed. It may be that the type of jobs available for older men was very different from those for younger workers. Such was the case for John Isaac Staples, an engineer in Victoria; when he 'applied for [the] Vacant Engineer's Job at the Vancouver Cement Company ... they told me I was too old!!! Why? Is there not enough profit in me? Then where is my pension, for I have a right to live.'[65] In specific industries employers may have used ageing as an excuse to lower both wages and employ-ment duration; older workers were perhaps relegated increasingly to 'injured,' or technologically obsolescent trades, thereby missing job opportunities in occupations where new skills earned both a wage premium and relative stability of employment. The jobs held by men aged sixty and over in 1901 did, in fact, differ in significant ways from the jobs held by younger workers. Twenty-eight per cent of men sixty and over who stated an occupation worked as a janitor, watchman, labourer, or servant. Only 16 per cent of those men between fifteen and fifty-nine years of age who stated an occupation worked in those sectors. Moreover, older workers were overrepresented in injured trades (barrel-making, blacksmithing, and the like). Also revealing, older workers were almost twice as likely to work in their homes as were workers under sixty. These contrasts suggest that, as men aged, they very often lost the jobs at which they had worked for most of their lives and had to settle for work of a secondary sort, which, as we see in chapter 6, was not only more vulnerable to unemployment but also paid less. Our results are tentative, but they tend to support an older, more pessimistic interpretation of the relationship between ageing and industrialization.[66]

Why was birthplace significant in 1901? Donald Avery has shown that Canada's immigration policy in this period 'served, above all else, the dictates of the capitalist labour market.' Business leaders argued successfully for the importation of an unskilled industrial proletariat, drawn most often from continental Europe and Asia. As one mine owner put it, 'We need immigrant workers ... for the jobs Canadians won't do.'[67] And they got them. While the proportion of Canadians born outside Canada did not change during the 1890s (it was about 13 per cent in 1891 and 1901), the country of origin did. In 1891 just over three-quarters of all foreign born immigrated from the British Isles; in 1901 that figure had dropped to three-fifths. The proportion born in continental Europe more than doubled, from 8.4 to 17.9 per cent. Those from Asia increased at a similar rate.[68]

As Table 3.11 indicates, the odds of being unemployed rise for immigrants, who were more likely than the native born to work for eight months or less in the year. Only 9.1 per cent of the native born worked for eight months or less, compared to 16.7 per cent of the recent immigrants. Whatever their stated occupation, immigrants were likely to be laid off before the native born. Moreover, immigrants were overrepresented in the primary sector and general labouring, occupations with the highest unemployment rates.[69] The fact that birthplace was significant in 1901 and not in 1891 results directly from intensifying labour-

TABLE 3.11
Immigrants and non-immigrants underemployed and fully employed,
six cities, 1901

Months worked	Not an immigrant (%)	Arrived 1898–1901 (%)	Arrived before 1898 (%)
8 or less	9.1	16.7	14.6
9 to 11	10.2	7.2	9.0
12	80.7	76.1	76.4
Total	100.0	100.0	100.0

Note: Non-immigrants were 69.5 per cent of the sample in this table.

market recruitment of and discrimination against continental Europeans and Asians.[70]

This result needs to be qualified, however: immigrants were almost as likely to be working twelve months as were non-immigrants. There was a relationship between immigration and unemployment, but it is not a simple one, and over three-quarters of immigrant wage earners worked for twelve months in the year, albeit on average at lower-paying and less desirable jobs than the native born. Unemployment was a condition of both native-born and immigrant workers.[71]

As in 1891, religion is connected to birthplace in the construction of ethnic identity in 1901. The significance of religion in Table 3.9, however, does not stem from an overlap between Catholicism and French Canadians. Furthermore, employment prospects in Montreal were better in 1901 than in 1891, for both French Canadians and others.[72] The significance of religion relates rather to the overlap between specific religions and specific birthplaces (Confucians and Asians, for instance) and the overrepresentation of the unemployed among these overlapping groups.[73] There is an obvious problem of collinearity between the religion and birthplace variables: the extent of the overlap means that significance levels suggested in Table 3.9 cannot be understood as a measure of the effect of religion, independent of the effect of birthplace.

Did religion have an independent influence on the chances of being unemployed? We summarize briefly a laborious effort to answer the question. For some groups (such as Confucians and Chinese, or Catho-

TABLE 3.12
Probability of severe unemployment and distribution of
unemployment by ethno-religious group, six cities, 1901

Group	UQ*	% of all severely unemployed
French-Canadian Catholic	.74	21.4
British Catholic	.96	13.8
British Protestant	.95	39.7
European Catholic	1.50	3.4
European Protestant	1.42	5.8
Asian-origin Confucian	2.26	4.1
Asian-origin Protestant	.90	0.8
Asian-origin other	4.25	6.5

*The percentage of all severely underemployed (those
working less than nine months) accounted for by this
group, divided by that group's percentage of all wage
earners. If the group is underrepresented among the
severely underemployed, the quotient is less than one.
Asian-origin others were mainly Muslims, Buddhists, and
Hindus.

lics and French-speaking Quebecers) it remains impossible and point-
less to test the relative importance of religion and birthplace or racial
origin (as defined by the census), since religion and racial origin were so
tightly connected. For other national groups possessing more than one
religion it is possible to estimate the effect of religion, while controlling
for other variables such as birthplace or origin, city, sex, age, and occupation. The results are conclusive: except for a few groups (such as the
English and Scots in Winnipeg) religion does not have a significant association with the chances of being unemployed.[74]

The concentration of unemployed by occupation was much greater
than any concentration by ethno-religious group. The point becomes
clearer if we shift the focus of analysis. So far we have focused on the
changes in the odds of being unemployed as one moves between various characteristics of individuals. But how much does this tell us about
the extent and distribution of unemployment in the population as a
whole? Table 3.12 offers the telling reminder that, while the probability
of being unemployed was high among people of Asian origin, the
majority of the severely unemployed were of British origin. To explain

TABLE 3.13
Likelihood-ratio (LR) assessment of relative importance of variables in
contributing to unemployment, six cities, 1901

Variable	−2 log LR	d.f.	Sig.
Occupation category	355.9	8	.0000
City	126.9	5	.0000
Birthplace	50.1	4	.0000
Average monthly earnings	30.1	1	.0000
Relationship to head	28.1	5	.0000
Age	10.7	1	.0011
Household type	7.8	3	.0507
Marital status	3.2	2	.1989
Sex	.9	1	.3339

unemployment as a condition affecting the Canadian working class, one
must look at the conditions that affected not only Asians but also French
and British Canadians, both Catholic and Protestant.

As in 1891, occupation affected the chances of being unemployed
more than did any other variable. The procedure used in Table 3.7 to
assess the relative importance of variables in 1891 again confirms the
priority of occupation over all other variables, including even city (Table
3.13).[75] Workers in the primary sector, in manufacturing, and in general
labouring were particularly vulnerable to unemployment. No less than
56 per cent of those who worked for less than twelve months in the year
were in industrial production (both craft and larger-scale manufacturing). A further 16.4 per cent were general labourers. If one encountered
an unemployed worker in a Canadian city of 1901, the chances were
very high that that worker was, by his or her own account, normally
employed in manufacturing or in unskilled general labouring.

Our findings on occupation for both 1891 and 1901 suggest that unemployment was not random. Even within the working class, the odds of
being unemployed shifted among groups, and particularly at risk were
the unskilled. Keyssar concluded that 'there was ... surprisingly little
relationship between the degree of skill demanded by a man's job and
the odds of his ending up out of work.'[76] More recent literature has been
less certain. Relying on company-level data, Carter and Sutch, for
instance, found that in Connecticut in the 1890s plants requiring high
proportions of skilled workers, tended to reduce hours rather than shut

down in order to keep workers in their vicinity. Plants requiring fewer skilled workers tended to lay off all employees. In this sense, then, Carter and Sutch qualify Keyssar's claims about the relationship between skill and the odds of unemployment.[77] In all of this, skill is assumed to be significant, but its importance in explaining the incidence and extent of unemployment remains unconfirmed.

In the Canadian urban economy there were many workers labelled simply 'labourers' (over 11 per cent of our male urban workforce in 1891 and slightly less in 1901). There can be no doubt that these people were neither craft workers nor workers having skills specific to new industrial workplaces. They were a disproportionate number of the total unemployed in urban Canada. One other variable may relate to this point about skill: the odds of being unemployed were much higher among the illiterate than among the literate.[78] Finally, the census under-enumerated those at the bottom of the socioeconomic ladder, many of whom would doubtless be general labourers.

It is essential to be clear about what we are stating. For several reasons, skill level cannot explain much about the overall level of unemployment or the unemployment 'rate' in the economy. First, the majority of the unemployed were in the production and transport sectors; whatever definition of skill one uses, many in those categories possessed skill. Second, many skilled workers in those categories were as likely to be unemployed as were general labourers. Third, skill is itself a highly problematic concept. The notion that it is an objective property of either individuals or jobs has long since been overthrown. Skill is a value-laden quality assigned variously to tasks, jobs, women, or men. In industrial capitalist society, 'unskilled' became a convenient label for persons who were at a disadvantage in labour markets. It became a potent tool for further mystifying the reality of unemployment – a means used by those who had jobs to separate themselves from those who did not. Nevertheless, the putative skill level of the male general labourer did affect his odds of being unemployed.

We now know, more completely than before, who the unemployed were. They were not a specific subset of the adult population, but a mass of workers subject to varying degrees of vulnerability in developing capitalist labour markets. Unemployment was not really random, because there are combinations of variables that improve one's ability to predict whether or not people will be unemployed. Unemployment was not the result of a lottery, or chance unaffected by specific historical conditions. Occupation, skill, social class, and location influenced the chances of being unemployed far more than did such personal characteristics as age, sex, and birthplace. Unemployment was related most strongly to one's social class and to the type of occupation that one held prior to being unemployed. Especially vulnerable were any workers who possessed more than one in a series of characteristics: the non-white, the recent immigrant, the illiterate, the older worker, and the general labourer.[79] For some, including specific groups such as the illiterate, lack of skills was a problem, and general labourers were especially likely to be unemployed. There were also concentrations of the unemployed in a specific household type – those with no marriage. Add one more variable, and the odds rise even more, embracing a much wider range of groups: primary-sector, manufacturing, and general labouring jobs affected one's chances more than any other factor.

Yet the conjunction of characteristics that affected the chances of being 'out of work' should not obscure the many ways in which the unemployed resembled the employed. The unemployed were not a group suffering from personal or cultural disadvantages, still less were they a visible minority. Any solution to unemployment that began by treating the condition as a form of individual disability was bound to fail. The army of unemployed was recruited from the ranks of the employed.

4

Seasonality, Occupations, and Labour Markets

Where did the unemployed work in the period before they were laid off? As we have seen, most had held jobs, however briefly, in manufacturing, construction, transportation, or general labouring. They were laid off from these jobs; then they were not rehired at all, or they were rehired only after a spell of joblessness. Finding and losing jobs took place in labour markets different from those of today. In this chapter we look at the nature of labour markets in late Victorian Canada. We then examine how specific characteristics of those markets – seasonality, technological change, and the emergence of factories and new workplace hierarchies – related to unemployment. An argument is that unemployment was no longer merely a condition of seasonal change. It had become a condition of industrialization and its effect on workplaces, the structure of occupations, and relations between employers and workers.

How did labour markets function a century ago? Many economic historians have argued that 'the industrial labor market prior to 1915 was a market of movement, characterized by high rates of mobility.' Turnover rates were relatively high, and the attachment between employer and employee was weak. Workers were often hired at the factory gate by foremen whose choices were dictated by personal preference, ethnic prejudices, and favouritism. The rate of dismissal was also high, and lay-offs occurred without notice and without respect for seniority. Turnover rates were high because of dismissals and also because the quit rate was high. High quit rates can be seen as a form of labour protest and bargaining: workers quit in response to poor working conditions and in the hopes of finding a better job elsewhere.[1] These conditions encouraged high rates of geographical mobility. Labour markets were therefore more fluid and more localized than today. Hiring was done in very localized 'spot markets,' in which wages and working conditions varied enormously over time and between places. Despite high labour mobility, labour markets were not well integrated at the national or even provincial level.[2]

Though the literature on the history of labour markets is scanty in Canada compared to that in the United States, there is evidence to suggest that Canadian labour markets conformed to the general picture outlined here. In his analysis of Italian immigrants working for the Canadian Pacific Railway (CPR) between 1900 and 1930, Bruno Ramirez discovered that 60 per cent of employment durations were less than six months; only one of three Italian workers was rehired by the company after a spell of joblessness.[3] Barton Hamilton and Mary MacKinnon, focusing on a sample of all CPR workers, have also concluded that long employment spells were uncommon in the early twentieth century.[4] Peter Bischoff has found very high rates of mobility among the iron moulders of Quebec and Ontario in the 1870s and 1880s.[5]

Workers 'are moving around continually,' J.W. Wilkinson, of the Vancouver Trades and Labor Council, assured the commissioners investigating the state of labour in British Columbia in 1912.[6] In 1901, just under one-third of all wage earners in our six sample cities had immigrated from other countries. Those workers born in Canada also moved in large numbers.[7] Internal migration rates increased dramatically between Confederation and 1901.[8] In Canada as a whole by 1901, 6.4 per cent of all Canadian born were living in a province other than that of their birth. The urban working class of 1901 was particularly mobile: of Canadian-born adult workers in our six cities, 16.6 per cent were living outside the province of their birth.[9] Those born outside Canada and those Canadian born who were living in cities in a province different from that of their birth represent a substantial 43.8 per cent of our urban workforce.

Yet this figure understates the extent to which mobility characterized the life of workers and their families: it provides no indication of the prevalence of intraprovincial movement. Fortunately the 1901 census allows us to uncover some of this movement. While we cannot know the number of urban workers born in other cities in the same province we can calculate the number of workers living in cities in their native province who had been born in rural areas of that province. Census enumerators asked whether a person had been born in a rural or urban locale. While neither term was rigidly defined, the distinction is clear enough for our purposes: a worker born in Hamilton would not be likely to give his or her origin as rural! Close to 98 per cent of the workers in our sample who were born in Canada answered this question. Of those urban workers living in the province of their birth, 37 per cent had been born in a rural area. When one adds this figure to the number of workers born outside Canada and to those living in cities outside their native province, a remarkable 64.3 per cent of urban workers had migrated from the place of their birth.[10]

Mobility was common among both skilled and unskilled workers and their families. Mobility rates differed, however, and the differences tell us even more about these labour markets. Despite what we might expect, workers most vulnerable to unemployment were the least likely to move. One in four of Canadian-born workers in the occupations least threatened by unemployment lived outside their native province; only one in seven of those in the most vulnerable occupations had made a similar move.[11] Why would this have been the case? The answer in part is that the unskilled poor were least able to afford the cost of moving (a point we develop in chapter 7). The data are consistent with the idea of what economists call 'segmented labour markets.' Unskilled workers were hired for short periods and had little prospect of upward mobility within their workplace. Employers, in other words, were taking advantage of the relative immobility of the poor. The skilled, in contrast, were hired for longer periods, if only because it was not easy for employers to find replacements. From the workers' point of view, the market offered differential opportunities: skilled workers could both afford to move and expect to find suitable employment. Unskilled workers were more tied to place and more easily exploited by employers or left to depend on municipal relief or non-wage forms of survival. Though we do not have company-level evidence, our data suggest that late Victorian labour markets were both localized and segmented. Unemployment existed in this context – part of the 'market of movement' experienced by a 'permanent floating proletariat' that included workers from all sectors of the economy.[12]

The little we know about the social characteristics of the transient unemployed, vilified by contemporaries as 'tramps,' underlines the points made above. Tramps tended to reflect a segmented labour force, at least to the extent that the floating proletariat included a very high proportion of craft or skilled workers. As J.J. McCook, compiler of the 1893 census of American tramps, put it, 'The sedentary clerk was just as numerous as the nomadic peddler.' Three-fifths of the men he surveyed were skilled workmen.[13] The *Toronto World* reported that in March 1889 the inmates at the local House of Industry included skilled as well as unskilled workers: labourers rubbed elbows with an engineer, a stone mason, a clerk, a fuller, and a baker, among others.[14]

Many contemporaries understood that these men were in search of, not in flight from, work. As the *Western Clarion* observed in 1904, commenting on workers' frequent changes of address: 'Capitalism surely cultivates incentive to look for a job.'[15] The insight is nicely corroborated by Richard Anderson's careful reconstruction of tramp movements in southern Ontario in the 1870s. 'Tramps were not a distinct and perennial class of wanderers,' he concludes. 'Most were unemployed and their movements were those we would expect of men seeking work.'[16] Anderson's conclusion is consistent with at least one working-class definition of tramps in 1904, which neatly contradicts the condescending bourgeois view of tramps as 'professional idlers': 'What the tramp is today ... is a working man for whom there is no place in industry.'[17]

Most scholars who have analysed the tramp phenomenon have concluded that they represented a growing reserve army of disposable labour, men who in their desperate search for work smoothed over the 'fluctuations of an expanding economy.'[18] Recent studies of labour mobility and employment duration lend support to this interpretation. Jacoby and Sharma, for example, have demonstrated that 'most industrial jobs and workers were unstable during the decades around the turn of the century.'[19] In these circumstances, for most employers, the notion of paternalism was outmoded. People who had been laid off, or others, would always be available for rehire at the appropriate time. T. Turnbull of the Amalgamated Society of Carpenters and Joiners in Vancouver put the matter succinctly in his testimony before the British Columbia Royal Commission on Labour: 'Capitalism always fixes things so that labourers will be able to get around where they [capitalists] want it. They see to that.'[20]

Late Victorian labour markets fluctuated with the seasons, and even in the cities economic activity slowed in winter. There is plenty of evidence that both employers and commentators viewed seasonal lay-offs as normal and even inconsequential. As Samuel Landers, the *Labour Gazette*'s Hamilton correspondent, stated in the autumn of 1901: 'In the trades, many are just now "between seasons" and are a little slack. ... This by many of the men is looked forward to as an annual rest.'[21]

In the late nineteenth century it was easy to see seasonality as an ubiquitous and inevitable condition of work in Canada. Comforting as the view may have been for contemporaries, it missed the significance of changes unrelated to seasonality within the economy.

'Seasonality' is not an unambiguous term, and we use it here in two precise senses, to refer either to changes in productive activity caused directly by weather conditions or to the effect of seasonal fluctuations in the supply of raw materials or natural products.[22] How many of the unemployed had occupations affected by seasonality in either of these senses? It is not always easy to distinguish seasonal from non-seasonal occupations, but here we err on the side of caution by including among the seasonal trades even those where we know that some workers could be employed year-round. Thus seasonal trades include all building trades, since weather conditions in winter caused most urban construction to grind to a halt, though some people in these trades did work eleven or twelve months in the year. Not all unemployment in these trades, however, can be attributed to seasonality. Walter Dodd, a New Westminster carpenter, explained to the British Columbia Royal Commission on Labour in 1912, that, despite 'a greater amount' in winter, 'at nearly all times of the year there is a certain amount of unemployment.'[23] Seasonal trades also include ship masters and other workers in ships, even though many could find work in ships all year.[24]

Take, for example, the incidence of unemployment reported by people in specific occupations in Vancouver and Victoria in 1891. Estimating the quotients (as in Table 3.2) for specific occupations yields a short list of extremely vulnerable jobs: brickmakers (twelve times the expected rate, given their share of the workforce); fish cannery workers (eight times); loggers (seven times); farm hands (six times); ordinary seamen (five times); coopers (four times); watchmakers (four times); longshoremen (four times); nurses (three times); and railway engineers (three times).

Seasonality explains the high unemployment for some of these workers, but not for all. Some jobs (such as coopers) were vulnerable to technological change and the obsolescence of a traditional craft skill. For others there is no apparent explanation. There were also 111 distinct occupations in Vancouver and Victoria that do not appear among the unemployed at all. In the census week of 1891, these occupations, which spanned all occupational categories in Table 3.2, enjoyed an apparently complete immunity to unemployment.

Of the severely underemployed in 1901 – those who said that they worked less than nine months in the year – between 29 and 38 per cent held occupations directly affected by seasonality.[25] Seasonality was clearly one major condition of unemployment in the Canadian city. It affected not only fishing and farming and other types of work in the primary sector, but also many manufacturing occupations. Thus cannery workers, dependent on seasonal output from fishing and farming, were prominent among the unemployed.

Nevertheless, seasonality does not account for the majority of unemployment. And there is another, perhaps even more useful observation about employment in the Canadian city that comes from our analysis of seasonality. The data suggest that occupational pluralism must have been even more extensive than enumerators realized (or were able to report in the columns of the census relating to employment status). Perhaps sensitive to this situation, one enumerator in Victoria in 1901 recorded the occupation of Herbert Whitfield, an unemployed eighteen-year-old who lived with his parents, as 'anything!'[26] When given the opportunity, workers such as Andrew McAinsh of Halifax testified to the extent of movement between occupations:

Q. Do you know if painters during the idle season go to other occupations?
A. I believe some of them do.
Q. Where do they find employment?
A. They work on the wharves and steamers, drive cabs and trucks, and do anything they can get to do.[27]

What is surprising is the number of workers in highly seasonal occupations who reported that they worked twelve months in the year. Loggers did not work in logging all year round; but eleven of sixteen in this occupation in our census sample reported working twelve months! Half of the fishermen reported the same. Sixteen of thirty-three stone cutters, and seven of nine roofers, did likewise. People obviously did not do fishing, logging, stone cutting, or roofing for twelve months of the year. Respondents most probably understated the extent of their movement between jobs. Possession of a highly seasonal occupation did not prevent many people from working all the months of the year – indeed, in our sample of employees, 55 per cent of seasonals claimed to work twelve months in the year!

There was certainly a relationship between seasonality and unemployment, but it was complex. First, a significant minority of urban employees found themselves in occupations subject to seasonal fluctuations. These people suffered a high risk of lay-off, and they probably accounted for over one-third of all the unemployed. Second, seasonality was compounded when lay-offs overlapped: in winter, laid-off roofers and stone cutters found themselves looking for work at a time when farm employment was scarce and when laid-off farm hands were also looking. Third, seasonal downturns had a rippling effect, often causing lost time and lay-offs throughout the economy.

Nevertheless, the chances of remaining unemployed after lay-off from a seasonally affected occupation depended on other things. Many individuals found other jobs; some did not. Even for workers in seasonal occupations, unemployment was also the result of failure to find jobs in non-seasonal occupations. Seasonality and the business cycle now exerted powerfully combined effects on labour markets.

Since unemployment was not simply a condition of winter, other influences were at work, and one of these was technological change. Most of the unemployed had held jobs in industrial production and general labouring, where lay-offs could be related to technological changes and the shift to machine-based production. 'Science, steam, and machinery have done nothing for me,' explained one embittered worker in 1883.[28] Was technology displacing workers' skills at such a rate that workers with obsolete skills were being laid off? It is probably impossible to categorize occupations by skill content, but we can isolate the 'injured trades' – crafts such as shoemaking, cigarmaking, and blacksmithing, in which technological innovations and related changes in the organization of work were altering job content and displacing workers.[29]

William Byers, a fifty-four-year-old Victoria blacksmith, is a case in point. His was a skilled trade, but it was a skill less and less in demand. He found only five months of work during the year, earning $325, far short of the bare minimum necessary to maintain his wife, Harriet (who had no recorded occupation), and their six children, only one of whom was over the age of fourteen. That child, Elizabeth, was fifteen, and, as her father told the census enumerator, she had only 'just started work' as an ironer in a laundry, so she had yet to bring any money into the household.[30] The economic future for the family would increasingly depend on the labour-force participation of the children. How typical was William Byer's plight? It is surprising to find how little can be explained by reference to 'injured trades': it is likely that only about 18 per cent of those who were unemployed at some time during the year were in such occupations.

TABLE 4.1
Percentage of workers by employment duration, by city, 1901

| City | Months | | | |
	1–5	6–8	9–11	12
Victoria	7.7	10.1	6.2	76.1
Vancouver	8.0	11.5	7.6	72.9
Winnipeg	2.7	10.7	8.2	78.4
Hamilton	3.1	11.3	18.6	67.0
Montreal	1.5	5.7	7.9	84.9
Halifax	2.3	8.8	12.1	76.8

The causes of unemployment at the turn of the century were a mixture of seasonality, technological change, and cyclical and structural conditions reflected in growing capitalist labour markets. If, as most of the literature suggests, labour markets functioned differently a century ago, and were highly localized, then we would expect to find significant variations in unemployment rates, wage rates, and occupational mixes across cities. We resist a direct comparison of unemployment rates between 1891 and the 1990s, because the methods of estimation were so different, but it is clear that the *variation* in rates among cities was greater a century ago than today.[31] Our analysis of the earnings data in the 1901 census suggests extreme variations in wage rates for the same occupations, and considerable variations even after wages are adjusted for the different costs of living in our six cities.[32]

The 1901 data on work duration also suggest considerable variation among cities. Table 4.1 shows for each city the proportion of employees working twelve months, nine to eleven months, six to eight months, and five months or less. Montreal stands out as having the lowest frequency of unemployment. In Vancouver, about one of every five workers claimed to work less than nine months, and in Montreal only one out of every fourteen did so. The ratios in the other cities fall between these extremes.[33] These results tend to confirm the conclusion that labour markets differed significantly among cities and that there was no well-integrated national labour market, despite the mobility of workers themselves.

The differences among cities may relate somewhat to seasonality. Vancouver, for instance, may have had more unemployed because it had the highest proportion of workers in the primary sector (see Table 4.2).

TABLE 4.2
Occupation distributions, by city, 1901

Occupation	Victoria	Vancouver	Winnipeg	Hamilton	Montreal	Halifax
Professional	8.8	6.9	7.1	3.9	4.5	4.3
Manager/gov't	2.3	1.9	2.9	2.3	1.8	0.7
Clerical	10.0	12.7	17.5	12.3	15.0	14.8
Sales	8.1	5.5	6.6	5.6	6.1	5.5
Service	21.5	17.0	16.6	12.7	16.5	15.1
Primary	4.3	4.8	1.8	1.2	0.7	1.9
Industrial	27.0	31.5	28.4	51.7	39.5	33.7
Transport	9.3	6.8	9.4	4.5	5.9	15.8
Labourer	8.7	12.5	9.1	4.8	9.3	7.8

Even in Vancouver, however, such people were a small proportion of the overall workforce and of the unemployed. A more complete explanation must relate to occupational mixes: a high proportion of general labourers tended to produce a high unemployment frequency. Vancouver had relatively more general labourers than other cities and the highest proportion of those working less than nine months in the year.

We already know, however, that a large proportion of the unemployed were in the industrial production sector. To understand the variation in unemployment frequencies among cities, we must focus on this sector. Table 4.2 points to a clear variation in industrial employment: the proportion employed in industry was smaller in the west than in the east. Why would a smaller industrial base coincide with high unemployment? One might have expected that a low proportion of workers in industrial production would coincide with a low unemployment frequency. This is clearly not the case.

As the data in Table 4.3 suggest, a regional condition was affecting the relationship between occupation mix and unemployment frequency. Not only did Victoria and Vancouver have relatively low proportions of workers in the industrial sector; they also suffered from high rates of unemployment within that sector. Both conditions are consistent with ongoing deindustrialization, a process documented by several historians.[34] Indeed, over the 1890s, the proportion of Victoria's workers employed in the industrial sector declined from over 40 per cent to less than 30 per cent. In Vancouver deindustrialization was merely beginning. By contrast in central Canada industrial employment remained fairly stable between 1891 and 1901.[35]

TABLE 4.3
Unemployment in industrial production occupations, by city, 1901

City	Industrial production workers as % of all employees	% of industrial workers employed less than 9 months	Unemployed industrial workers as % of all unemployed
Victoria	27.0	32.1	51.9
Vancouver	31.5	27.5	46.7
Winnipeg	28.4	21.3	46.2
Hamilton	51.7	17.7	64.9
Montreal	39.5	8.3	51.3
Halifax	33.7	14.2	45.3

Clearly the overall frequency of unemployment depended on both the size of the industrial sector and the proportion of industrial workers in each city who were unemployed. We can be more precise about industrialization, deindustrialization, and unemployment because the 1901 census distinguished factory workers from those employed at home and in small non-factory workshops. In column 22 of the census, enumerators were required to indicate whether an employee was 'working at trade in factory or in home.' In practice enumerators often failed to fill this column. They were more consistent, however, in columns 23, 24, and 25 for wage earners, where they entered the number of months employed in a 'factory' (column 23), 'in home' (column 24), and 'in other occupation than trade in factory or home' (column 25).[36] Unfortunately their instructions for schedule 1 of the census did not offer enumerators a precise definition of 'factory.' Column 25 is not, however, about the number of months employed in some occupation other than the informant's primary job: very few enumerators entered information in more than one of these three columns. Since occupational pluralism was not being measured, it is reasonable to assume that enumerators were making the same distinction as was applied to schedule 8, the manufacturing schedule: a factory was a larger manufacturing establishment, having five or more employees. It seems likely that column 25 recorded months worked in non-factory establishments: small workshops with fewer than five workers.

Unemployment in 1901 was a reflection, in part, of an uneven transition from traditional craft workplaces to factory production. In 1891 some

TABLE 4.4
Workplaces of industrial production employees, by city, 1901

City	Factory (%)	Home (%)	Other (%)	Residual* (%)
Victoria	28.8	8.2	61.8	1.2
Vancouver	47.3	12.0	39.8	0.9
Winnipeg	25.1	1.7	71.4	1.8
Hamilton	78.2	4.4	17.1	0.3
Montreal	73.5	10.4	15.4	0.7
Halifax	46.2	11.8	42.0	0.0

*Workers for whom months worked were entered in more than one of the three columns. Their very small number indicates that enumerators were not allowing for occupational pluralism in these columns; they were entering months worked by type of workplace for employees' principal occupation in the year.

26.4 per cent of all manufacturing employees in Canada worked in shops having fewer than five employees. In 1916 such workers represented under 7 per cent of all manufacturing employees.[37] The 1901 census suggests that in our six cities 24.5 per cent of industrial production employees worked in small workshops. How far did the pace of industrialization, and the reduction of small workshops, explain unemployment in each city?

Table 4.4 shows the proportion of industrial production workers in each city who worked in each of three settings. The shift to factory employment was furthest advanced in Montreal and Hamilton. Deindustrialization in Victoria led to a diminishing number of industrial employees, and those who remained were concentrated in small workshops. In Winnipeg the shift to factories had only begun.[38]

As Table 4.5 indicates, in all six cities the proportion of workers who were severely underemployed was highest in small workshops. The relationship between industrialization and unemployment holds for all our cities: factory output was capturing a greater share of markets, and those who worked in small workshops suffered. Not all six cities participated to the same degree in this transition. In Vancouver, for instance, those who called themselves factory workers endured an extremely high unemployment frequency. By contrast, their counterparts in Montreal and Hamilton not only made up a larger proportion of the overall workforce but were also relatively immune to unemployment.

There were other differences between those who worked in a factory and those who laboured in more traditional workshops. The size of the

TABLE 4.5
Severely underemployed* industrial
production employees, by city, 1901

City	% in factory	% in other
Victoria	14.3	42.9
Vancouver	30.6	30.8
Winnipeg	9.3	24.9
Hamilton	14.4	31.1
Montreal	7.9	10.9
Halifax	14.1	15.5

*Less than nine months' work in the year.

TABLE 4.6
Work duration and earnings by type of workplace, industrial production occupations,
six cities, 1901

Workplace	Months worked	Annual earnings ($)	Monthly wages ($)	No. of cases
Factory	11.05	386	35.17	3,003
Home	11.22	357	31.99	381
Other	10.45	459	44.54	1,096
F ratio	36.43	45.70	81.86	
Significance	.0000	.0000	.0000	

earnings advantage in favour of non-factory workers, as shown in Table 4.6, is something of a surprise, and it is consistent across most industries experiencing rapid change in scale, technology, and management.[39] The advantage in wages was offset, however, by the greater risk of being unemployed. As factory output captured a greater share of markets, the smaller workshops responded by shutting down, either seasonally or permanently, and laying off their relatively well-paid workers. This evidence helps to make sense of the craft workers' enduring defence of the small workshop. Workers there tended to be older than factory workers; almost all were male.[40] Their higher monthly wage might come close to the desired 'family wage' and to offer some protection against the effect of seasonal lay-off. This wage advantage, however, was being eroded by the effects of competition and prolonged periods without work. Unemployment affected the older artisanate first, and among its members fear

TABLE 4.7
Likelihood-ratio (LR) assessment of the relative importance
of several variables as contributors to the unemployment of
industrial workers, six cities, 1901

Variable	−2 log LR	d.f.	Sig.
City	90.0	5	.0000
Birthplace	52.7	3	.0000
Age	24.7	2	.0000
Place of work	20.4	2	.0000
Family earnings	18.6	1	.0000

of unemployment was most keen. Labour markets in the late nineteenth century were being flooded not only with unskilled labourers but also with craft workers experiencing repeated spells of short-term unemployment.

Wages were lower in factories than in small workshops, but people who took a factory job worked more months in the year. The pattern shown in Table 4.6 is repeated, with small variations, in all our cities except Vancouver and Victoria, where factory workers enjoyed both higher earnings and longer work duration.[41] The advantage of longer work duration should not be exaggerated, however: factories offered more stable employment than non-factories, but the advantage to workers was small. The new factories often ran on 'short time,' curtailing production and laying off parts of their workforce in response to commodity markets.[42] Furthermore, the majority (53.2 per cent) of the severely underemployed – those working less than nine months in the year – were employed in factories. It would be a mistake to conclude that most unemployment was a short-term condition among workers in transit from small to large workshops.

Table 4.7 provides a clearer picture of how moving from a small workshop to a factory affected an industrial worker's chances of being unemployed. As we did in chapter 3, here we indicate the relative importance of a series of variables through use of the likelihood ratio. In this regression we include only workers in the industrial sector. When measured against other variables, place of work remains very significant, but it is far from the principal determinant of unemployment in this period. In 1901 the factories of central Canadian cities, at the forefront of the industrial transition, offered limited stability, while contributing to the reduction of employment in other workplaces and in other regions.

The role of structural changes associated with industrialization becomes clearer if we shift away from individuals and look at occupations. Among adult employees in our sample, enumerators recorded 784 occupations. If we examine high-risk jobs (those in which 10 per cent or more worked less than nine months), there is only one obvious pattern: over 81 per cent of the occupations were in manufacturing, transportation, and general labour.[43] At the other extreme, in 421 occupations nobody reported less than twelve months of work.[44] Perhaps people in these occupations did not report a second occupation that allowed them to work the full twelve months; it is also possible, however, that their primary occupation alone ensured twelve months of work. Over half of the occupations carrying full immunity from unemployment (and two-thirds of all workers in such occupations) were in 'white collar' sectors – professional, managerial, clerical, and service sectors.

A distinction between 'blue collar' and 'white collar' work is rather crude and serves only as a step towards a more important distinction. In this working class there was an occupational elite, distinguished by stability of employment and by relatively high annual earnings. We refer not to a craft elite but to a new supervisory elite of workers that appears at this stage of industrialization: managers, inspectors, superintendents, and supervisors. People in such occupations made up a mere 1.5 per cent of all employees but their immunity from unemployment appears to have been virtually certain.[45]

These conclusions derive from our six-city sample, but it is possible to extend the analysis to the country as a whole. In 1907 the dominion government's Census and Statistics Office published *Bulletin I: Wage-Earners by Occupations*, which includes a list of all occupations reported by wage earners in the 1901 census. For each occupation the document reports average number of months worked, average annual earnings, and total number of workers.[46] Occupations are organized into nine 'classes.' For the country as a whole, two classes were clearly affected by seasonality: the average months worked for fisheries occupations was 7.55; the average for forestry and lumbering was 9.27 (compared to the national average for all occupations of 10.53). Agricultural occupations (10.00 months) were also below the national average. One group – professional occupations (11.29) – was significantly higher than the national average.

The bulletin lists 1,592 occupations for the whole of the country. Of these, no less than 592 appear to have involved full employment – the average number of months worked was twelve! The statistic is less impressive than it might seem, however, for there were only 2,450 men and 516 women in this category in the whole of the country. Clearly, jobs that guaranteed year-round employment for all who worked at them were reserved for a tiny minority of the working class.

In the list of 592 occupations, one obvious pattern emerges. In 322 there appear one of the following words: 'manager,' 'superintendent,' 'foreman,' 'overseer,' or 'inspector.' Here again is the supervisory elite that we encountered in our six-city sample. Of course, not all people having such occupation designations worked twelve months in the year. Nevertheless, they clearly enjoyed a very low risk of lay-off. Managers, supervisors, foremen, overseers, and inspectors made up a small group in Canada – 11,039 men and 292 women, or less than two in every one hundred male employees and two in every one thousand women. Particularly numerous in the manufacturing sector, this elite earned more than twice as much as the overall average earnings in manufacturing.[47]

The supervisory elite was part of a larger subset of waged or salaried occupations emerging at this stage in the development of industrial capitalism. We refer not to the labour aristocracy of the older Marxian definition, which too easily shades into an amorphous mass of 'skilled' workers. Instead we are observing the emergence of a managerial and supervisory elite, smaller than any labour aristocracy, but more sharply distinguished as part of the movement towards scientific management occurring in the United States, which would have varying influences on industry in Canada.

The managerial and supervisory elite includes those who held disciplinary authority over other wage earners in manufacturing, construction, transportation, and mining. It includes also those who were acquiring other kinds of authority over the work process: the small number of highly trained professionals, hired by private capital and sometimes by government, to apply scientific knowledge to production and to economic development. Our elite numbers among its members engineers, chemists, metallurgists, draughtsmen, designers, accountants, lawyers, insurance and advertising agents, railway agents, and railway 'officials.' It also encompasses those government employees who clearly held managerial or supervisory responsibility, either within government itself or over sections of the population as a whole – not the clerks, but 'officials,' police, and prison and asylum guards.

This broadly defined managerial and supervisory elite (26,733 persons) was 3.3 per cent of the Canadian labour force. It was disproportionately male (less than 2 per cent were women). Average annual earnings for men was $850 (compared to an overall workforce average

TABLE 4.8

Occupations of machinists, printers, sawmill workers, and coal miners, Canada, 1901

Occupation	Aggregate wage earners		Average months worked		Average yearly earnings ($)	
	Male	Female	Male	Female	Male	Female
Machinists	12,622	0	11.23	–	485	–
Apprentices	800	0	11.17	–	172	–
Foremen	35	0	11.59	–	902	–
Managers	7	0	12.00	–	1,008	–
Superintendents	6	0	12.00	–	1,500	–
Printers, etc.	6,476	489	11.43	11.12	452	206
Compositors and pressmen						
Apprentices	453	9	11.04	10.22	129	86
Foremen	27	0	11.88	–	707	–
Managers	23	0	12.00	–	1,307	–
Superintendents	2	0	12.00	–	1,825	–
Sawmill employees	5,219	0	9.53	–	305	–
Foremen	99	0	10.03	–	685	–
Managers	34	0	11.48	–	1,305	–
Superintendents	2	0	12.00	–	1,300	–
Coal miners	7,856	0	10.74	–	468	–
Labourers	1,780	0	10.46	–	304	–
Foremen	126	0	11.51	–	483	–
Managers	26	0	11.85	–	1,164	–
Inspectors	9	0	11.89	–	609	–
Superintendents	2	0	12.00	–	1,800	–

of $387). Key to developments in manufacturing were not only the fore-men, but those further removed from the shop floor – male managers or superintendents. Very few of them worked less than twelve months in the year; they took home, on average, $1,256 in 1901. Table 4.8 gives four examples of the very common occupational hierarchy at the turn of the century: workers, foremen, managers, and superintendents.

Stable employment was a privilege, and a rare one, within the structure of industrial capitalism. Skill was one part of achieving this privilege: managerial workers possessed types of knowledge, often the result of lengthy training and even expensive education, which was reserved for a tiny minority. Training, however, meant more than simply the acquisition of knowledge. It involved also acceptance of values and ideology: these were the reliable workers whose loyalty was rewarded when employers paid a premium to retain their services. The demand for managers and engineers might fluctuate, but the knowledge they possessed was restricted to a few, and so companies ensured access to their knowledge through long-term contractual employment. These were the new brainworkers and supervisory taskmasters: full employment was a reward, but also a mark of their status within the new authority structure of industrial capitalism. A further reward came in the form of wages, increasingly dignified as an annual 'salary.' The work of the managerial elite was sheltered from the effects of both season and markets.

At the other extreme from the managerial elite were workers in jobs that did not guarantee year-round work. Almost one-quarter of Canadian 'employees' held jobs for which the average months worked was less than ten.[48] Most of these vulnerable jobs were in manufacturing.[49] The average annual earnings in such occupations was a mere $297. In these occupations were the most vulnerable of Canadian workers, for whom the lack of waged work compounded the problem of low wages.

Among these vulnerable occupations, how far was unemployment the result of seasonality? The Census Offices *Bulletin I* of 1907 allows a cautious answer at the national level. At least 60 per cent of employees in occupations averaging under ten months' work were in seasonal occupations.[50] In the urban context, of course, the proportion was much lower (between 29 and 38 per cent). In rural Canada in 1901 few occupations could guarantee year-round employment, and very few rural workers would have expected year-round work in a single job. In this context unemployment was slow to appear as a social problem. The predominantly seasonal nature of rural work overshadowed the emerging urban reality, making it more difficult for contemporaries to dissociate seasonal from structural unemployment.

There were thus two kinds of unemployment in Canada – the absence of work caused by change of seasons and the joblessness due to the nature of emerging capitalist labour markets. The former obscured the latter and so helped to preserve the myth that the unemployed were 'between seasons.' The two forms of unemployment overlapped in labour markets that were highly localized and fluid. In their families and their organizations, wage workers struggled to limit the impact of labour-market uncertainty. Stabilizing wage rates and controlling hiring practices became central issues for the labour movement. When older seasonal fluctuations overlapped with the wage system's weak attachment between employer and employee, the result was widespread fear of enforced idleness, which fuelled a long struggle to control the labour markets of industrial capitalism.

5

Dimensions of Space and Community

Canadians in the last half of the twentieth century associate unemployment with region. We know that certain parts of our country have extraordinarily high rates of unemployment. Some analysts assume that removing barriers to mobility is a key to solving the problem. Though in recent years the heartland of central Canada appears to have lost its relative immunity to unemployment, we still tend to assume that joblessness is a regional phenomenon.[1]

We need to rethink both the temporal and the spatial dimensions of unemployment. In 1891 and 1901, as we have shown, the probability that a worker would be unemployed depended much more on occupation than on city of residence. This conclusion cannot, however, be the last word on the spatial context of unemployment. Since a major purpose of this book is to understand the context of unemployment at the turn of the century, we must ask not only who the unemployed were and where they worked, but also where they lived. Some scholars have suggested that spatial segregation has a direct effect on the development of collective consciousness, and in this chapter we comment, where possible, on how location might have affected one's perception of, and ability to deal with, unemployment.[2]

Factories began to appear in certain cities, and in parts of those cities. At a time when most people still walked to work, residential patterns were influenced by the location of factories. Residential segregation also related to ethnicity, and important American studies by Olivier Zunz and others argue that class-based segregation eventually superseded older patterns based on ethnicity. Were the unemployed being sorted and concentrated in space, even as they were concentrated by occupation? Did a spatial concentration of the unemployed emerge at the same time as the problem itself? Was family unemployment part of the emergence of pockets of poverty – the slums that so alarmed urban reformers?

We look first at the smallest spatial unit in which working-class families lived: the family dwelling place. If the unemployed were segregated into slum neighbourhoods, we would expect to find them in relatively substandard and overcrowded households. From the 1891 census it is possible to construct one widely used measure of relative well-being: the ratio of people to rooms within households. As the authors of a study of household space in late-nineteenth-century Montreal wrote: 'Space per person is a fundamental measure of equity in urban society.'[3] Most literature on household crowding suggests that a ratio of one person per room (minus the bathroom) can be seen as reasonable living conditions. That literature also suggests that well-being is very much tied to expectations, and it is clear that British and European immigrants moved on average from relatively crowded to relatively uncrowded households and may therefore have been quite satisfied with their new living space. What we attempt to measure here is less the degree of satisfaction felt by individuals and their families and more the differences in living conditions experienced by households with and households without unemployed people.

As Table 5.1 indicates, people who lived with an unemployed person were likely to live in more crowded conditions than did people in households without any unemployed. The relative differences are amazingly constant across the six cities in our sample. Overall, one was less likely to live in crowded conditions in Hamilton and more likely to do so in Montreal whether one lived with or without an unemployed person. But even in Hamilton and Montreal, the difference between the two household types was very similar to that found in the other cities. Unemployment affected more than simply the individual who was out of work. To live in the same house as an unemployed person meant a higher probability of living in substandard conditions.

Moreover, if Hamilton is any indication, not only did the unemployed dwell in relatively overcrowded conditions, but they also lived in accommodation worth considerably less than those houses without unemployed people.[4] These costs varied according to the size of frame and brick dwellings. In Hamilton, close to three-fifths of all one-storey wooden dwellings – the cheapest housing in the city – were inhabited by families with unemployed people; close to 70 per cent of all brick and stone houses in excess of one storey were inhabited by families without any unemployed people.[5] The unemployed may not have stood out in

TABLE 5.1
Household space: households with and without unemployed
people, by city, 1891

| City | % fewer rooms than people | |
	Households with unemployed	Households with no unemployed
Victoria	45.7	30.1
Vancouver	45.2	30.9
Winnipeg	47.8	31.4
Hamilton	33.4	19.1
Montreal	58.0	42.6
Halifax	48.8	37.6

terms of their personal characteristics, but they certainly were differentiated by their living conditions. When a worker told the 1891 census enumerator that he or she lacked work during the previous week, that response signalled a social reality that stretched far beyond a seven-day holiday. In fact, this analysis of housing conditions suggests that most of those who admitted to being without work during that week were far from strangers to unemployment.

In Victoria in 1901 families with high unemployed or non-waged time continued to live in relatively crowded conditions. Close to three-fifths of families with ten or more months of unused labour time lived in houses with fewer rooms than people. Only one-quarter of families with less than ten months of non-waged time lived in similar crowded conditions. Underemployment on the part of the household head (eight months or less of employment in the year) also affected a family's chances of owning a home: in Victoria, 34 per cent of families whose head worked nine or more months owned their homes; only 22 per cent of families whose head worked less than nine months did so. For Hamilton the relevant percentages are 29 and 21.[6]

Clearly there was a relationship between ownership and unemployment, but it is not dramatic: a strong majority of working-class families, whether or not the head was unemployed, rented and did not own their homes. In part this reflects the unpredictable and often sudden nature of being out of work. It may be that working-class families adjusted to the omnipresent threat of unemployment by renting rather than owning. In this way they were less tied to a particular location and were better able to move in search of a new job. Gilliland and Olson argue that this was true for workers in late-nineteenth-century Montreal.[7] Yet literature on the working class and housing has more often pointed to the strong desire exhibited by members of that class to own their homes.[8] Both as a threat and as a reality, unemployment stood firmly in the way of that goal.

To what extent were the dwellings of working-class families, especially those of families that experienced high levels of unemployment, concentrated in slum neighbourhoods? Urban geographers have documented the social geography of major Canadian cities in the late nineteenth and early twentieth centuries.[9] They have paid particular attention to the development of working-class neighbourhoods and to the intersection of ethnicity, occupation, and social class. We can build on much of this work in two ways. First, we introduce employment duration as a variable in the process of residential differentiation. Second, our database allows levels of comparative analysis that few historical geographers have been able to attempt. We have comprehensive evidence on ethnicity, class, and occupation for the adult populations of several cities across the country. We do not need to use surrogates, such as occupation category for class, or birthplace for ethnicity. The census takers' distinctions among employers, employees, and those 'working on own account' allow us to separate the working class from employers and from petite bourgeoisie. Since respondents were asked to state their 'racial or tribal origin,' the census allows us to know individuals' own definition of their ethnicity as well as it can ever be known. We do not need to focus simply on heads of households, as many geographers do. Finally, we can move beyond the level of the city ward to the finer levels of sub-ward analysis achieved by such geographers as Daniel Hiebert, Larry McCann, and Sherry Olson. We can analyse spatial patterns at the very fine level of the census subdistrict. For Montreal, for instance, there are 141 subdistricts in our analysis. Subdistricts are of comparable size in all cities except Montreal (where they are somewhat larger), and this similarity in size facilitates analysis across cities.[10]

The simplest way to show how far workers and the unemployed were concentrated by district is to use a standard measure of segregation, known as the dissimilarity index. This index measures the degree to which a particular group was spread evenly among districts in a city. Evenness is defined with respect to that group's share of the total city population. If 20 per cent of all adults in a city were factory workers, then an even pattern means that in each ward 20 per cent will be factory workers. The index of dissimilarity gives the percentage of all factory workers in the city who would have to move in order to achieve an even residential pattern.[11] Though there are no exact benchmarks of significance, an index number of 25 and above is generally considered important.[12]

To demonstrate how the method is used, we begin by looking at Hamilton, the city in which industrialization had advanced furthest. The 1901 census divided the city into seven districts, corresponding to the seven city wards, and sixty-four subdistricts. Table 5.2 compares ward- and subdistrict-level segregation by social class and by work duration. We break down the working class into four broad categories: white collar (mainly sales, service, and clerical workers), blue collar (mainly industrial and transport employees), the unskilled (general labourers), and housewives. The last are a separate category, under both class and work duration. Their inclusion lowers very slightly our weighted index for each variable. Since they were part of the adult labouring population it would be a serious mistake to omit them; their form of non-waged labour gave them a class position arguably different from that of others, and their work duration was certainly of a different order from that of others.[13] To leave them out would be to take a part of the population (such as heads of households) as reflective of the whole.[14]

Table 5.2 demonstrates that the extent of segregation, when measured at the level of ward, is understated. For instance, those living on their own means and the self-employed were distributed relatively evenly across wards. The subdistrict indices reveal, however, that members of these classes did tend to cluster spatially. In only one class category did ward- and subdistrict-level analyses turn up similar results: labouring employees were clustered within subdistricts, which were also located within particular wards. Those wards were two east-end areas where much of the city's new industrial growth was taking place.[15] The spatial segregation of social classes should not be exaggerated, however: both ward and subdistrict analyses demonstrate that skilled blue-collar workers lived throughout Hamilton. At a finer level, even a majority of factory workers lived outside the two east-end industrial wards.[16]

Table 5.2 suggests that the unemployed – those working less than twelve months – were spread unevenly among subdistricts. Their segregation appears only at the subdistrict level. Of the severely unemployed – those working less than nine months – two-thirds lived in twenty of the city's sixty-four subdistricts. In these subdistricts 28.5 per cent of all employees were severely unemployed; the rate for Hamilton as a whole was 14.4 per cent. There is one other notable characteristic of these subdistricts: the fully employed – those working twelve months – were

TABLE 5.2
Spatial segregation of adults by social class and by work duration,
Hamilton ward and subdistrict levels, 1901

	Indices of dissimilarity	
	---	---
	Seven wards	Sixty-four subdistricts
Class		
Living on own means	13.8	39.4
Employer	22.9	48.3
Self-employed	10.9	24.9
White-collar employee	13.9	21.1
Blue-collar employee	10.0	15.7
Labourer	40.8	42.7
Housewife	5.8	11.9
No occupation	7.6	17.9
Weighted index	10.6	18.6
Work duration		
Housewife	5.6	9.7
Work time not reported*	10.6	26.6
No occupation	7.8	18.6
Working 1–8 months	9.2	32.1
Working 9–11 months	15.8	26.2
Working 12 months	5.0	12.5
Weighted index	7.5	17.0

*Includes people who did have an occupation but reported no
months; most were employers, self-employed, and professionals.

underrepresented. The 'internal' index of dissimilarity measures the
extent to which two groups – the fully employed and the severely
underemployed – were evenly distributed with respect to each other
throughout Hamilton's subdistricts. What proportion of these two
groups would have to move in order to have even distribution? The
answer is that 40.6 per cent of each group, or 81.2 per cent of one group,
would have to relocate. Clearly the fully employed tended to live in
neighbourhoods other than those inhabited by the severely unemployed. This spatial separation is an important dimension of difference
within the working class.

There are many possible dimensions of segregation in the urban environment. Geographers such as Hiebert have argued persuasively that

TABLE 5.3
Indices of dissimilarity for six cities, 1901

	Victoria	Vancouver	Winnipeg	Hamilton	Montreal	Halifax
Birthplace	27.3	23.1	20.2	11.4	12.5	9.2
Ethnic origin	27.3	26.1	23.3	18.8	24.1	21.5
Immigrant	15.5	16.0	15.8	9.2	10.1	8.2
Class	19.0	21.4	21.0	18.6	15.2	18.8
Occupation	22.7	26.6	23.0	18.5	16.8	21.6
Work duration	20.6	22.7	14.7	17.0	14.2	28.6

Note: Birthplace was divided into six categories: Canada, the United Kingdom, Ireland, continental Europe, Asia, and other. We took ethnic origin from the 'racial or tribal origin' column in the census and divided it into seven categories: French, English, Scottish, Irish, European, Asian, and other. 'Immigrant' refers to three groups: recent immigrants (since 1890 for Hamilton and since 1897 for all other cities), all other immigrants, and non-immigrants. 'Occupation' refers to ten categories by economic sector: professional/managerial, clerical, sales, service, primary industry, industrial production, transportation, general labour, housewives, and people of working age with no listed occupation. For class and work duration see Table 5.2 and the text.

class segregation and ethnic segregation interact with each other. Similarly, work duration cannot stand alone as an independent agent of spatial distancing. Before considering the implications of our results for Hamilton, we need to ask what other variables entered into the social geography of the city and whether our results for Hamilton are unique to that city. Segregation by class was not significant in Hamilton, the most industrialized of our six cities. Were other variables more important there? Was class more or less significant in other cities? The easiest way to answer these questions is to use weighted indices of the kind presented in Table 5.2. These indices are measures of the degree to which each category (class and work duration), taken as a whole, accounted for spatial segregation in the city.

Table 5.3 presents weighted indices for six key variables for six cities. The results call into question the idea that there was 'great variation in the degree and nature of residential differentiation' among cities.[17] Most indices fall within a narrow range, and most are below 25 (though there were interesting and important variations within each category). In all six cities the index for ethnicity is higher than the index for class. There appears to be no simple relationship between stage of industrialization and extent of segregation, by class or by any other variable. The class

TABLE 5.4
Indices of dissimilarity: the fully employed
and the unemployed, by city, 1901

City	Index
Victoria	26.6
Vancouver	58.0
Winnipeg	39.4
Hamilton	40.6
Montreal	35.4
Halifax	39.5

Note: Fully employed: working twelve
months; unemployed: less than nine
months.

indices are slightly lower in the eastern industrial cities than in the western cities. This result is consistent with Hiebert's conclusions in his studies of Winnipeg and Toronto. Where Zunz argued for Detroit that class superseded ethnicity as the 'salient feature' of urban segregation, Hiebert argues that Zunz's conclusion cannot be applied to Canada. In Canada class and ethnicity were thoroughly interwoven in cities, where most industry remained small in scale compared to industry in Detroit and other large American cities.[18]

Unemployment also conditioned the spatial fabric of the city. The distancing of the unemployed from the fully employed occurred in all six cities (Table 5.4). The separation was most dramatic in Vancouver, where the unemployed were concentrated in the growing east end of the city, east of Cambie Street and adjacent to the docks on Burrard Inlet. Ten of thirty-one subdistricts contained 78 per cent of all the severely underemployed in the city (these subdistricts contained only 34 per cent of the city's working class). In these ten subdistricts, no less than 45 per cent of all workers stated that they worked less than nine months in the year.[19]

What does this distancing of the unemployed from the fully employed mean? Until now, analyses of social segregation have taken as their primary unit of analysis the occupation of the head of household and a measure of class position derived from those occupations. Sherry Olson, for instance, has constructed neighbourhoods on the basis of similarities in occupational profile.[20] We propose to select neighbourhoods on the basis

of work duration and to discover what other characteristics are associated with high-unemployment neighbourhoods. It could be that the
majority of the severely underemployed were separated spatially from
others in the working class and that spatial separation overlapped with
and reinforced other lines of difference. Or perhaps the chronically
unemployed were indeed 'other' from the perspective of most of the
working class – concentrated in neighbourhoods where joblessness was
subsumed into wider conditions of inequality.

It could follow that spatial distancing had implications for the politics
and class consciousness of the working class. Several years ago the geographer Richard Harris challenged both historians and urban geographers
to tackle directly the interaction between spatial segregation and political
consciousness. From the work of urban historians and geographers he
drew the hypothesis that segregation played 'a positive role in articulating dissent, not because it fosters intolerance ... but because neighbourly
proximity fosters action.'[21] As Hiebert has shown for Winnipeg in 1919,
the argument is persuasive for certain times and places. Whatever urban
geographers may do with the hypothesis, however, there was certainly
little opportunity for cohesion over the problem of unemployment if the
unemployed were spatially segregated from the rest of the working
class.[22]

To test these hypotheses, we begin with Vancouver, where the segregation of the unemployed seems to have been most extreme. We focus on
two clusters of subdistricts: first, the seven having marked overrepresentation of severely underemployed workers; second, the eight where all
workers stated that they were fully employed.[23] Both clusters exhibited a
wide mix of occupations. Nevertheless, the unemployed were living in
subdistricts having definable characteristics. The most marked difference
was that of income level: family per-person income was well below the
city average in the 'unemployed' subdistricts and even further below
the average for the subdistricts that had no unemployed. This income difference was related to the wide gap in average annual earnings of household heads: $499 for the 'unemployed' cluster and $866 for the 'fully
employed.'

A few other characteristics distinguished the subdistrict clusters from
each other. The 'unemployed' cluster tended to have fewer Canadian-
born workers and many more Asians. Those of 'English' ethnic origin
were overrepresented in the 'fully employed' cluster. In fact the 'unemployed' neighbourhoods were characterized by a profound racial cleav-
age: almost half of the residents were Asian. By contrast, there was

relative homogeneity in the 'fully employed' neighbourhoods: 72 per cent were English, Scots, or Irish. These ethnic differences overlapped with class differences: wage-earning employees were overrepresented in the 'unemployed' cluster. In the 'fully employed' cluster more prosperous workers found themselves living in some proximity to employers and to those 'living on own means' (of whom there were none in the 'unemployed' cluster). Particularly noteworthy, the 'fully employed' neighbourhoods contained many individuals who crossed class lines: those who were both self-employed and 'living on own means'; those who were both employees and self-employed. The 'unemployed' neighbourhoods contained no individuals who crossed class lines in this way. Compared to the more prosperous 'fully employed' neighbourhoods, the neighbourhoods sheltering the unemployed had proportionately more young people, more men, and more unmarried people. Also overrepresented there were lodgers and recent immigrants.

At several levels these patterns of difference made it difficult for the working class to act as a unified whole on the issue of unemployment, or on any other issue. Vancouver's working class was divided internally by race, by income level, and by living spaces. The more stable and prosperous lived in close proximity to employers and the self-employed, in the more ethnically homogeneous British neighbourhoods. By contrast, most of the unemployed found themselves among less-rooted groups (lodgers, recent immigrants, Asians, single men), disconnected from labour's social and economic leaders.[24]

Vancouver's heaviest concentrations of unemployed were in subdistricts that included Chinatown, on Dupont and Carrall streets. Kay Anderson has explored Chinatown as both a physical place and an imagined geography, a cultural construct rooted in the symbolic system of European observers. Europeans saw Chinatown as a noxious mix of moral, social, and economic evils. One of the defining elements of that imagined Chinatown was unemployment, which was directly related to 'John Chinaman's' descent into depravity.[25] 'Many of the discharged railway hands are plunged in poverty, and as they can neither work nor borrow must either beg, steal or starve.'[26] Many labour leaders ignored, or failed to see, the Chinese workers' capacity for strikes and organized resistance and instead projected onto Chinatown their fear of surplus labour. Chinatown was the place where a 'surplus slave population' was 'thrown into our labour market against, and in unequal competition with our own people.'[27] By the early twentieth century a few labour writers, notably among the socialists, began to see Chinese immigrants as victims of capitalist exploitation.[28]

Concentrations of non-Chinese unemployed lived in streets adjacent to Dupont and Carrall, but neighbourly proximity did not foster collective action. Within the 'unemployed' cluster of subdistricts, the unemployed were split along racial lines: over 60 per cent were Asian. At this stage in the history of class and race in British Columbia, cultural and racial distancing divided workers who lived so near to each other that they must have walked the same streets and seen each other regularly. It was therefore unlikely that the unemployed themselves would generate common understandings and their own leadership from within their neighbourhoods. Some of the most virulent anti-Asian sentiment in Vancouver came from white workers who were at risk of being unemployed. Much of the argument against Asian immigrants was a defence of the *unskilled* white workers who lived near to the Asian enclaves: 'His garden produce would stand no chance as against Chinese competition, nor [would] his daughters find domestic work with families, or remunerative laundry work at home, from the like cause. ... The white is simply being crushed out of the manual labor market in British Columbia by the Chinamen.'[29]

Was it likely that the non-Asian unemployed would produce their own leadership through connections with the existing trade-union leadership of the city? Labour historians have not yet told us where every trade union leader lived, but they have provided an occupational and ethnic profile of the leadership. This elite tended to be of British origin, and from several, mainly craft occupations.[30] Our first hypothesis was that more prosperous workers in the categories from which the labour leadership emerged lived apart from the unemployed. In fact such categories were not underrepresented in the 'unemployed' neighbourhoods. A few carpenters, engineers, machinists, and other skilled workers who enjoyed above-average annual earnings did live there.

It is very unlikely, however, that these workers, who were most likely to be connected to trade unions or other organizations, made contact with the unemployed. Spatial distance is a highly relative and problematic concept, even when race is not a primary element in the construction of space, and especially when one attempts to make inferences about consciousness or action on the basis of space. It is quite possible for people to live in adjacent streets, or even in the same street, and disregard each other. Between the labour elite of our 'unemployed' neighbourhoods and the unemployed in the same streets, spatial distance still existed, and it was interwoven with other forms of separation. The severely unemployed were concentrated spatially, even within their own neighbourhoods. Of the 101 dwelling places in our 'unemployed' cluster, forty-six did not house any unemployed; four contained fifty-nine unemployed, or 44 per cent of all the severely unemployed in the cluster. This spatial distance overlapped with other differences that rendered the severely unemployed even less visible to the skilled labour elite living nearby. Two-thirds of members of that elite were heads of households; most were of British origin. The severely underemployed tended to be lodgers; 80 per cent were immigrants; most were Asian. For the British carpenters and machinists living between Dupont Street and the docks, success would mean moving to another neighbourhood, rather than taking collective action with the unemployed who lived next door.

At certain times and in certain places 'neighbourly proximity favours action,' but more than physical proximity is required for the act of resistance to register in the wider society. Within micro-social and small physical spaces 'a shared critique of domination' may well have existed, of course. James C. Scott has correctly pointed to hidden transcripts – 'critique[s] of power spoken behind the back of the dominant.' Self-help within Vancouver's Asian communities permitted material existence at some level, fostered social interaction, and encouraged forms of resistance. As a writer in the *Industrial News* put it, 'Here in the far West we join hands with a neighboring and friendly people *of our own blood*.'[31] The unemployed, however, rarely acted together as unemployed, to '[speak] directly and publicly in the teeth of power.'[32] The site of unemployment was itself 'contested terrain.'[33] The unemployed were isolated behind several overlapping barriers of physical and social distance. There were many such barriers, both between and within neighbourhoods. Far from uniting on the basis of a shared condition of joblessness, west-coast workers turned inward and fought bitterly among themselves, fracturing along lines of race, ethnicity, gender, and even intraclass status.[34]

The location of the unemployed in space could take different forms in different cities, depending on local social and economic structures. In Hamilton, the most industrialized of our six cities, just over half of all employees were in industrial production, compared to just under one third in Vancouver (Table 4.2). In Hamilton, almost three-quarters of industrial workers toiled in factories; in Vancouver, less than half (Table 4.4). Hamilton was a factory city, at the forefront of central Canada's industrial development: yet as Table 5.3 indicates, social and economic groups were more evenly dispersed than in Vancouver. Where one might have expected people to be more concentrated by class, ethnicity, birthplace, or occupation, they were less so.

As we have seen above, however, the unemployed in Hamilton were spatially concentrated. Fifty-six percent of the severely underemployed lived in thirteen of the city's sixty-four subdistricts.[35] By contrast, eight subdistricts had no people working less than nine months. As in Vancouver, per-person earnings and earnings of household heads varied dramatically between the two subdistrict clusters.[36] Yet social differences seem more muted than in Vancouver. Measured by the distributions of sex, household positions, marital status, family cycle, age, ethnicity, birthplace, and proportion of immigrants, the two clusters were virtually identical. The unemployed subdistricts had a slightly higher proportion of employees and a lower proportion of employers. The only measurable difference in occupational distribution was the higher proportion of general labourers in the unemployed subdistricts. Even more striking, both clusters contained the same proportion of factory workers.

Hamilton's unemployed were concentrated, and, apart from income differences, they and their neighbours had much in common with people in fully employed neighbourhoods. Unlike Vancouver, Hamilton in 1901 was not riven by ethnic divisions (see chapter 1). As we have seen, the interplay of ethnicity and class underlay the distancing of unemployed from fully employed in Vancouver. Given Hamilton's relative ethnic homogeneity, the unemployed could not be so easily segregated and defined as 'others.' Moreover, the thirteen subdistricts where the unemployed were overrepresented were more widely dispersed throughout the city's wards than was the case in Vancouver. Unemployment could not be so easily isolated as a condition of a working-class east end. Even in their own neighbourhoods, the unemployed were not easily identified or distinguished, and hence isolated, by personal characteristics. The comment of a sympathetic journalist, writing about the unemployed of Toronto in 1891, might as well be applied to Hamilton: 'If you want to learn where these people are, you will find them not clustered together in one spot, but scattered over the whole city and its suburbs, in the north some, but mainly in the centre, and in the east and west.'[37]

Unemployment in Hamilton was much more a family condition than was the case in Vancouver. It was not so easy to distance unemployment, to refer to it as a condition of single men, or recent immigrants, or lodgers. Almost one of every two families in the unemployed subdistricts sheltered a severely underemployed person. In fact 78.8 per cent of the unemployed in Hamilton were members of a nuclear family: husbands, wives, sons or daughters. Only 43.9 per cent of the unemployed in Vancouver were members of a co-resident nuclear family.

In Vancouver the severely unemployed could be distanced in a number of ways from the skilled labour elite and from those specific occupations from which trade union leaders were recruited. Workers in Vancouver's skilled occupations were relatively immune to unemployment; they might easily consider extended joblessness to be a condition of 'others.'[38] In Hamilton such distancing was more difficult. Among those who held such skilled occupations, including household heads, the probability of being unemployed was higher than for the rest of the working class.[39] In Hamilton, the more industrialized city, unemployment was more fully integrated into the experience of stable, co-resident working-class families. It was a pervasive condition of working-class experience there, affecting family relationships, expectations, and ambitions at every stage of the family cycle.

Despite substantial ethnic segregation in Winnipeg and Montreal, the patterns in those cities and in Victoria and Halifax resemble those of Hamilton rather than those of Vancouver (Table 5.3). The unemployed were overrepresented in certain subdistricts, but these were scattered through several wards. As in Hamilton, the most distinct characteristic of the neighbourhoods where the unemployed were gathered was the low average income of families. The unemployed could not be marginalized, even from the perspective of skilled industrial workers. In those cities, being without a paying job for more than a few months in the year was something that all workers, outside a narrow supervisory elite, had to fear.

Spatial analysis cannot tell us how consciousness of a problem was articulated. The various patterns of segregation evident in the cities under review here, however, impeded more than they facilitated the emergence of a collective expression of grievance on the part of the unemployed. In Vancouver, to be sure, the unemployed were concentrated to a degree not evident in the other cities. Yet, as we have pointed out, within such concentrations other barriers separated the unemployed from each other and from their neighbours. Different patterns of spatial and social division were evident in Hamilton, Montreal, Halifax, Victoria, and Winnipeg. In 1901, social characteristics did not, as in Vancouver, sharply separate the employed from the unemployed in these cities. The subdistricts within which the unemployed concentrated were not themselves as closely clustered as was the case in Vancouver. Equally important was the low level of segregation of the working class as a whole. Working-class voters were spread through many city wards; politicians were more likely to make pan-class than class-specific appeals.[40] Gathering together to articulate grievances and to consider collective action required transcending barriers of space: having incurred the costs of travel to and from their workplaces, workers had to travel again to meet each other during evenings or weekends. They did not live in the same streets; for a majority, the union hall was in another neighbourhood.

Working-class responses to unemployment occurred within these various spatial contexts. Their responses, while shrill, personal, and often insightful, were bounded by the social and physical spaces within which they lived their lives. Though the unemployed were concentrated to a degree, the spatial dispersal of both the working class and the unemployed was unlikely to yield a shared consciousness or a concerted campaign of resistance. There was no community of the unemployed. Whatever labour leaders may have foreseen, there could be no 'army of the unemployed.' Workers responded to the threat and the reality of unemployment, but in a fragmented manner. For many, the first response occurred within the family and household, and it is to these contexts that we now turn.

6

Family, Work, and Income in 1901

The unemployed who carried their black flags through the streets of Canada's cities in the 1890s spoke of the suffering of their families. Charity workers and social investigators also emphasized the distress of families when breadwinners were idle. Unemployment was a family condition, and family was a crucial line of defence against the impersonal tyranny of labour markets. 'In the same district, in a very neat house, a carpenter was found, a big, strong man, eager to work, who had done nothing for months. The signs of poverty were only too apparent, and on being questioned he admitted that his family were in want. His wife, by going out to work, earned enough to provide food, but not enough to buy fuel or pay rent. A neighbor gave him some shutters to mend, the first work he had had for a long time.'[1]

There are many such stories from the 1890s: responses to unemployment occurred not simply within the trade union, the friendly society, or the charity. The carpenter and his wife responded to unemployment by finding work, not through any institutions, but on their own. Together they provided for the survival of their family. In previous chapters we have asked who the unemployed were, where they worked, and where they lived. In this chapter we focus more closely on the people with whom they lived, a focus that encompasses the unemployed both as individual workers and as family members.

By situating the unemployed within a family we hope to provide a new perspective on the meaning of unemployment for the Canadian working class at the turn of the century and to add to the many links between family history and labour history. We hope also to add to the literature on the history of living standards. Few studies of unemployment have attempted to estimate standards of living for unemployed people. Conversely, the literature on living standards has provided only rough approximations of the impact of unemployment, or duration of work, on conditions for the working class as a whole. In this chapter we propose to build a bridge between these related bodies of literature. We provide, for the first time, a measure of family income that takes into account duration of work over the entire family cycle. In chapter 7 we expand the discussion to include costs of living in our sample of Canadian cities.

Most literature dealing with family income and living standards, while not ignoring unemployment, has been limited by the 'paucity of data' to which Michael Piva referred in 1979.[2] Michael Haines was reduced to categorizing unemployment in the following way: heads of households who had some income were employed; those with no income were unemployed. It is little wonder (but an inevitable consequence of data limitations) that he could suggest only that 'the decline in adult male earnings with age is clear, but an explanation remains obscure.'[3] Patricia Van den Eeckhout, in her study of the family income of working-class families in Ghent, Belgium, appears to ignore duration of work as a variable that might explain the variation in husbands' contributions to family income, even though her data source contained information on 'the total number of days lost by unemployment in the week considered by the inquiry.'[4] David and Rosemary Gagan, in their study of working-class living standards in late-nineteenth-century Ontario, have provided the most systematic effort to link earnings to duration of work. In so doing they have underlined the reality that known weekly or monthly wages have little to do with actual or potential annual incomes for individuals, because wage levels say nothing about the number of weeks worked in a year. The Gagans conclude that work duration was 'the essential determinant of standards of living for working-class families.'[5]

Unfortunately, as Bettina Bradbury has noted, the Gagans 'hardly mention the possibility of families having more than one earner or of other ways of getting by.'[6] Bradbury herself is most sensitive to the role of multiple breadwinners in a family. Her study of working families in Montreal demonstrates convincingly that few families survived on the income of the family head. Survival for working-class families was a collective endeavour. Her study shows the necessity of broadening the unit of analysis from family head to family as a whole, if income and standards of living are to be understood. Yet Bradbury, in part because her analysis stops in 1891, and because provincial sources on patterns of work are less rich in Quebec than in Ontario, deals less effectively with unemployment. She was unable to estimate the effect of joblessness on the living standard of Montreal families.

Ideally, what is required is a combination of the approaches of the Gagans and Bradbury. Equal concern for wages, duration of work, and family economy is required if we are to understand living conditions in major Canadian cities at the dawn of the twentieth century. The 1901 census allows us to explore precisely these variables. Of course the enumerators sometimes had a difficult task, and some newspapers reported general public reluctance to answer questions on income and other private matters. One noted the case of a 'maiden lady' who, even under the threat of court proceedings, refused to divulge her age, ancestry, and resources, considering such questions 'a piece of insufferable impertinence.'[7] Such resistance was, in fact, not widespread.[8] Of the 17,339 individuals who reported an occupation in our 1901 sample, 81.9 per cent provided information on earnings. Those who did not do so tended to be people of least immediate concern to enumerators – employers, people working on their own account, or people living on their own means. Only 7 per cent of employees failed to state their earnings. Moreover, 10,958, or 80.9 per cent, of the 13,537 people who called themselves 'employees' provided information on both earnings and months worked. The database allows us a fresh look at work duration, income, and the working-class family in early industrializing Canada.[9]

We begin with the earnings of the male household heads in our six cities, if only because heads contributed the largest proportion of family incomes. Their annual earnings, broken down by the age of the head, show a similar pattern to earnings of heads in the United States and Europe (compare Figures 6.1 and 6.2). In Canada, however, the average annual earnings of household heads dropped later – when heads were in their fifties. Furthermore, the decline was much less steep in Canada.[10] When heads were older, other family members began to compensate for the decline in heads' earnings.

Why did the heads' earnings decline at all? Two factors contributed to the decline: average monthly wages fell, and heads were increasingly vulnerable to unemployment. Which factor was the more important? Certainly the decline in work duration (or rise in unemployment) began first: average months worked in the year peaked for heads in their thirties, whereas average monthly wages peaked when heads were in their forties. But the decline in average monthly wages was more steep: aver-

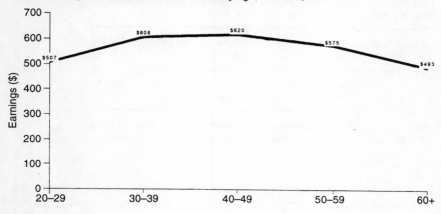

FIGURE 6.1

Annual earnings of male heads of household by age, six cities, 1901

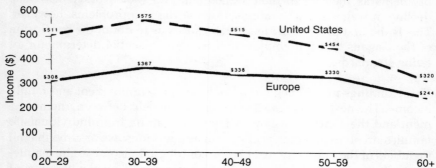

FIGURE 6.2

Annual incomes of husbands by husband's age, United States and Europe, 1889–90

age wages for heads in their sixties were 20.5 per cent lower than those for heads in their forties. The decline in average months worked was much less dramatic: a 5 per cent decline between heads in their thirties and heads in their sixties.

Perhaps the simplest way to show the relative significance of wages and unemployment is to ask the following question: which would have done more to maintain the annual earnings of heads, as heads aged – stable average wages, or stable employment? The answer is stable wages. If we leave average months worked as they were and hold average wages at their peak level, then annual earnings of heads would have

TABLE 6.1
Percentage of nuclear-family income contributed by family members
(where heads were employees), six cities, 1901

Sample type*	Heads %	Wives %	Sons %	Daughters %	Others %
I	76.8	0.6	13.4	4.7	4.5
II	78.0	0.7	13.2	4.5	3.7

*Sample type I includes families without wives as well as those where a
wife was present; sample II includes only families where a wife was
present.

been 20 per cent higher than they actually were when heads were aged
sixty or over. If, in contrast, we do nothing to average wages and keep
average months worked at their peak level, then heads' annual earnings
would have been 5 per cent higher. In other words, heads faced two
problems as they aged: their wages fell, and they worked less. The
decline in wages was the more serious of the two problems, however.
This is the first piece of evidence that causes us to doubt the conclusion
of the Gagans that full employment was 'the essential determinant' of
living standards.

These findings merely begin our analysis of unemployment and family
income. The next step is to look at the relationship between unemployment and the annual earnings of families. Shifting from individuals to
families involves acceptance of certain assumptions: we assume that all
members of the family living at home contributed income to the maintenance of the family.[11] It follows that when we add up the earnings of
individuals to arrive at family income, we offer an upper estimate of the
family's income potential. In adopting this procedure we do not imply
that the family was uncontested terrain or that exploitation within the
family did not occur.[12]

   Table 6.1 indicates the extent to which family income was a shared
enterprise in our six cities. For every dollar earned by the head of the
household, an additional thirty cents was contributed, on average, by
other family members. This places the Canadian family closer to the pattern in the United States than to that among families in many European
cities.[13] In one major way, however, Canadian urban families appear to
have differed from their U.S. and European counterparts: the contribu-

tions of wives in Canada were significantly lower than those of wives elsewhere.

There can be no doubt but that the Canadian census underenumerated women workers: the family of the carpenter who finally found 'some shutters to mend' had survived, after all, by his wife's 'going out to work.' Newspaper reports suggest that such practice was quite common: 'Where is your wife?' a reporter asked Mr Gloynes, a general labourer who was without work. 'She is out working,' was the reply. 'She makes eight or ten dollars a month scrubbing and doing chores.'[14] There is growing evidence that working-class families recognized the importance of married women's wage earnings.[15] Until somebody proves, however, that the Canadian census was unique in this underenumeration, we think it likely that the difference between Canadian families, and families elsewhere, was a real one.[16] Of course, wives in Canada, as Bettina Bradbury found for Montreal, made critical non-waged contributions to the family economy. For the wife of one wage worker, such efforts varied from 'putting the children to bed,' to dispensing 'with a doctor for reasons of economy' when 'in delicate health,' to helping her husband keep track of weekly expenditures.[17] It appears, however, that in so far as wage income was concerned, Canadian urban families relied more on children and others than on wives than did U.S. families for which comparable data exist.[18]

The relative contributions of family members were not static. Both family income and the contributions of family members depended critically on the nature and composition of the particular family. Here we find the concept of family cycle useful, and certainly more pertinent than age of household head. The concept highlights the severe differences in the household economy during the five stages of the family cycle (listed in Table 6.2): differences in average family income (column 6), in average per-person income in the family (column 7), and in earnings contributed by various family members. Table 6.2 confirms that the general patterns demonstrated by observers of American and European families also occurred in Canada. The data also underline the role of 'Others' and of teenaged workers, as the family matured and as the earnings of the head declined in both absolute and relative terms.[19] Clearly families deployed children into the labour force as those children became teenagers; prior to that, when the children were young, families depended rather more on the contributions of 'others.'[20]

Sending other workers apart from the household head into the labour force was a very common survival strategy. 'I think,' Herbert Bishop,

TABLE 6.2
Contributions to nuclear-family income by family members, by stages of family cycle, six cities, 1901

	1 Head (%)	2 Wife (%)	3 Son (%)	4 Daughter (%)	5 Others (%)	6 Average family income ($)	7 Average income per person in family* ($)	8 Number of families
1 Wife <45, no children	92.0	1.6	0.0	0.0	6.5	681	310	559
2 All children <10	94.5	0.4	0.0	0.0	4.4	619	197	1,362
3 Some children 10–14, none 14+	92.2	0.4	1.3	0.5	5.7	644	145	679
4 Some children 14+	57.5	0.5	29.8	10.4	1.8	986	187	1,566
5 Wife ≥45, no children	91.8	2.6	0.0	0.0	5.6	515	227	224

*In estimating per-person income by family, we divide the sum of annual earnings contributed by all wage earners in each family by the number of persons in each family, where all children under ten count as half a person.

TABLE 6.3
Unemployment by stage of family cycle, six cities, 1901

Stage	Families having at least one underemployed person*	
	%	No.
1 Wife <45, no children	9.6	581
2 All children <10	9.2	1,416
3 Some children 10–14, none 14+	11.1	703
4 Some children 14+	19.6	1,609
5 Wife ≥45, no children	20.2	243

*An underemployed person here is a person who reported working less than nine months in the year.

superintendent of a large Vancouver department store, noted in 1912, 'you will find where there is a family, there are others [besides the head] contributing to the support of the home.'[21] But what was the connection with unemployment? Was the deployment of second and third wage earners a means of coping with unemployment? It could be that the unemployed were clustered in certain types of family and that the family served as a kind of 'safe haven' in which waged and unwaged work of the majority compensated for the recurring joblessness of a few. If the family had such a function then we might more easily understand why it took so long for unemployment to be discovered and identified as a social problem.

To answer these questions, we need to know how unemployment was distributed among family cycles. Clearly the probability of finding underemployed people was highest in the last two cycles (Table 6.3). Furthermore, of all families having at least one severely underemployed person, no less than 50 per cent were in stage 4 of the family cycle. Moreover, in 52.4 per cent of those stage 4 families having a severely underemployed person, the head of the household was severely underemployed![22] Were families compensating for unemployment? Stage 4 suggests that some were: this is the stage when total family incomes peaked and when children contributed a larger share of family incomes than they did in any other stage.

An example of a family in stage 4 that coped with unemployment would be the Charland family, living in the St James Ward of Montreal in 1901. Edmund Charland was a sixty-two–year-old shoemaker who worked only six months and earned $312 in the year. Edmund was not the only underemployed member of this household: his son Arthur, a plumber, also worked only six months in the year. Here, in one household, were two common types of unemployment: that of the older craftsman and that of the worker in the highly seasonal building trades. Yet the family deployed other wage earners: Charland's thirty-three-year-old daughter worked for twelve months as a hairdresser, and another daughter worked in the home for twelve months as a milliner. The six-person household, including a sister of Edmund who reported no earnings at all, had a total annual income of $1,608. It was not among the poorest of working-class families, despite the underemployment of the household head and his son.[23]

The Charland family was probably better off in 1901 than it would have been ten years earlier, when two of the children were non-working dependants. In 1901 the per-person income in the family was $268 (this is merely the total earnings of all wage earners, divided by the number of consumers in the family, where children under ten are counted as half a person). Ten years before, when the family was in stage 3, per-person incomes were likely to have been lower, even if Edmund had been employed all year. This pattern was a general one: as Table 6.2 indicates, average per-person incomes were at their lowest in stage 3 and recovered somewhat in stage 4, when the family deployed more wage earners. Furthermore, when we group families into income quintiles (by per-person income) we find that, while stage 3 families were dramatically overrepresented in the lowest income quintile, stage 4 families were only very slightly overrepresented in the poorest two income quintiles. To this extent, the 'safe haven' hypothesis is confirmed.

There were, however, limits to the hypothesis. The sheltering effects of family existed, but they were fragile. The odds were very high that a family sheltering an underemployed person would find itself in the lowest family-income quintile. As the number of severely underemployed persons in a family rises, the probability of finding the family in a low-income category also rises.[24] Moreover 49 per cent of the severely underemployed were lone wage earners: while other family members must have worked in the home or in the informal economy, none earned wages. Even where the unemployed lived with other wage earners in their nuclear family, there were limits to the family's ability to compensate for the lost earnings of the unemployed. Compared to families with heads who worked nine or more months in the year, families with severely underemployed heads were not as successful in sending other family members into waged work.[25]

TABLE 6.4
Wages and months worked by stage in family cycle,* six cities, 1901

Stage	Average monthly wages	Average no. of months
1 Wife <45, no children	53.97	11.5
2 All children <10	51.50	11.2
3 Some children 10–14, none 14+	51.50	11.0
4 Some children 14+	42.79	10.5
5 Wife ≥45, no children	41.07	10.6

*Average monthly wages is the result of dividing total annual earnings of all family members by total months worked by all family members; average no. of months is the result of dividing total months worked by all family members by the number of employed persons in the family.

Furthermore, even as 'mature' families deployed more workers into the labour force, earnings did not keep pace with the number of mouths to be fed. Perhaps the most striking data in Table 6.2 are the figures for 'average income per person in the family.' Clearly per-capita family incomes never returned to the levels of the first family cycle, when younger couples had no children. Per-capita incomes in stage 4 did not return even to the levels of stage 2, when all the children were under ten. Particularly vulnerable were families in stages 2, 3, or 4 where the head was underemployed. An example was the family of Antoine Lepine, living in a rented house of four rooms on Avenue Taillefer in the St Antoine district of Montreal. Lepine was a labourer who earned $300 over nine months. No other family member earned wages, and probably his wife, Cécile, was fully occupied with the care of their three children, aged eight, seven, and one. Here was a poor family that could ill afford three months with no wage income at all.

The poverty of the Lepine family was the result of two conditions – both unemployment and the low wages that Lepine earned at his labouring jobs. As time passed and his family grew, Lepine could not expect to earn more: we already know that as heads aged, their monthly earnings and months worked declined. The vulnerability of many mature families results from the fact that the family as a whole experienced similar declines! As the family matured, the average monthly earnings of all workers declined, and the average work duration also fell (Table 6.4).

A good example is the Chorette family – ten people sharing five rooms in a house on rue Poupart in the Ste Marie district of Montreal in

1901. Louis Chorette, aged fifty-five, was a labourer who worked for four months in the year. His wife was not in the measured labour force, but his four older children were. Unfortunately all four were underemployed: the son, a carter, worked only five months in the year; two daughters were employed in a cigar factory for nine months, earning only $100 each; another daughter worked for only four months. Five wage earners in this family, all experiencing extended periods of 'lost time,' managed to bring in a total cash income of only $416. There were four dependent children aged between five and twelve.[26] Here is a dramatic example of a wider trend among stage 4 families: families put their older children into the labour force, but the younger workers, critical as their earnings must have been, earned a much lower wage than did their older kin.

As the Chorette family suggests, wage levels were the primary determinant of poverty. The average monthly wages of all five workers in this family was only $13.42. The low average wages of stage 4 families also reflected the way in which gender affected labour markets: many of the younger wage earners were women, and when they entered the labour force they might earn half or less as much as their male kin. Between stage 1 and stage 4 of the family cycle, therefore, the decline in average monthly wages was dramatic: monthly earnings fell by 20.7 per cent. Average months worked fell by only 8.7 per cent. Unemployment was a problem for working-class families, since, for whatever reason, they did not increase the total of working months to keep pace with family size.[27] But wage levels were still the more important issue: as families matured, the new wage earners they deployed could not earn enough to maintain per-person incomes in the family.

For families in stage 5 the incidence of unemployment was high, and there was a further problem: the family no longer had co-resident children in the labour force. Offspring living elsewhere may have contributed income to their needy parents, but their ability to do so was limited – this was precisely the time when they were trying to save for the future of their own families. Just when older parents were most vulnerable to unemployment and to lower wages (see chapter 3), their ability to rely on family support was limited. Annie McGregor of Victoria was the head of her household in 1901. She was a sixty-three-year-old midwife who told the census enumerator that she had 'not worked during [the] past year.' Her sixty-one-year-old husband James, a carpenter by trade, admitted that he too had made 'no earnings during past year.'[28] In the 1890s James had been employed by the Albion Iron Works, a major manufacturing firm in Victoria.[29] His lay-off reflects the general discrimination against older workers that we pointed to in chapter 3. Yet the McGregors were probably more fortunate than many in stage 5: they jointly owned their own house as well as one other city lot and a further four lots outside Victoria (though they owned no buildings on these lots); they had space in their house to take in a lodger (a common response for many in stage 5, as we note below in chapter 7). Clearly they had accumulated assets on which they could draw for a limited period.[30] Equally clearly, however, their words indicate a concern about joblessness. And well they should. Their city property was not worth much, and their joblessness was in all likelihood to be a long-term problem.[31]

A less secure, and probably more typical situation was that of Joseph and Julia Buckley of Victoria, aged fifty-one and fifty-eight, respectively. Neither brought in any earnings during the year. Joseph told the enumerator that he was 'looking for work of any kind.' The Buckleys did not own any property; they rented a five-room wooden house, and they had no lodger.[32] Even less secure was Alice Lawrenson, an eighty-year old widow, who lived alone in a three-room rented house in Victoria. As she told the enumerator, her 'living [was] almost entirely derived from charity.'[33]

The absence of co-resident wage-earners was likely to have been a problem for many, but we should not exaggerate the advantages that came from their presence. Having multiple wage earners often coincided with the presence of dependants in families. The figures for 'average income per person' in Table 6.2 suggested that low per-person incomes were associated with the appearance of children. What we need is a more sensitive measure of the presence of dependants. Unemployment, after all, was not a singular or unambiguous condition – something that individuals did or did not suffer from. It was also a relative condition: it was a lack of something needed or desired, and needs or desire existed in the context of one's relations to others. It follows that unemployment existed, and should be measured, in terms of an absence of gainful employment needed both by individuals and by families. Families were attempting to support members whose connection to labour markets was varied and fluctuating: there were adult workers who were employed for twelve months, adults employed for a small part of the year, children in school, children who helped the family in various ways, older adults who had left the labour force, and sometimes younger adults who, for reasons not appearing in the census, lacked a wage-paying occupation and were not 'living on their own means.'

In other words, families had wage earners and dependants. The word 'dependant' does not refer to people who did no work: children and older adults often worked very hard in support of the household, and their labour should not be interpreted simply as a means of releasing other family members to earn wages. 'Dependant' refers instead to those who benefited from some part of the wage income earned by others in conditions of increasing wage dependence by the family as a whole. Unemployment existed as a problem where the number of wage earners, or the amount of their returns, did not keep pace with the number of dependants.

The most accurate measure of unemployment therefore is not some artificial measure of unemployment 'rate,' but rather a measure of the ability of families to maintain per-person incomes as the number of dependants increased. By any measure that we can construct from the 1901 census, large numbers of families did not have this ability. In 59 per cent of working-class families, the number of dependants exceeded the number of wage earners.[34] Could these wage earners, outnumbered as they were, maintain the family's per-capita income as the number of dependants increased? The answer is no (Table 6.5).

It is not self-evident that per-person incomes should fall as they do in Table 6.5, because at the same time as families acquired more dependants they also deployed more wage earners.[35] These extra wage earners were not able to maintain per-person incomes in the family for two reasons: first, the number of workers in the family did not rise as fast as the number of dependants; second, and more significant, the extra wage earners worked fewer months and earned less on average than did the family's first wage earner (normally the head).[36]

To summarize the relationship among unemployment, wages, and family incomes, we move beyond the simple category 'severely under-employed' and construct a measure of 'family unemployment.' For every family, of whatever size, there was a rate of potential labour-force participation, which we may compare to its actual participation rate. Potential labour-force participation is the total months that all adults (aged fifteen and over) in the family might have worked in the year, if they had all been employed for twelve months. We construct this estimate in the following way: we subtract adults said to be living on their own means, and we subtract housewives on the grounds that they were already fully employed in domestic (non-waged) labour; we assume

TABLE 6.5
Per-person incomes by number of dependants
in the working-class family,* six cities, 1901

No. of dependants	Per-person income ($)	No. of families
0	368	281
0.5–1	281	908
1.5	240	479
2	211	776
2.5	172	415
3	169	475
3.5	157	289
4	134	250
4.5	119	162
5	135	136
5.5	122	80
6 +	109	122

*Dependants are the sum of persons in the
family, of whatever age, who had no
stated occupation, minus persons said to
be living on their own means; children under
ten count as half a dependant. Average
per-person incomes is the result of dividing
total annual family income by the number of
persons in the family, where children under
ten count as half a person.

that all other adults were eligible to participate in a wage-paid occupation. Thus the Chorette family, mentioned above, had five wage earners
in addition to the housewife: actual months employed were thirty-one;
potential months were sixty. The difference between potential and
actual months worked can be seen in two ways: it is a measure of the
extent of underemployment in wage labour; it is also a potential indicator of the extent of non-waged labour, or participation in the informal
economy.

Table 6.6 points to the three primary conditions associated with low
family incomes: average monthly salaries, family unemployment, and
the number of dependants. The gap between potential and actual
labour-force time was very high for families in the lowest per-person
incomes quintile. Similarly, families in the lowest income quintiles had
the most dependants.

TABLE 6.6
Labour-force participation, wages, and number of dependants by income quintiles, six cities, 1901

Per-person income ($)	Months worked		% difference	Monthly wages ($)*	No. of dependants
	Potential	Actual			
0–102.86	23.0	14.4	59.7	29.71	3.55
103–149.50	22.5	17.4	29.3	35.94	2.79
150–199.53	23.8	19.5	22.1	40.23	2.22
200–275	23.0	18.7	23.0	48.01	1.82
276–highest	21.4	17.8	20.2	84.01	1.49

*This is total annual earnings for each family, divided by the sum of months worked by family members.

Which factor is most helpful in explaining income differentials? Regression analysis suggests that average monthly wages by themselves explain 52 per cent of the variation in family incomes. Family unemployment explains at most another 5 per cent of the variation.[37] This does not mean that unemployment was not a serious problem for working-class families. Conditions of low wages, high unemployment, and numerous dependants went hand in hand; the converse was also true.

To explain this result even more simply, let us ask what it would take to solve the problem of poverty for those in the lowest per-person income quintile. First, if all adults were fully employed, but their average monthly wage remained the same, what would happen to families in the lowest income quintile? The result is a measure of the effect of full employment on the family, assuming no other change. The result is that 52.8 per cent remain in the same income quintile (where per-person incomes were below $102.86 a year). Twenty-eight per cent of families would have improved their incomes significantly – rising into one of the top three income quintiles.

Instead of changing a poor family's labour-force participation, let us change average wages earned by the family's breadwinners. Leaving unchanged the total months worked by family members, we alter only the average monthly wage for workers in the lowest income quintile, raising it to the average level for all workers in the higher quintiles. The result is a more substantial change in income status: only 22.4 per cent now remain in the lowest income quintile, and 42.4 per cent make it into the top three income quintiles. Here then is our best measure of the importance of unemployment to income-based standards of living. Unemployment was a serious problem for poor families, but it was a distant second to the problem of low average wages. These findings help to make sense of the priority that workers gave to wages in their bargaining with employers (a theme to which we return in chapters 7 and 8). A 'living wage' or a 'family wage' meant earnings sufficient to see the family through the anticipated times of joblessness and to allow the family to save for the time when there were more mouths to feed. Bargaining for permanent employment was less likely to succeed than was bargaining for a stable wage. 'Full employment' did not become the focal point of labour organizing and bargaining. It was instead a major force behind collective action over wages.

We have presented evidence on working-class incomes that takes into

account both duration of work and the presence of multiple wage earners in working-class families. The results are benchmarks for urban Canada in 1901. Unemployment cannot be understood simply as an
individual problem. One out of every seven Canadian families in 1901
sheltered at least one severely underemployed person – a person lacking waged work for at least four months of the year. Many other families had members out of work for one or two months of the year.
Unemployment was a condition the Canadian working-class family
during the nation's transition to industrial capitalism.

A more complete study of standards of living must recognize variation among cities in both wages and costs of living. A per-person
income of $102 would buy much less in Vancouver than it would in
Montreal. Furthermore, the relative importance of average wages and
unemployment, as contributors to family poverty, may vary considerably among cities. We examine these issues in the following chapter.

7

Living Standards and Survival Strategies

Unemployment was a condition of industrial capitalism, and it was part of the experience of life and work in the city. In this chapter we explore the relationships among city, unemployment, and family standards of living. The central issue of this chapter is how the unemployed coped. Were the patterns described in chapter 6 common to all six of our sample cities? Did unemployment have a greater effect on family incomes in certain cities? Historians in Canada are rightly sensitive to regional variations in incomes, unemployment, and economic structures as a whole. In contemporary neoclassical analysis, regional unemployment levels are critical, and barriers to labour mobility even become a cause of unemployment itself. There is, however, an even more obvious reason for a city-level analysis: to measure real living standards we must estimate living costs, and these varied among cities to such an extent that a national-level analysis would make little sense. After providing estimates of the number of families in each city that lived below the poverty line, we then examine how these families struggled to survive.

In chapter 6 we observed that average monthly earnings, work duration, and family cycle were key determinants of the income levels of urban families. The next question relates to city: how did income disparities vary among cities? Did families in certain cities avoid poverty despite unemployment? The 1901 census offers a unique opportunity to answer these questions. Our census sample permits an analysis of the distribution of annual income across urban space.

Previous studies of wealth distribution point to substantial inequities in the population as a whole.[1] These inequities did not go unnoticed by workers at the time: 'If a man drinks no beer, eats no meat, wears no clothes, he may get along. But he would get along just as well – better –

TABLE 7.1
Annual earnings of employees, by city, 1901

City	Men Mean ($)	Std. dev.	No.	Women Mean ($)	Std. dev.	No.
Victoria	559	463	540	294	239	73
Vancouver	546	418	904	353	220	110
Winnipeg	651	508	905	277	227	259
Hamilton	441	340	1,306	207	112	497
Montreal	484	353	4,740	217	176	1,838
Halifax	407	293	657	171	113	231

if he were dead. The capitalist swigs his bottle of Champagne in his opera box, and abuses the son of toil for his extravagance, forgetting all the time his wine and his box for that one evening would support a family for a week in comparative luxury.'[2]

This speaker nicely captures the differences in living standards among classes; in what follows we focus on the disparities within cities and on the variations in income within the working class itself. All historians of standards of living agree that there were marked differences in living standards among Canadian cities. Our evidence confirms the differences among cities and indicates in a dramatic way the disparities within cities. In contrast to most other calculations of urban living standards, however, our data permit a more specific delineation of variations within the wage-earning, or working, class. Our measurements reveal more clearly than ever before the material basis for well-known distinctions within the working class.

Table 7.1 presents average annual earnings of all employees by city, before we adjust for differences in living costs. While the difference among cities is obvious enough, more important are the standard deviations, which point to large variations within each city and underline the ubiquitous income differences between men and women.

Much more revealing than individual earnings is family income. We could show income disparities among working-class families in a number of ways. We could divide families into groups by total family income: the disadvantage of this method is that one- or two-person families might dominate the lowest income quintile, simply because such

TABLE 7.2
Working-class family-income distribution,* by city, 1901

City	Poorest 20%	2nd 20%	3rd 20%	4th 20%	Top 20%	Top 10%
Victoria	11.0	15.8	15.1	26.2	31.9	21.3
Vancouver	10.1	16.3	17.4	25.7	31.6	16.9
Winnipeg	9.4	14.1	19.3	22.0	35.2	21.5
Hamilton	12.4	13.8	18.9	23.0	31.7	19.6
Montreal	10.6	14.5	18.2	21.2	35.4	21.8
Halifax	8.6	16.8	18.6	19.9	36.0	21.3

*The income quintiles are the result of dividing total family income by the number of persons in the family, where children under ten count as half.

families had fewer earners. A better method is to group families, as we did in chapter 6, by their per-person incomes – the total incomes of each family divided by the number of family members. This method is more realistic because it takes into account the number of consumers within the family.[3] A poor family was poor precisely because its disposable income was low relative to the number of its members requiring food, clothing, and shelter.

Table 7.2 groups families into income quintiles for each city. The poorest 20 per cent were those one-fifth of all families having the smallest ratio of earnings to consumers. The table should be read as follows: in Vancouver, the poorest fifth of families had only 10.1 per cent of all incomes in the working-class population. The most affluent 20 per cent had 31.6 per cent of all incomes. Given that the data relate only to working-class families, the income disparities within each city are striking. The truly remarkable point about Table 7.2, however, is the symmetry across cities: in all cities the income disparities were very similar. Whatever the differences among cities, in their economic and social structures and labour markets, income disparities remained remarkably constant.

How did unemployment relate to these income disparities? We return to our measure of family underemployment in waged work, which we used in chapter 6: this is the difference between potential number of months in waged work, assuming full employment on the part of all adults in the family, and the actual number of months worked by those adults. This difference we refer to as non-waged time or unemployed time, with the understanding that family members experiencing such unemployed time may have been working inside the household or in the informal economy outside the household. In all cities but one there was a strong relationship between unemployed time and income quintile. The strongest relationship was for Vancouver, where the average unemployed time was 10.9 months for those families in the lowest income quintile. Those families in the highest-income quintile used virtually all available labour time (average unemployed time per family was only 0.8 months).[4] Among the poorest families, those who did participate in the labour force were not earning enough to compensate for the unemployed time of those outside the labour force. The 10.9 months outside the labour force was not therefore time that the family could afford for leisure or schooling. It was a cost to the family, which would have to be met by participation in non-waged work and by an ongoing search for remunerated work.

A different result might have been found, as was the case for Halifax: in this city there was no relationship between unemployed time and family-income quintile. The most prosperous working-class families had an average of 10 months of unemployed time on the part of their adults. Only here might this time outside the labour force be construed as a matter of choice or a benefit that the family enjoyed as the result of adequate earnings on the part of a principal breadwinner. The other possibility is that those in the labour force managed to command a significant wage premium from seasonal work, sufficient to allow longer holidays for themselves or other adults in the family. But only a very small minority of families could entertain such flexibility: most suffered significantly from the absence of income from potential waged workers, a point that can be established even more dramatically by an examination of the relationship between real income and unemployed time.

Income disparities were similar across cities, but how much does this tell us about real standards of living in each city? It remains possible that the poorest fifth in Vancouver had a higher real income than the poorest fifth in Montreal. We must now introduce costs of living, which varied considerably from city to city. The literature on costs of living is voluminous. The details of our cost estimates appear in Appendix B. The principles underlying the cost estimates can be stated briefly. The purpose here is not to estimate changes in living standards over time, as many others have done. It is rather to estimate differences in real living standards and to relate these differences to the extent of unemployment. It follows that we are interested less in the incomes and costs of 'average' families of specified sizes than in defining a minimum material standard necessary for the family to survive and reproduce itself in specific cities in 1901. In defining a minimum standard, we cannot borrow the family budgets presented by the dominion Department of Labour. The more detailed of these budgets appeared after 1901. More seriously, the Department of Labour, in common with government departments in other countries, was interested less in showing the minimum costs necessary for the survival of a family than in charting changes in the prices of commodities regularly purchased by working-class families.[5]

How then do we define a minimum standard of living? In common with other authors, we assume four main categories of living costs: food, shelter (including fuel and lighting), clothing, and other essential items. Our food allocations differ from those of the Department of Labour and are much less generous. We begin, as did Bettina Bradbury in her study of Montreal, with Seebohm Rowntree's adaptation of England's Local Government Board workhouse diet of 1901 for an adult male. Rowntree was attempting to create a diet of about 3,500 calories a day, one sufficient to sustain a man performing 'moderate muscular work.'[6] The diet is frugal and culturally specific; cheese rather than meat is the main protein source. We adjust the diet to North American conditions by substituting meat for cheese twice a week and making a few minor substitutions for such items as treacle and dumpling.[7] The cost of food for a woman aged fifteen and over is estimated at 80 per cent of that for an adult male; boys aged fifteen and nineteen are weighted at 85 per cent; children under fifteen are weighted at 55 per cent. The result is not a representative working-class diet, but a diet sufficient only for bare survival – for what, as one Victoria worker said, 'is rather short commons but it keeps us alive.'[8]

In estimating minimum housing requirements we assume modest rental accommodation varying according to family size, and we allow for overcrowding. The amounts and costs of fuel varied by city but made up a relatively large portion of family budgets in the Canadian climate; again our estimates are frugal. We allow for the purchase of a modest amount of clothing every two years. Survival in the Canadian city required other essentials, sometimes forgotten in estimates of living costs: water, soap, and replacement of some household equipment. Our budget allows nothing for medical care, schooling, newspapers, tobacco, or recreation, and we assume that all laundry was done in the home.

For each working-class family (nuclear family and kin, excluding lodgers and others, as well as single-person households) we subtract the

TABLE 7.3
Families and the estimated minimum living standard, by city, 1901

City	Real income		
	% below $0	% $0–$70	% above $70
Victoria	9.3	3.5	87.2
Vancouver	15.2	7.0	77.8
Winnipeg	15.3	8.1	76.6
Hamilton	12.6	9.2	78.2
Montreal	13.3	10.4	76.3
Halifax	26.2	11.2	62.6
All	14.4	9.5	76.1

sum of costs of living for all family members from the sum of earnings by all family members. The result is the real income standard for all families. The first column of Table 7.3 gives the proportion of families in each city where the total of family earnings was less than the minimum amount required for food, shelter, clothing, and other essentials. The second column includes families at the margin of subsistence.

There can be little doubt that for those under the minimum real income level the word 'poverty' applies. Two qualifications are necessary. First, 'measures of real income define the relationship between actual income and the cost of commodities; they do not measure individual decisions on the allocation of resources.'[9] Second, the difference between income and costs may also measure the extent of non-waged economic activity, or participation in the informal economy by family members. Certainly work by Bettina Bradbury on Montreal has demonstrated that working-class families raised pigs, cows, and poultry to help make ends meet. As she notes, however, the city passed by-laws against the keeping of animals, and such activities had declined sharply by the early 1870s.[10] Many families continued to cultivate small garden plots. There is evidence that keeping animals continued in other urban places. In Hamilton in June 1881 'ten head of cattle were grazing along Main Street and no person in charge.'[11] It was not until 1937 that the city council of London, Ontario, passed a by-law prohibiting cows from the precincts of the city.[12] The large proportion of people in Halifax under the poverty line (see Table 7.3) reflects in part the greater persistence of rural traditions. Halifax was slower than other centres to restrict the raising of animals within city limits. As late as the 1920s, families regularly kept pigs and cows in the working-class neighbourhood of Richmond Heights. Moreover, the ubiquitous street sellers hawking their fish and vegetables suggest the presence of a substantial barter economy in that city.[13]

What our procedure does clearly measure is the inability of the capitalist labour market to provide employment and incomes adequate for the survival of one in seven urban working-class families. Those families faced a situation similar to that which confronted Malcolm Douglas, his wife, and their twenty-year-old daughter. In April 1901, Douglas admitted to the census enumerator in Victoria that they 'have lost more than have made' over the past year.[14] To survive, a significant proportion of families had to draw on savings or function outside the wage labour market.

In every city a significant proportion of families had inadequate incomes. In only two cities was the proportion very different from one in seven: in Victoria only one in every eleven families lived below our 'poverty line'; in Halifax the proportion reached a remarkable one in four.[15] Our estimate of the extent of poverty in terms of real incomes is consistent with the measure of relative poverty in Table 7.2: the more narrow income disparities in Hamilton, Vancouver, and Victoria did not protect families there from the problem of inadequate incomes. Montreal, once assumed to be unique in the extent of its poverty, does not stand out in this comparative context. Relative poverty was symmetrical across cities; absolute poverty was not symmetrical but it was extensive.

Despite this overall structure of inequality, upward mobility on the part of both individuals and families may have taken place. Darroch and Soltow have argued that a structure of severe inequality in land ownership in late-nineteenth-century Ontario was mediated by life-cycle effects. Home ownership and landed wealth in general rose systematically with age up to about sixty years. They have suggested that even within a structure of inequality, where the top 10 per cent owned 60 per cent of all real estate wealth and the bottom 50 per cent 1 per cent, there was yet a real possibility for young men to acquire property at some point in their lives. As proof, they note that 86 per cent of all household heads owned some real property. Their analysis tends to confirm the image of Ontario as a society in which easy acquisition of land was the key to independence and security. Inequality did not prevent upward mobility: the latter cannot exist without the former. If Darroch and Soltow found that inequality was mediated by life-course effects in late-nineteenth-century rural Ontario, did a similar process take place in urban environments?[16]

There is a strong relationship between stage in the family cycle and the real income level of the family.[17] It suggests, however, that the hypothesis of Darroch and Soltow for rural Ontario does not apply to real income inequalities in urban Canada in 1901. Prosperity, as measured by real income, was most likely among young families – those in stage 1. As a Toronto carpenter put it in 1883, 'It was far easier to live 30 years ago, when I was courting my wife.'[18] The vulnerable phase in the family cycle was stage 3 (as we noted in chapter 6): just under one-third of families having only young children were below the 'poverty line.' Some families may have escaped from the problem of low real incomes in later stages of the family cycle, but in stage 5 more than one in five remained below or barely above the poverty line. There is no evidence here that movement through the family cycle was accompanied by upward mobility.

Security required stable employment, and, as we have seen, no stage in the family cycle was immune to unemployment (see Table 7.4). Unemployment was a common condition of the poor family: of all families below the minimum real income level, 32.3 per cent had at least one severely underemployed member; by contrast, only 10.5 per cent of those families earning more than $70 of real income contained a severely underemployed person. For all cities except Halifax, there was a strong relationship between having unemployed time and being above or below the poverty line.[19] Poor families were poor because they sheltered adults who could not find regular employment and because those with work could not earn enough to compensate for the non-waged time of others.

Poor families lived therefore in a condition of double jeopardy, struggling against the combined effects of joblessness and low wages. Not only did they lack stable year-round employment for all adult members; their jobs also yielded low average wages. The case of a Victoria carpenter who had been out of work for some three months underlines this point. When asked by a local reporter how he kept warm and what he ate, he replied, with 'a weary smile,' 'We don't keep warm. I haven't been real warm at home in six weeks, and as for the cooking, why there is very little to cook. I wouldn't care so much if it wasn't for my wife and little girl. They feel it most when a body is out of work. Still, I get an odd job occasionally.'[20] Such were the overlapping conditions of poverty: the worker was unemployed, and when he did find work it consisted of a low-paying 'odd job.'

Average monthly wages of those in families below the poverty line were only 55 per cent of average wages of those above. Living in poverty was the result of a short list of key conditions: the average monthly wages of all family workers, unemployed months, stage in the family

TABLE 7.4
Families and the estimated minimum living standard in each stage of family cycle, six cities, 1901

Stage	Real income			
	% below $0	% $0–$70	% above $70	% in each stage
1 Wife <45, no children	3.2	5.5	91.2	12.2
2 All children <10	14.7	12.4	72.9	29.7
3 Some children 10–14, none 14+	29.6	11.9	58.5	14.8
4 Some children 14+	12.4	5.7	81.9	34.1
5 Wife ≥45, no children	7.6	14.7	77.7	4.9
6 One-person families	19.0	17.0	64.0	4.4
All families	14.6	9.5	75.9	100

cycle, city, and occupation of the household head. Which of these variables were most important in determining the real income level of a family? If we turn each of them into category variables, analysis of variance (with real income as the dependent variable) suggests at least some order of causal priority. Average monthly wage and family cycle were the most important main effects. Number of unemployed months was also significant, and clearly more so than city, which was the least influential of the main effects.[21]

City, while significant, had less influence than the other factors. In urban Canada in 1901 one's chances of escaping poverty simply by moving from one centre to another were not high. Where the conditions of poverty were so similar across cities, poverty cannot be reduced to a regional problem, and the movement of surplus labour from one city to another was no panacea. The impact of industrialization worked itself out in various ways in different cities, but for many wage earners the effect was the same – high risks of unemployment most often coupled with low monthly wage rates.

More important than city was the association of low wages, specific occupations, and a high risk of unemployment – a link that existed in all six cities. Low wages were associated with particular occupations, which were overrepresented in families below the poverty line – none more so than that of general labourer, and being a labourer was not associated with any stage in the family cycle. There is no evidence of movement out of the vulnerable labouring occupations in later stages of the family cycle.

Yet family cycle, as analysis of variance confirmed, mattered a great deal. Family mediated the material conditions of individuals. Labourers are to be found in all cities, and in all types of family – but it was family condition that plunged them below the poverty line. Most families headed by labourers were able to meet the costs of living in the early stages of the family cycle. In stage 2, as soon as the family acquired dependants, most fell into poverty, as did the family of twenty-two-year-old James Fryon, a general labourer who had found eight months of work in Hamilton during the 1901 census year. James made only $240, and he and his wife, Martha, were the new parents of a seven-month-old son. The only way that they eked out a living on that sum was to share the costs of renting a five-room wooden house with another family of three. Just how Sam Hill of Hamilton, a thirty-five-year-old general labourer who worked for ten months and his thirty-four-year-old wife Bridgett, who had no recorded occupation, were able to feed and clothe their five children, all under seven, must remain a mystery. It is certain that they could not have done so simply on his $36-a-month income.[22] In stage 3, when there were no children over the age of fourteen, almost two-thirds of labourers' families were living below the poverty line.[23] They did so even though the average wages of their heads actually increased slightly in those vulnerable stages of the family life cycle.[24]

Only when we place individuals within the family can we understand their relationship to labour markets and to the material requirements of urban life. Occupation and family were key parts of a bundle of interacting effects. To assign primacy to any one is to oversimplify the reality of urban working-class life. Living in poverty was not random and unpredictable; it was a condition of family cycle, occupation, and employment duration among urban working-class families.

How did working-class families attempt to deal with the interrelated effects of unemployment and poverty? We begin by accepting, as a useful hypothesis, that there existed a 'family adaptive strategy,' or a collective response to changing economic and social conditions. As a recent review of the literature on family strategies has concluded, 'Depicting families and households as role allocating, income pooling, and income spending units is both intuitively compelling and empirically valid.'[25] The problems in using this analytical tool are, however, formidable. The

TABLE 7.5
Percentage of family income contributed by
nuclear-family members, six cities, 1901

Family members	Real income	
	Below $0	Above $70
Head of household	89.7	74.8
Sons	6.2	14.7
Daughters	3.0	5.0
Wives	0.2	0.7
Others	1.0	4.9

evidence for actions and their outcomes is available; the evidence for prior decision making is slender. The evidence for short-term responses is usually more abundant than that for long-term or cross-generational strategies. It is almost impossible to unravel the precise inputs to decision making of all family members, and in the late nineteenth century all members of the family did not have equal input into the process. Nevertheless, a shared problem was likely to prompt some form of shared response. Tentative as our test of the 'family strategy' hypothesis must be, we can offer some evidence about the interaction between family composition and opportunities in the local economic environment.

Most families attempted to supplement income, and in fully 70 per cent of families, both above and below the poverty line, every available adult person was in the labour force at some time during the year (housewives are again assumed to be working full-time at home). The opportunity to deploy wage earners other than the head varied, however. Having two or more wage earners was a characteristic of families above the poverty line: 38 per cent of such families had more than one income earner, compared to only 22 per cent of families below the line. Being above the line was in part a family-cycle effect: it was related to being in stage 1, when there were no dependants. It was also related to having more teenaged children capable of working compared to families in poverty, and this advantage was an effect of being at a more mature stage in the family cycle.[26] It follows that families above the poverty line were less dependent on the earnings of the head than were those below the line (Table 7.5). Put another way, moving above the poverty line depended very much on the availability of others, especially sons, who could find jobs.

For families with more daughters than sons of employable age, the capitalist labour market placed severe limits on deploying additional wage earners. As the Reverend William Stevenson of Victoria declared, the practice of paying young women low wages is 'compelling the female to make a contribution indirectly to the store. The remuneration is not sufficient to keep body and soul together. The parent has to come in and provide the surplus necessary for a living wage.' Mrs Mitchell, an executive member of the Women's Council in Victoria, was equally blunt: 'A great many employers pride themselves on not taking girls except they live at home. They're simply taxing the home for that girl's livelihood.'[27] In families below the poverty line the ratio of employable daughters (those aged fifteen and over) to employable sons was 1.7 to 1. In families above $70 real income there were more employable sons than daughters.[28] Sex ratios intersected with labour-market discrimination against women: the very presence of sons rather than daughters increased the chances that a family would not be in poverty.[29]

Many of the important contributions made by children, especially younger ones, to the family economy cannot be measured in a precise way: such activities as gathering wood and coal cinders for fuel, scrubbing doorsteps, rummaging in garbage heaps, and begging on street corners.[30] In this period working-class families also sent children under the age of fifteen into the formal workforce. Much of the literature on child labour begins by showing changes in the proportion of child workers in the total labour force. In Ontario's industrial establishments, for instance, children under sixteen made up 3.6 per cent of the workforce in 1901.[31] The 1901 census allows us to measure child labour differently: of all families having offspring under a specific age, what proportion sent them into the labour force? Despite truancy laws and legislation restricting child labour in factories, and despite the inevitable under-counting of working children, our six-city sample reveals that one of every ten families having children aged ten to fourteen sent at least one of those young people into waged labour. This finding would not have seemed remarkable to contemporaries such as Mrs William Forbes Macdonald of Vancouver, author of a paper on 'Employments for Women.' When asked by the Royal Commission on Labour in British Columbia in 1912, 'Do you find that many parents turn their children out to work at a low age?' she responded, 'They do. ... The Education law is not enforced about children going to school up to fourteen years of age.' 'The prices of food and living,' she continued, 'are so high that they are glad to get the few dollars a week.'[32] The employment of these children kept some families above the poverty line, a condition associated not only with the presence of sons but also with sending a higher proportion of available children aged ten to fourteen into the labour force.[33]

Sending youngsters into the workforce was, however, a double-edged sword. The need to supplement family earnings collided with the desire to keep children in school and to protect adult labour from cheap competition. Craft workers and the unskilled shared the fear of competition from other workers. In many industries the threat came from children: Montreal's garment workers regularly complained of being 'undercut' by farmer's daughters doing their work for half the wages.[34] In other sectors the threat came from boys. 'There are too many apprentices in a shop,' W. Johnston, a Halifax housepainter, complained. 'We have known two men to be in a shop and nine apprentices, and good mechanics with families, walking about in fine weather, and when the men are discharged the boys are kept on.' 'Work is very uncertain,' Arthur Marrion, a Victoria plumber, stated. 'The shops employ one or two good plumbers, according to amount of work, to do the intricate work and employ handy lads to do other work, by which means skilled workmen are not wanted much.'[35]

Clearly families below the poverty line had to employ other survival strategies. One obvious possibility was the taking in of lodgers and boarders.[36] Much has been written about boarding and lodging in the late nineteenth and early twentieth centuries.[37] Most authors have found it difficult to distinguish between those who did and those who did not accept lodgers and boarders.[38] Yet the process of accepting lodgers may not have been as random as many have implied. Our family income variables allow us to connect the presence of lodgers with family income levels. The ability of poor families to take in a lodger would have been limited by the size of their dwelling places. Nevertheless, many families below the poverty line made the effort, and, no matter the city in which they resided, poor families were more likely to have a lodger than were other families (Table 7.6). And despite probable space constraints, such families were more likely to accommodate multiple lodgers.

The benefit of lodgers should not be exaggerated.[39] Taking them in helped alleviate poverty for only a minority of families: four out of five poor families had no lodger at all. Poorer families in the western cities tended to adopt this strategy more than did their eastern counterparts – a reflection of preference and, given the larger number of recent arrivals, opportunity.[40] As well, more families in the west were in family-cycle stages that could facilitate accommodation of lodgers. It was easier to

TABLE 7.6
Lodgers and families below, at, and above minimum living standard, six cities, 1901

	Real income		
	% below $0	% $0–$70	% above $70
One or more lodgers	20.1	16.4	13.9
Two or more lodgers	11.2	8.6	5.9
Of families with lodgers,			
% having two or more	55.7	52.2	41.3

have lodgers in stage 1, before the arrival of dependants, and in the last stage, when dependants had left. The proportion of families with lodgers fell as the family grew, and presumably space constraints limited the ability to take in a lodger.[41]

It might be assumed that families with daughters would be more likely to take in lodgers or boarders: cleaning and cooking might be of greater economic benefit to the working-class family than underpaid wage work outside the home. The fact that more families below the poverty line took in lodgers and that such families had, on average, more daughters than other families might indicate that they were indeed using the labour potential of their daughters in that way. Some historians have found, however, that such families were in fact less likely to take in lodgers. Fears concerning the possible predatory behaviour of male lodgers may have motivated such decisions.[42] Our data tend to support the second of the two alternatives outlined above: only 15.1 per cent of families below the poverty line with daughters took in boarders; 40 per cent of families without daughters did so.

Taking in lodgers promised only limited returns, especially when their care and feeding required effort by one or more family members.[43] It is clear, for example, that Jill Stewart, a fifty-five-year-old married woman in Hamilton whose husband no longer lived with her, could not have made ends meet simply through her stated occupation of 'boarding mistress.' Though she had no other family members living with her and at the time of the census rented to seven lodgers, her declared annual income was only $200. This sum fell short of what it would have cost her to rent, furnish, and heat the thirteen-room, brick house in which she lived. She may have adopted the same strategy as Mrs Jane Saunders, a thirty-nine-year-old widow with two children aged twelve and thirteen, who operated a boarding-house in Victoria in the early

1890s. She looked to the British Columbia Benevolent Society, a local charitable organization, for assistance in her family's struggle to survive.[44] So, too, did Annie Glover, a thirty-year-old widow with three children under age thirteen, who, though she operated a small boarding-house, needed help from the Benevolent Society.[45]

The $1,500 grossed by Agnes Symonds, a seventy-year-old widowed landlady in Halifax, who fed and provided rooms for fourteen lodgers, might suggest that a larger-scale operation could result in a comfortable income. Perhaps, but when the expenses of hiring four domestic helpers, including a cook, of renting a sixteen-room wooden house, and of feeding her lodgers are deducted, Mrs Symonds would have been left with about seven per cent of her gross income for her own use – barely enough to meet her own food, clothing, and health needs.[46] The preferred strategy adopted by poor families was clearly to deploy a wage earner other than the head whenever possible. A few tried to do both: 16.2 per cent deployed a wage earner other than the head and took in a lodger as well.[47]

Until now we have looked at immediate or short-term strategies for survival. Are there indications that families attempted a more long-term approach? It is possible that young couples, at the least vulnerable stage of the family cycle, were able to save or invest earnings so as to mediate the material pressures incurred in later stages of the life cycle.[48] It would have required substantial foresight, conscious savings, and much sacrifice, over a number of years, for families to compensate for the income shortfall so common in stage 3. As Elyce Rotella and George Alter have suggested, there will be some working-class families who had the capacity to accumulate sufficient savings to help cover deficits incurred in later stages of the family cycle.[49] Clearly, too, some Canadian working-class families were able to put funds in postal and government savings banks.

It is probably impossible to know how many young couples saved portions of their earnings for later use.[50] The capacity to save was limited. Paul Johnson, in his classic study of the working-class economy in Britain in this period, has concluded that there was 'an insignificant amount of aggregate working class hoarding' of money in shoe boxes and the like at home. Moreover, he states, when workers saved they did so for short term reasons: most believed that they would never live to retirement age. His analysis shows that workers were a minority of those who deposited money in saving institutions.[51]

'Yes, I did put money in the bank, thirty dollars, the summer before last,' a thirty-nine-year-old day labourer and father of six told a *Globe* reporter, 'but I drew it out in three instalments last winter to pay for rent and coal.' When the same reporter commented to an independent tradesman that 'sober, industrious labourers who have earned but a dollar a day own their own homes and have money in the saving banks,' the tradesman was quick to reply: 'You don't say so; I don't believe it.' He thought that such a possibility may have existed twenty years earlier, but not under current conditions.[52]

The most detailed study of the operations of a government savings bank in Canada – that by Bunbury on Halifax – concludes that few of Halifax's working poor could afford to use the bank and that even that small number declined as industrialization advanced.[53] Even the data of Rotella and Alter for the United States in 1889–90 suggest that the capacity to save was limited to workers in high-wage occupations or families benefitting from substantial employment of children at early ages. Our data also indicate that the ability to save was limited by time and by occupation. The stage of relative prosperity was short for the overwhelming majority: stage 1, when couples had no children, was much briefer than stages 2 and 3. The phase prior to marriage offered no relief either: almost a third of young unattached individuals (single-person families) were living below the poverty line.[54] For many families the life cycle was a roller-coaster, not a ladder: a brief period of security was followed by uncertainty and the need to provide for dependants. Security in old age depended on whatever one might have saved and/or the ability of children to provide assistance at the same time as they were forming their own young families.

Long-term security could depend on the ability of sons to obtain better jobs than those of their fathers. For families headed by labourers there is clear evidence of occupational mobility across generations. Of all sons of heads in general labouring, 87 per cent aged fifteen and above had an occupation, and only 23 per cent of those occupied sons were labourers. The rest were in other occupations, especially manufacturing.[55] Where household heads were in the most vulnerable of occupations, sons were clearly attempting to break out of an occupational ghetto.

The Kidd family of Hamilton is one example of a family making a concerted effort to raise their status within society.[56] Their experience also provides some support for the argument that even though a degree of altruism may have existed when parents made sacrifices for the sake of their children, it was limited by a powerful desire to benefit from their children's paid work.[57] Samuel Kidd, the household head, was a forty-nine-year-old general labourer who found only seven months of wage work during the year. Neither he nor his wife, Elizabeth, could read or write. But all seven of their children could do so. William, their oldest son, was a machinist who worked twelve months during the year, as did their twenty-year-old daughter, Martha, who worked as a packer. Thomas, aged seventeen, worked for twelve months as a general labourer. Three of the other four children were under thirteen and were in school, a fifteen-year-old daughter was not at school and did not have an occupation. The evidence of a search for upward mobility is clear: the children had more schooling than the parents; the eldest son had a more skilled occupation than the father. Perhaps more remarkable, the family lived in a brick house; it had a female domestic servant, whom it paid $150 a year; and Elizabeth, Samuel's wife, had no occupation outside the home. Both the presence of a servant (extremely rare among families where the head was unemployed), and the absence of a labour-force occupation for the wife, are conditions that historians have traditionally associated with middle-class status.[58] Here was a family that compensated for the unemployment of the head, and did even more – invested in the future of the children. Yet there was a price to be paid for the marks of status, and it was paid by the children. All earnings of the children had to go into family revenues to cover minimal living costs, the rental of a brick home, and the cost of a servant.[59]

This family illustrates a convergence of tensions and ambitions on the part of the patriarchal working-class family. At what point would the sons and daughters be able to save for their own family formation? Who determined that individual discretionary spending would be forgone in order to hire a maidservant and to live in a relatively expensive brick home? The internal decision-making process is hidden, but unemployment certainly affected it, because the lost earnings of the underemployed head must have cut deeply into all decisions on revenues and expenditures. Family survival strategies were not simply a response to material need; they were also, at times, a function of social ambition and pride.

Finding a more stable occupation was one response to unemployment; a related response to the overlapping threats of unemployment and poverty was spatial mobility. Perhaps the clearest testimony to the determination to find work lies, as we have indicated in chapter 4, in the willingness of Canadian workers to move in search of work. Though informal networks for the transmission of employment information existed throughout the working class, workers were also aware that such networks did not always solve the problem. 'I have friends all over the Coast,' an unskilled labourer in Victoria explained, 'and from what they tell me I can't see the use of jumping from the frying pan into the fire by moving just now.'[60] A skilled tradesmen echoed this appraisal: 'I wrote away several times last winter to find out how times were elsewhere, but I could not see they were much different in other places.'[61]

For other reasons, too, geographical mobility was an imperfect answer to unemployment and poverty. It was difficult for those workers who did move, and especially for those who did so often, to take full advantage of their right to effect political change. As Wilkinson noted in 1912 in British Columbia, the result of moving around 'is that whilst we have adult male suffrage a man may register in a certain electoral district and may be fully qualified in every way, and yet by reason of the occupations which men have to follow when election day comes he may be a long way from the place where he could exercise his franchise.'[62] The approaches employed by workers to better their positions in society overlapped: the exercise of one could weaken the utility of others.

Finally workers testifying before the dominion Royal Commission on Labor in 1887 state that mobility was costly and uncertain:

Q. What I say is, if longshoremen are so badly treated in Montreal, why do they remain here?
A. They cannot help it, because a man has his wife and his family.
Q. It does not cost much to go away?
A. It costs a good deal. If a man is able to go away he may have to leave his family behind him, and may not be able to take them with him.[63]

It is not surprising, then, as we noted in chapter 4, that those in occupational groups most vulnerable to unemployment were the least able to hit the road in search of work. Those in the most vulnerable occupations were also those who, on average, could ill afford to move any considerable distance in search of alternative employment.

Family survival depended more than ever on adaptation to the vicissitudes of wage labour: the most obvious methods of survival occurred in the formal and informal negotiation with employers. The fear of lay-off affected that bargaining, since workers expected wages sufficient to tide them through periods of unemployment. 'The carpenter stores up for the winter like the squirrels,' declared J.A. Key, of the Amalgamated Society of Carpenters and Joiners of Vancouver.[64] 'I have like many others of my trade been out of work. But this is rather to be expected,' a skilled brick-layer in Victoria explained in March 1893. 'You see we get big wages, gen-erally $5 per day when we do work, and that is because we are not supposed to have steady work as some other trades would afford.'[65]

When we control for variables (such as sex, age, and occupation) that could have affected average monthly wages, we find that the latter were indeed *higher* for those who faced the prospect of prolonged unemploy-ment during the year. This result actually appears above in Table 3.9, where the exponent for average monthly earnings was slightly above one (1.01), when we controlled for the other variables. Thus a unit increase in average monthly earnings was accompanied by a small but significant increase in the odds of being unemployed.

The pattern is not ubiquitous in our Canadian urban sample of 1901. It appears among male manufacturing workers in Montreal and among specific occupations (masons, house builders, machinists, and long-shoremen, for instance). It is noticeable also among male general labour-ers in Montreal. It is weaker, for whatever reason, outside Montreal, among women, and in white-collar occupations. A few results of a lengthy comparison of mean monthly wages appear in Table 7.7.

These findings are consistent with the results of a study of Michigan workers in the 1890s which showed that workers were often aware of the risks of seasonal lay-off in certain jobs. Either they avoided jobs car-rying a high risk of lay-off, or they accepted such positions only after a process of informal bargaining: they demanded and received a wage premium if the lay-off risk was high.[66] The bargaining occurred on both sides, of course: some employers were offering lower monthly wages when they knew that they were likely to want to employ people for a full eleven or twelve months in the year.

Whatever the wage premium some workers might have won to com-pensate for the risk of lay-off, the victory was small. The occasional gain in monthly earnings, achieved through either a union or informal bar-gaining, was rarely enough to offset the effects of unemployment over the year. As the Victoria bricklayer quoted above admitted: 'I don't say they got much ahead.'[67] The presence of a wage premium for jobs subject to lay-off is important, however, for what it suggests about worker-employer interactions and understandings. The fear of unemployment and the risk of lay-off fuelled the drive for a 'living wage' at the end of the nineteenth century.

Survival depended on much more than wage bargaining. Many families

TABLE 7.7
Monthly wages of underemployed and more fully employed (selected subsets of workers), 1901

Subset	Mean ($)	Std. dev.	F	Sig.
Montreal manufacturing employees:				
French-Canadian male heads aged 20–45				
Working 1–9 months	49.18	20.93	8.41	.004
Working 10–12 months	41.58	16.04		
Montreal general labourers:				
French-Canadian male heads aged 20–45				
Working 1–9 months	37.26	11.80	8.27	.005
Working 10–12 months	31.72	7.62		
Montreal general labourers:				
male heads of British origin aged 20–45				
Working 1–9 months	35.15	8.25	7.29	.009
Working 10–12 months	30.26	5.30		
Montreal transport workers:				
French-Canadian male heads aged 20–45				
Working 1–9 months	62.19	56.74	12.44	.001
Working 10–12 months	35.42	7.68		
Montreal masons and brickmasons:				
Working 1–10 months	63.04	38.50	7.82	.008
Working 11–12 months	33.21	16.51		
Hamilton manufacturing employees:				
male heads born outside Canada aged 20–45				
Working 1–9 months	57.07	23.89	9.94	.002
Working 10–12 months	43.57	15.48		
Winnipeg manufacturing employees:				
male heads of British origin aged 20–45				
Working 1–9 months	67.27	20.79	1.96	.166
Working 10–12 months	59.21	21.66		
Vancouver general labourers:				
male workers of British-origin aged 20–45				
Working 1–9 months	48.28	10.06	2.45	.131
Working 10–12 months	41.24	11.56		

attempted to make use of resources within the wider community, severely limited as those were. Though this period saw the decline of retail credit and its replacement by cash sales, local shopkeepers continued to be counted on for support. In order to make it 'over a space when times are dull,' workers depended on the accommodation of businessmen who, according to one Victoria artisan, 'are usually willing to do the best they can.' In 1886 a character in an anti-Chinese 'farce' in Victoria voiced the concerns of creditors: 'Already the boarding-house and saloon-keepers in this city, and throughout the country, lead anxious lives over the credit they give to half destitute men; and only a big gold find in the spring can avoid a crisis.'[68]

Members of local communities were willing to extend credit, albeit reluctantly. Those who lived elsewhere, like absentee landlords, had different attitudes. In January 1890, William Moore, of Moore and Davis, a Hamilton-based real estate firm, informed W.J. Aitken, of Detroit, that one of his Hamilton renters 'is considerably behind with his rent,' having been unemployed 'for five weeks.' Moore, the local agent, advised Aitken that since the renter had 'been there a long time we do not want to distrain if we can help it.' Aitken disagreed, and the bailiff was called. In other economic sectors, too, traditional community networks were dissolving in the face of competition from larger, more centrally based manufacturers and retail outlets, many of which, like Eaton's, attempted to do a cash-only business.[69]

Working-class families had little hope of borrowing from banks and trust and loan companies. As in Britain, pawnshops in Canada probably provided cash to many hard-pressed working-class families, though to date there have been no systematic studies of such activity.[70] Moreover, as in Britain, the household goods of Canadian working-class families served as collateral to raise capital during times of unemployment. In fact, lending and borrowing on such collateral were widespread in Victoria and Vancouver and undoubtedly in other cities. In Victoria in October 1892, William Henry, a twenty-six-year-old unemployed expressman and his wife, Laura, mortgaged their household goods and assorted chattels for $302. In August 1894, Ed Adams, an unemployed clerk, used his piano as collateral for a $200 loan. In New Westminster, in August 1888, Mabel Claire, a woman whom the registering clerk called 'a hook,' mortgaged her mattress, bedroom suite, and household furniture for $373.[71] A preliminary examination of the government records relating to such activity reveals that a significant number of working-class men and women borrowed in this manner, but most of those who did so were from occupations that were among the least likely to be affected by unemployment. Those most at risk of job loss were the least desirable from the point of view of discerning lenders.

Colonial and provincial governments permitted municipalities to provide outdoor relief, and this form of seasonal opportunity certainly provided some assistance to the unemployed, especially in winter. As our discussion of the Ottawa demonstrations in the latter 1870s indicated (see chapter 2), workers did not hesitate to petition city councils for such employment. Working-class families also showed considerable ingenuity in using local institutions, such as houses of industry and orphanages, to shelter children or the elderly when the family faced unemployment and starvation.[72] Municipal responses were increasingly seen by the working class and others, however, to be insufficient. A comprehensive social welfare system did not exist in any of the jurisdictions under review in this book. Moreover, throughout the century public and private philanthropy carefully distinguished between the deserving and the undeserving poor. When Mary Dowling and her husband applied to Toronto's House of Industry for relief in 1882, the interviewer was clearly unimpressed and recommended 'a little starvation until self help [is] engendered.'[73] And even for the deserving, the principle of 'less eligibility' underlay the provision of aid: work conditions were to be worse and income levels lower than those of the least attractive and lowest-paid occupation.

Faced with unprecedented numbers of people without work in the early 1890s, local councils were sometimes persuaded to offer modest additional support. We offer the following case study of public philanthropy and the unemployed and destitute in Victoria as probably being representative of activity in the other cities considered in this book.[74] Victoria's council went so far as to replace a machine with men: it put the city-owned rock crusher in mothballs and allocated $1,500 for the hiring of unemployed men to work in parks and break rocks for $1 per day.[75] When some men protested that such a sum was hardly sufficient to feed a family and that it was less than half what a regular outdoor city worker received, the local paper could not conceal its contempt for such ingratitude and was 'pleased to know that the meddlers have not been successful in upsetting the arrangements.'[76]

Yet, as in Ottawa some twenty years previously, it was those very same 'meddlers' who, by organizing public meetings of the unemployed and presenting petitions to the council, had forced the city to take at least some token action. The names of the organizers never appeared in the public press, though some are preserved on the petitions they sent to council.[77] Appearing in the press instead were the names of the city elite, who wanted the public to see that they were in control of the situation. Thus a Citizen's Relief Committee, composed of many of the community's leading men, was formed to deal with the unemployed. Even its members were unhappy with the council's piecemeal response. When T.J. Burnes, president of the oldest and most

prominent local charitable organization, the British Columbia Benevolent Society (founded 1872), learned that the city's charter required the
municipality to 'make suitable provision for its poor and destitute' and
that the city was reimbursed for 25 per cent of such charitable expenditures by the provincial government, he complained that 'the corporation
should have given more help than they had.' The mayor argued that it
had done enough and that to do more would 'advertise for people outside of the city to come and register themselves as paupers.'[78]

In fact the city had established a budget item called the 'Charitable
Aid Fund' in 1892 and was quite diligent in its attempts to recoup the 25
per cent from the province. Given that provincial governments required
municipalities to look after their resident poor, it is no surprise that cities such as Victoria became more active in dispensing charity. That city's
Charitable Aid Fund rose from $511 in 1892 to a peak of $2,508 in 1895,
averaging about $1,100 a year from that point through 1901. The fund
helped to underwrite the philanthropic activity of several local charitable agencies as well as directly providing a few individuals with small
grants of money for food and lodging. In addition, the city, as we have
seen, created make-work projects to alleviate the distress of some workers in 1894. Finally, council also underwrote the establishment of an Old
Man's Home in 1891 and a Home for Aged and Infirm Women in 1897.[79]

The fact that the president of a prominent charitable organization
which appealed each year for a donation from the city was unaware of
the legal context the city's involvement in charity provides yet another
instance of the uncoordinated and haphazard nature of the relief process. For its part, the British Columbia Benevolent Society struggled
valiantly to meet the growing demands on its limited resources. In
December 1890, it had a surplus of $1,611, the largest in its history.
Between January 1890 and December 1894, it had expended $7,147 on
relief. Subscriptions from the wider community, on which the society
depended for its activities, had 'fallen off' by two-thirds from the level
of 1891. In October 1895, because of insufficient contributions, the society was unable to provide any relief.[80]

Given an economic downturn and declining subscriptions, the criti-
cisms of the city council made by the society's president, T.J. Burnes,
could be read as reflecting a desire to overhaul the existing system of
relief. Far from it. He and the organization he represented were, in fact,
quite wary of too great a presence for the state in charitable matters. In
1896, the Benevolent Society's annual report noted that, though private
'subscriptions have materially fallen off,' state support was not the solu-

tion. Such support, 'if persistently adopted must tend to curtail and dry up charitable and philanthropic feelings amongst the people for love and charity which are spontaneous and voluntary are incompatible with forced contributions levied by law.'[81]

It was to this very same spirit of 'love and charity' that the Citizen's Relief Committee appealed in February 1894. The committee solicited private donations, offers of work, and gifts of food to alleviate the growing distress. In response, several major employers hired men at $1 per day, for which they received copious public thanks from the committee and from the local paper. Even over hirings, committee members complained of a lack of coordination between the city council and itself; the hiring of the same individuals by both groups prevented the widest distribution of relief. The committee's 'intention,' one member explained, 'was to employ as many men as possible one week, and lay them off so as to give another set of men a chance the next week, and so in some measure evenly distribute the relief.' Implicit, but unstated, such a strategy conformed nicely to the principle of 'less eligibility.' The necessity for such a strategy also underlines the limited resources forthcoming for unemployment relief. Indeed, cash contributions were meagre, totalling only $127.90, of which $111 came from the employees of the Canadian Pacific Navigation Company, a group that received no special thanks from either the committee or the local press.[82]

In the depressed conditions of the 1890s the scope of 'love and charity' narrowed. The British Columbia Benevolent Society had long prided itself on its ability to meet the pressing needs of any worthy poor in the local community, no matter their 'creed, colour or nationality.'[83] Surviving records suggest that the society attempted to alleviate the needs of single as well as married men, of women, of families, and of young and old. The events of the 1890s quickly overwhelmed this liberal attitude towards aid giving. New participants began to appear in charity efforts, who, by redefining somewhat the definition of needy, shunted the Benevolent Society and its principles to the sidelines.

In Victoria the dispensation of aid became increasingly feminized. Local women felt that the city was unfairly ignoring elderly women in favour of elderly men. Thus, on the heels of the establishment of an Old Man's Home, women successfully petitioned the city for construction of an equivalent home for women. Though some in the wider community wondered if impoverished women were somewhat reluctant to approach the male-run Benevolent Society for aid, such was not the

TABLE 7.8
Relief given by the British Columbia Benevolent Society, 1890–5

Sex of receivers	No. of individuals	Benefits received		Amount received	
		No.	No. per person	Total	Per person
Men	307	675	2.2	2,405	7.83
Women	277	873	3.2	3,690	13.32
Unknown	233	260	1.1	1,548	6.64
Total	817	1,808	2.2	7,643	9.35

Source: All receivers of aid as listed in the society's monthly returns have been entered into a computer file for the period examined. BCARS, N/D/B77, British Columbia Benevolent Society, Minute Book, vol. 1.

case.[84] Between 1890 and 1895 a greater number of men received benefits than did women, but in isolation this statistic is deceiving. The case of Mrs Bessie Rosson is more revealing. She had four children. The eldest, Annie, worked as a nurse maid, and her husband was a general labourer. Bessie, not her husband, George, went to the Benevolent Society twice in 1891 for money for groceries.[85]

As Table 7.8 indicates, individual women went to the Benevolent Society more often than men and received on average a much higher dollar value in benefits. As Table 7.9 shows, these differences were fairly constant throughout the period under review; women, not men, were the primary receivers of aid. When several women affiliated with the recently established Provincial Council of Women of British Columbia established the Friendly Help Society in Victoria in February 1895 they were paralleling a process of feminization already in place at the level of receiver. As Pitsula has noted in his study of Toronto's House of Industry in the early 1880s, poor families relied when possible on women to solicit aid from charitable organizations.[86]

The Friendly Help Society's aims were significantly different from, if not at odds with, those of the male-run Benevolent Society. At the outset the Friendly Help Society wished to receive and repair old clothes and then, since 'our object was to make people independent + help them to keep their self respect, + not make paupers of them [they sold] the articles at a very low price rather than giving them away.' By comparison, the Benevolent Society gave cash or vouchers to needy applicants for the purchase of clothes and other essential goods. Unlike the Benevolent

TABLE 7.9
Recipients of relief from the British Columbia Benevolent Society by gender (where known) and by year, 1890–5

	Men			Women		
Year	No. of persons	No. of benefits	Amount ($)	No. of persons*	No. of benefits	Amount ($)
1890	29	70	294	42	113	531
1891	58	116	473	52	103	491
1892	61	110	441	48	107	514
1893	74	154	568	88	231	944
1894	108	175	481	102	216	851
1895	34	50	148	58	103	353

Source: See Table 7.8.
*These figures include repeaters from a previous year; therefore the total will be larger than that found in Table 7.8.

Society, the Friendly Help Society did not set up an employment registry, and it early decided that 'no single man be helped ... as the Association had as much as they could do in helping families.' Finally it took systematic measures to ascertain the worthiness of all applicants for aid. It divided the city into districts and appointed 'visitors' for each area.[87]

Discussions did occur about possible amalgamation with the Benevolent Society, but the men agreed with the Reverend Canon Beanlands, who 'while approving of working in harmony with the Ladies Society thought the proposed arrangement should be one of segregation than of amalgamation and so that the women would look after women's work and the men after mens.' Pressed by the women, they did agree to exchange monthly lists of applicants in order, as the Friendly Society put it, 'to prevent a repetition of alms be[ing] given to any one individual.'[88]

Of what relevance is this minor turf war between men and women to the needs of the unemployed poor? In fact, Reverend Beanlands and the Benevolent Society men failed to understand that what was really at stake was less a matter of gender and more an issue of redefining the needy poor. On this central issue the women correctly divined the attitude of the wider community, on which they, as did the men, depended for funds. The needs of single men, by far the largest group of applicants for aid at the depth of the economic disruptions of 1893 and 1894,[89] were significantly downgraded: women and families were now to have priority; and much more rigorous investigation would precede the giving of any charity. This redefinition and altered modus operandi clearly struck a sympathetic cord with the community: charitable donations to the venerable Benevolent Society slowly dwindled, while subscriptions from the city as well as from private individuals to the Friendly Society increased. Many of those aided in the past would find Victoria a much less sympathetic environment in the future. Less eligibility became more strongly entrenched.

Charitable aid could play only a modest role in the survival strategy of the unemployed. First, the amounts given were very small, considered as a proportion of the total needs of the poorest fifth of working-class families. Second, many or most of the recipients were not among the unemployed and underemployed identified by the censuses. Only 20 per cent of 209 individuals who used Benevolent Society relief between 1890 and 1892 could be found in the Victoria city directory and/or the 1891 census. Those using the charities and their aid were likely to have made up a minority of the mobile, unrecorded 'tramp' population; they were certainly a small proportion of the urban working class. Finally, the aid dispensed was clearly intended to be of a short-term nature, designed to prop up those in crisis. Fifty-five per cent of all monies spent by the Benevolent Society between 1890 and 1895 went towards purchase of food. The next closest item was 11 per cent for coal and wood.[90] The results were consistent with the intention; relief was never intended to cover unemployment, or be a system of income support for the poor. The fear of creating a dependent class of paupers underlay the pattern of giving: it even stood in the way of serious consideration of any alternative to short-term crisis management.

It is little wonder that the unemployed preferred self-help to charity. While some unemployed demonstrators still demanded 'work or bread,' by the 1890s the phrase was undergoing subtle but significant change: worker-led meetings in Victoria in the 1890s stressed the desire for 'work not charity.'[91] And, though the press rarely made much ado about it, it was often the employed workers who responded with the greatest generosity to the calls for donations and aid in times of crisis. In fact, the example of the Canadian Pacific Navigation workers providing 86 per cent of the donations received by the Citizen's Relief Committee in early February 1894 points to other possible sources for aid in times of distress.

Some trade unions were able to assist members who were unemployed, but limited resources prevented even the more stable unions from paying regular unemployment benefits.[92] Priority was given to death benefits. The best indication of union efforts in these areas appears in the annual reports of the Bureau of Industries in Ontario and, from 1900, in the annual reports of Ontario's Bureau of Labour. These agencies sent a questionnaire to unions each year. Among their questions was one about the amount of cash benefits paid to members or families of members in the event of 'lack of employment,' sickness, or death. In 1892, of the sixty-three locals submitting detailed responses, only six stated that they paid benefits to members during lack of employment. By 1901 the new Bureau of Labour was receiving more replies, but it knew that many union locals did not receive or return their surveys. The returns are representative probably only of more stable locals, or those with an official who had the time and the knowledge required to complete the form. In 1901 only twelve of 207 locals paid some form of unemployment benefit. The Cigarmakers were most consistent in doing so. Benefits were usually $3 a week, an amount that might have covered the food costs for a family of five. Other locals paying some unemployment benefit were the Engineers in Kingston, Stratford, and Toronto, the Carpenters in London, and the Iron Moulders in Smiths Falls.[93]

Unions were aware of the needs of unemployed members, and several indicated that they were trying to deal with the problem. 'It is intended to establish other benefits as soon as the union grows stronger,' said the Collingwood Carpenters. The Hamilton Tailors stated that their international organization was considering an 'out of work' benefit similar to that of the Cigarmakers.[94] Nevertheless, few unions made much progress, and by 1907 only the Cigarmakers, the Carpenters, and a few other locals were able to offer small unemployment benefits. Table 7.10 suggests the extent to which death benefits remained a priority. Death benefits were 60 per cent of all benefits paid in 1907; unemployed benefits were only 1.4 per cent of all benefits and only 6.3 per cent of benefits paid by the few unions that could afford unemployed benefits. Sickness benefits, of course, assisted families during unemployment caused by illness. Nevertheless, it is clear that unions could not afford much direct cash support for members who were simply laid off; in any case, they protected only a small portion of the working class as a whole.

It is likely that, even among unions, the more important support was informal and personal. Unions assisted members in finding jobs, in travelling to new locations, in making contact with locals in new locations, and in finding alternatives to waged employment. As one labourer told the dominion Royal Commission on the Relations of Capital and Labor:

TABLE 7.10
Benefits paid by international unions in Ontario, 1907

Union	Death benefit	Death benefit to members' wives	Sick benefit	Travelling benefit	Tool insurance	Unemployed benefit
Carpenters	1,775	–	6,843	–	7,257	11,326
Chainmakers	–	–	–	1,200	–	278
Cigarmakers	209,148	–	174,338	–	–	15,006
Compressed Air Workers	1,349	–	400	810	–	290
Jewelry Workers	100	–	262	–	–	50
Print cutters	600	–	–	–	–	35
Sub-total	212,972	–	181,843	2,010	7,257	26,985
All other unions	863,088	42,575	530,693	1,525	3,670	–

Source: *Eighth Report of the Bureau of Labor of the Province of Ontario ... 1907* (Toronto, 1908), 191–2. Figures are rounded to the nearest dollar.

Q. What advantage have you in belonging to the Knights of Labor?
A. One advantage I have is that it has helped to keep me in employment ... The brotherhood aids me to find work.[95]

A decade earlier, in the period of the Canadian Labor Union, some workers saw unions as a type of employment agency: 'Trade Unions are benefit societies in most cases. They are as well organizations through which men can locate jobs or, as important, find where the labor market is overstocked.'[96] Unions, like benevolent societies, extended individuals' support networks beyond those of neighbourhood and family. The unemployed must have often depended on economic exchanges now beyond our knowledge or measurement: union members gave food or fuel in return for small services given or useful labour performed by their needy friends. There are even occasional reports of union locals agreeing to shorten their working day in order to share work among their members.[97] Union locals communicated with each other across the country, sending information about labour-market conditions.[98]

It is impossible to measure the contribution of such union activity, but it is worth remembering that unions protected only a small proportion of the Canadian labour force before the end of the century, and a minority even after that. The most sophisticated American study of the process of 'getting work' in this period has concluded that employment agencies, unions, and other institutions were less useful than personal effort and family contacts. When it came to finding a job, most workers were on their own or depended on the assistance of family or ethnic networks.[99]

Fraternal societies were another potential source of aid and part of the survival strategy of many urban families. They flourished in Canada and elsewhere in the last half of the nineteenth century. One study has suggested that 37 per cent of all adult males in Ontario in 1901 belonged to a fraternal or benevolent society. By 1921 it has been estimated that a similar number of adult males belonged to such societies in British Columbia.[100] Fraternal charters made it clear that members were expected to help fellow members in need. Beyond that, however, organizations such as the Independent Order of Odd Fellows offered insurance for time off work due to sickness. In return for an annual fee, a member could receive up to $3 for each week off work. The International Order of Foresters offered funeral, old age, disability, and sick benefits as early as 1881. By the end of the century most other fraternal societies followed suit.[101] Some, such as the Ancient Order of Foresters, assisted unemployed members in their search for work.[102] The by-laws of a smaller society, the Sons of England, which restricted its membership to those of English heritage, made explicit the connection between unemployment and the benefits of fraternal membership: 'Sickness, though a terrible scourge, is not the only calamity a man has to dread. Many a noble upright man meets with adversity that he could not advert. Loss of employment is one; and is it not better and more noble – does not a man feel less degraded – when he can receive temporary aid from his own countrymen as a right, then when he has to slink along and live dependent on the charity of others?'[103] This concern with unemployment is understandable, since, according to one source, five of the eight founding members were without work when the Sons of England held its first meeting.[104]

It is clear that those who joined these associations could find some support for themselves and their families in times of need. It is also apparent that members were not a simple mirror image of the wider community. If the membership of the Independent Order of Oddfellows, one of the largest such groups in Ontario, is any indication of age distribution, then such members tended to be younger than Ontario males in the general population: in 1901, 18 per cent of all Ontario males twenty and older were between fifty-five and seventy-four; only 9.5 per cent of Ontario's Odd Fellow members were in that range.[105] This disparity reflected in part a fee schedule that required higher entrance payments for older applicants. But whatever the reasons, that population group most in need of assistance was underrepresented in those organizations that provided such help.

Fraternal membership was skewed in an even more dramatic fashion. Studies of such membership in various areas of the United States, in Great Britain, in Victoria and Vancouver, and in two small Ontario cities point to the severe underrepresentation of unskilled manual workers.[106] The unskilled 'found lodge fees an obstacle to joining.'[107] By the late nineteenth century, most lodges catered to the skilled and upwardly mobile working class. As Christopher Anstead has noted for Ontario, 'Men from the "Victorian middle class" forged the lodge into an instrument for creating and managing cultural consent.'[108] These findings are significant for our attempt to understand how working-class families coped with unemployment. Clearly those most vulnerable to 'enforced idleness'[109] had the least chance of taking advantage of the benefits offered by fraternal societies. Such societies thus played only a minimal role in ameliorating the lot of those most at risk of unemployment.

The conclusion about the fraternal societies applies to most other family strategies: some families were able to employ a strategy, but many were not. Just as the Canadian working class was characterized by severe income disparities, so also were there stark differences in the capacity of families to employ a full range of survival strategies. Social structural forces created the need for a range of methods, but at the same time constrained their success and limited their benefits.[110] Moreover, multiple approaches could work against each other and often enmeshed workers further in the structure of exploitation of which unemployment was a part. The evidence suggests that many families had strategies but that these approaches often failed. The poor survived, but as the appalling infant mortality rates in Canadian cities at this time reveal, many of the poor also died.[111]

To survive at all, a large proportion of the working class continued to depend on whatever could be scrounged from non-waged work. 'We manage to live on that,' said a Victoria worker in 1893. By 'that' he meant the short-term earnings of casual labour in the dockyards, which he estimated to be between 75 cents and $1.50 a week. But even by his own estimates he could not survive on those earnings, which would cover only his food. And he needed money for other things, too: 'Well a cabin will cost from $2.50 to $3.50 per month. The regular price ranges from $3.00 to $3.50. Lights, fuel, etc., will run up to 50c. to 75c. per week, no matter how careful one is. On $2 per week one manages very well, provided one is satisfied to exist and don't care very much for the rest of it.'[112] He did care to survive, however. It is clear that his stated earnings fell far short of covering his costs.

Together with a large proportion of the urban working class, he must have had recourse to the vast informal economy that grew together with industrial capitalism. Children scrounged for coal.[113] Boys sold fruit to sailors at the docks.[114] Men knocked on doors for money, bread, and work.[115] Recent immigrants took up hawking and peddling, filling gaps left in the nation's retailing system.[116] A 'respectable looking woman,' a mother of two young children, canvassed homes to do 'the family washing ... at the same rates as the Chinaman.'[117] The pedlar, the washerwoman, and the scrounger were commonplace figures on the streets of Canadian towns and cities. Getting and losing jobs, offering labour or goods as time and chance permitted, they were not marginal types relegated to the remote corners of late Victorian labour markets. They were part of the great parade of job seekers in an age of uncertainty.

8

The Working Class, Social Reform, and the State

Canadian workers took action to redress unemployment. Most responses occurred within family, a profoundly gendered space in which the effects of being laid off were first felt. Not all responses were personal and familial, however. Workers also took action by speaking about joblessness, loudly and frequently, if not with one voice. The fear of unemployment, even when not explicit, permeated all the causes espoused by workers and their organizations in late Victorian Canada. Their words expressed a class consciousness shaped and strengthened by experience in capitalist labour markets.

The words and the experience took place in a social and economic world that we have sought to define in the previous chapters. Unemployment was not exactly a random condition, but it did affect in varying degrees of frequency all groups within the working class, apart from a small elite. The unemployed were sometimes concentrated in certain urban spaces, but distance was an obstacle to united action. At any one point in time, the unemployed were an unstable, fluctuating, and mobile fragment of the working class. The working class's response to joblessness was therefore also fragmented and fluctuating. In the dialogue that workers opened with employers and with the state, workers were at a severe disadvantage. The same conditions that gave rise to the army of the unemployed militated against its mobilization on a single field of battle.

In all countries the voice of the unemployed was often muffled, but in Canada the unemployed suffered specific disadvantages stemming from the nature of the Canadian economy and the structure of political power. This chapter points to such disadvantages as we observe the opening cross-fire in the long verbal conflicts over unemployment that persist into our own time. We move from trade unions and labour intellectuals to social reformers and to politicians. We need not emphasize the many echoes of these old debates to be heard in Canada in the 1990s: readers will hear them for themselves. While the situation of the 1990s is different, there is little that is new in the principles and assumptions that underpin today's discussions of the problem.

As we have seen in chapter 2, workers spoke about unemployment and struggled to escape the language of reformers and city officials: the unemployed were not tramps, vagrants, beggars, or the casual poor. A new vocabularly was slow to catch on outside the working class and its leaders, however, and the noun 'unemployment' was rarely heard in Canada before 1900. Not until the relief crises in many cities in the winters of 1912–13 and 1913–14 did the word appear frequently in newspapers and in the mouths of politicians.[1] 'Unemployment' was preceded by 'unemployed,' applied frequently in the 1880s and 1890s to refer to people who were without work through no fault of their own. Canadian workers brought these words into Canadian political life, to indicate a structural feature of the industrial economy and a social problem of potentially overwhelming proportions.

Very often the unskilled were left to articulate the problem on their own, as they did in Hamilton every winter in the early 1900s, marching and petitioning the city for work, with little assistance from the craft union elite in their city.[2] Yet both craft workers and unskilled labourers had to respond to the same problem, and they shared the view that joblessness could be remedied by appropriate state intervention. It was the fear of being thrown among those petitioners for work that moved trade-union leaders to organize and to seek both wage and job stability.

Trade unions were, among other things, a response to the fear of unemployment and a central part of workers' campaign to influence labour markets. In chapter 7 we have seen how workers attempted to use trade unions to find work, to provide sickness benefits, and to negotiate a living wage sufficient to compensate for periods of unemployment. There was also a clear connection between strikes and fear of unemployment. Our studies of strikes in Canada cannot show how often motives for such action included concerns for work duration or job security, because these worries are often hidden behind the commonly stated motives – resisting wage cuts or fighting for shorter workdays or union recognition.[3]

The fear of unemployment was often present, however. Behind many wage-related demands was the need to earn and save enough to survive the 'idle season.' When the moulders of Hamilton went on strike in the summer of 1887 'we felt we should have more wages when we were working in order to be able to live during those portions of the year when there was nothing to do.'[4] When cotton-factory workers went on strike in Quebec City in 1908, they were not simply fighting against a cut in hourly and piece-rate wages in that year but also reacting against a reduction in the hours of work from sixty to forty a week and to longer seasonal shut-downs. It was the combination of wage cuts and 'the reduction in their working time' that led the cotton workers to strike.[5] Of the forty strikes in Quebec's cotton mills between 1900 and 1908, at least ten were related explicitly to job security; in many others, where wages were the key issue, 'lost time' was undoubtedly one of workers' grievances.[6] Strikes over wages were rarely, if ever, simply about the size of a pay packet. They were also related to stability of employment and to control of labour markets.

There was another connection between unemployment and trade unions. In 1894 the president of the Victoria Trades and Labour Council noted the effect of unemployment on trade unions' membership: 'It was a fact that a great number of families had gone away through the dearth of employment, because some of the trades unions that in good times had a large membership, now have barely sufficient to hold their charters; some of the unions could not even hold their meetings.'[7] In Ontario in the early 1900s, union organizing and strikes were more likely in times of economic growth, when the labour surplus had diminished and workers were more likely to believe that concessions could be wrung from employers. Widespread unemployment had a dampening effect on both organizing and bargaining.[8] Employers also played on the fear of unemployment: the threat to shut down a plant, and the threat to replace workers with machinery, were frequent bargaining tactics.[9] Workers responded by demanding union recognition. Behind this demand lay the chronic instability of unions; and behind that lay not only the opposition of employers but also the combined effects of unemployment and migration in search of work. Trade unions were agents of labour-market control and a response to the reality and the fear of 'lost time.'

From the beginning, the leaders of the Trades and Labor Congress (TLC) spoke about unemployment. One of the first motions passed by the TLC in 1886 – a motion passed again in subsequent years – objected to the use of public money to assist the immigration of 'paupers, indigents, and orphans' and urged the dominion to 'abolish the existing immigration system.'[10] The problem of unemployment reappeared in a motion calling for 'more stringent legislation ... in the direction of prohibiting the importation of Chinese labour.'[11] A related issue was imported contract labour, or 'alien labour.' In 1888 the TLC denounced certain employers, particularly Ontario's builders, for importing mechanics 'under false pretences,' thereby 'flooding the markets of our country with surplus mechanics.'[12] Assisted immigration and contract labour led to the artificial creation of a labour surplus that had the interrelated effects of limiting work duration and depressing wages throughout the economy.

Conceiving unemployment largely as a problem of excess workers, the TLC also opposed use of prison labour because it competed 'with that of honest laborers throughout the Dominion.'[13] The TLC urged governments to stop giving grants to any religious institution, reformatory, or penitentiary that put inmates into competition with 'free labor.'[14] TLC leaders discovered job poachers in many places: in 1887 and 1888 they protested against government employees supplementing their incomes by taking seasonal jobs with private employers. By working 'extra hours' they were 'competing in the labor market' and so depriving others of work.[15]

Even such unlikely events as the closing of canals for seasonal repair attracted the TLC's attention. The TLC supported the Knights of Labor in Ontario's Lincoln and Welland counties in their opposition to the 'unwatering' of the Welland Canal for five or six months in the year. What had this to do with unemployment? Shutting down the canal for so lengthy a period 'would throw over 2,500 working people out of employment.'[16] The problem also occurred elsewhere: in 1901 the seasonal closing of the Lachine Canal put 500 rolling-mill employees out of work.[17]

Responses to unemployment must be seen as part of the craft unionist's struggle for control. There was a radical edge to this struggle, as many labour historians have argued. Unemployment acted as a solvent of the older 'producer ideology,' which held that employers and workers shared common interests as producers. Echoes of this producer ideology can be heard in the argument that both employers and workers suffered when demand slackened and workers had to be laid off. Such echoes fade before the concerted blasts of labour reformers at the structure of labour markets that worked only in the interests of capitalists.

The ideas of the famous American social critic Henry George reverberated through the Canadian labour movement in these years. 'There should be nationalization of the land,' Mr Jury, an independent artisan, declared. 'Other remedies may alleviate, may improve the condition of the working classes, but to strike at the root, the land must be national-ized.'[18] The TLC's position on the taxation of land was also part of the wider assault on capitalist labour markets: 'The withholding of land from use causes a perpetual congestion of the labor market.'[19] A system of land taxation would cause 'a demand for labor, by preventing people holding land in idleness.'[20]

Labour reformers sought to transform the very nature of working-class life. The shorter-hours campaigns provide the best evidence for such a claim. In the U.S. context, David Roediger and Philip Foner argue that shorter hours was a leitmotif also of American working-class experience: 'The length of the workdays has historically been the central issue raised by the American labor movement during its most dynamic periods of organization.'[21] The shorter-hours movement was not merely a means of bargaining for higher wages; nor was it a simple demand for longer leisure-time escapes from harsh working conditions. It was about control of the quantity and quality of working time and of living time outside the workplace; it was about control of labour markets.

Workers tended to believe that there was enough work for all; the problem was inequitable distribution. Some people worked far too much, others, too little or not at all. This 'redistributionism' was consis-tent with workplace experience in the 1880s – industrial employees in Ontario averaged fifty-nine hours of work a week in 1889 but could expect several weeks or even months with no work at all.[22] Everywhere those with work had friends with none. 'There are four or five of our men unemployed. If we had the ten hour system they would all be employed. If a man works 17 or 18 hours he keeps them out of work.'[23] The speaker was a baker in Halifax. His observation was a simple one, based on a trade in which workdays could be exceptionally long.

Yet by the late 1880s this type of observation had become a political refrain, a commonplace justification for the shorter-hours movement which even royal commissioners learned to anticipate.[24]

Q. Have you ever thought what effect shortening the hours of labor would have on the labor market?
A. Yes; it would be an improvement; it would give more work.
Q. Absorb the surplus?
A. Yes; to a great extent.[25]

Another argument for shorter hours was also heard in the 1880s: there was a direct connection between 'absorbing the surplus' and the quest for a living wage. Fewer hours 'would reduce the production, and, so doing, you would increase the wages, because when you have an over-supply of labor on the market labor is always cheaper; and for that reason I think the hours of labor should be reduced.'[26] This line of argument was not consistent with other justifications, particularly the view that shorter hours would actually increase productivity and output. Workers also tended to ignore the possibility that shorter hours and full employment might accelerate employers' search for labour-displacing machinery. These possibilities, and even the argument that shorter hours would increase wages, were drowned out by the redistributionist refrain that shorter hours would spread work and so eliminate unemployment. Such a refrain was heard only rarely in the early 1870s' debates, but by the late 1880s the spectre of unemployment had changed the justification and given the movement a new lease on life.

Indeed, in 1886 the word 'unemployed' made its first appearance at a TLC Congress in a motion on shorter hours. The congress passed a motion:

That considering the increasing mass of unemployed labor in most branches of industry, particularly in that of unskilled labor, and considering also that it is the duty of the Government to further the welfare of the people in every possible way, and that the reduction of the hours of labor is an important means to that end, therefore this Congress petition the Government to enact a bill to regulate the hours of all workers in the employ of the State, and by all public bodies and companies obtaining contract or concession from Parliament, and that eight hours be the maximum time of the working day in these establishments.[27]

The TLC was articulating a complete argument about unemployment, and the logic was more apparent than it had been during the Nine Hours movement in Ontario in 1872, when the connection between unemployment and shorter hours was rarely mentioned. The TLC was repeating an argument well known among the Knights of Labor, even though the platform of the Knights did not include the words 'unemployed' or 'unemployment.' The *Palladium of Labor* put the case succinctly in 1886: 'The eight hour day would create vacancies for one-fourth the number of labourers and mechanics now employed. It would at one blow annihilate the army of the unemployed – the reserve force which is drawn upon by capitalism whenever a conflict between employers and employed takes place. By working ten and twelve hours a day the workingman not merely robs his fellow of the chance to earn a livelihood, but cuts a rod for his own back, by keeping up the number of unwilling idlers whose presence prevents the success of movements for bettering the condition of Labor.'[28] By the 1890s 'shorter hours' remained, as it had been in the 1870s, a movement to expand the family time of male breadwinners.[29] By the 1890s, however, proponents had added something new and remarkably durable to their movement, and their platform had now become a solution to a central problem of their existence – unemployment.

Workers challenged even the capitalist's prerogative to create work. Producer cooperatives were part of that challenge. As one observer put it, 'If the co-operative idea were pretty generally carried out, it would break the hump-back of monopoly.'[30] In 1901, the cigar makers of Montreal floated shares for a cooperative manufactory to be run by and for workers, and in the same year Montreal's moulders attempted to purchase a large city foundry in order to run it on a cooperative basis.[31] In 1908, the Trades and Labour Council of London, Ontario, established a cooperative toy factory to provide work for unemployed families.[32] The Knights of Labor and the TLC both endorsed cooperatives.[33] The co-op movement in Canada always had both rural and urban support, and it took direct aim at labour markets. One of the objects of the Co-operative Union of Canada, founded in 1909, was 'preventing the waste of labour now caused by unregulated competition.'[34]

Regulating competition also required state intervention in business and labour relations. 'If the obligation of employers to care for the welfare of dismissed workmen were once fully established, it would greatly check the injurious practice of taking on and turning off hands according to the so-called exigencies of trade, as though they were gas or water,' J.N.L. informed the editor of the Victoria *Colonist* in 1893.[35] This challenge was directed towards the state and its role in class relations. 'The Government most certainly has ... the duty to require that precautions must be taken and prudential institutions founded to secure the working people against the consequences of accidents and the stoppage of work.'[36]

Prudential action could also include the hiring by municipal governments of local residents, state encouragement of 'union label' production, and a government-mandated system of indentured apprenticeship. Such measures were intended to protect the jobs of union members and 'to prevent outside labour coming into places depriving skilled mechanics of work.'[37] Some argued that state-sponsored technical education would reduce unemployment because workers would then be 'in greater demand ... on account of their skill.'[38] Some form of arbitration or conciliation of labour disputes could reduce the 'lost time' resulting from strikes and lock-outs.

Demands for a bureau of labour statistics were part of the same campaign: the TLC wanted statistical ammunition to strengthen the campaign for control.[39] The TLC's report on the census followed: of the thirteen subjects on which the Congress wanted questions added to the census, the first related to the plight of the unemployed: 'If working, how many days unemployed during the year'?[40] Every major cause in labour politics at the end of the nineteenth century was connected directly to the problem of labour surplus and the campaign for labour-market control.

Control of labour markets was also linked to the 'woman question.' The reactions to women in the era of the Knights of Labor embraced many contradictions, and the fear of unemployment helps us to understand and to unravel those contradictions. On the one hand, women were the equals of men and were deserving of equal pay and equal political rights, or so the Knights insisted.[41] On the other hand, the labour market was 'flooded by unorganized female workers' who 'crowd out and displace men.'[42] Articles in the *Palladium of Labor* suggest that arguments for equality were sometimes a direct response to the fear of unemployment and the desire to contain the threat presented by women workers. The *Palladium* noted that until recently 'the feeling generally prevailed among trade unionists' that the way to deal with the problem was simply to exclude women from the labour force. But 'a more manly, reasonable and humane view of the subject now obtains': 'Instead of seeking to restrict the scope of female Labor, the demand is now for "equal *pay* for equal work." Only by granting full equality of rights to women at the polls as well as in the workshop and factory can justice to Labor be secured.'[43] The argument for equality emerged within the quest for labour-market control. It was quite consistent with the view that male access to labour markets must be different from that of women: 'his particular trade' was remote from 'women's sphere,' and his trade must be made 'secure from the invasion by the influx of underpaid female labor.'[44]

Even in the most progressive circles the quest for control of labour markets buttressed the assumption of male priority. Phillips Thompson's paper, *The Labor Advocate*, had a regular 'Woman' section and insisted that men must accept women as workers and as political equals. Yet women were 'competitors in the labor market' who 'generally can afford to take wages which would not support a single man.' 'It is hard to get working women to realize that they are committing almost a crime in driving their natural protectors and providers out of their occupations by accepting wages on which a man cannot live.'[45]

Among some trade-union supporters the exclusionist strategy persisted and coincided with a radical critique of capitalism. 'The labor[ing] woman in industrial pursuits means the total destruction of the family life of the working man.' The woman is 'torn from her family of little ones' and 'this condition of the family is begotten of capitalism.' In capitalism women become 'instruments of exploitation' because they help to create a labour surplus, or 'the increase of labor power in a market already overstocked.'[46] The quest for labour-market control reflected and reinforced gender divisions, privileged the wage of the male 'head,' and constrained the argument for equality.[47]

The variety of labour's reform causes, and the deeply gendered responses to labour markets, suggest how far the Canadian working class was from achieving consensus on unemployment. Trade-union leaders offered a plethora of solutions to an ubiquitous problem and in doing so gave reformers and politicians plenty of opportunity to seize on parts of the radical reform package rather than the whole. And workers threatened with unemployment were put in the invidious position of demanding waged work within the very system that created unemployment. As the emphasis on immigration, on alien contract labour, and on women as labour-market competitors suggests, trade-union leaders, in common with many of their rank and file, tended to interpret unemployment as a surfeit of people rather than a shortage of jobs. The absence of consensus made it very easy for the state to grant some reforms (an alien-labour law, restrictions on Chinese immigration, limited trade-union recognition) without addressing unemployment directly or even acknowledging the existence of the problem. In these circumstances employers or the state could easily set the terms of the discussion. An independent perspective was difficult to achieve.

Some became pessimistic: 'Can you suggest a remedy for the present state of things?,' a Toronto reporter asked Mr Jury in 1883. 'Lots of remedies,' Jury replied, 'but where is the use? The supply [of labour] in the market is greater than the demand, and therefore capitalists rejoice, while labour perishes.'[48]

Others, however, did attempt a wider analysis. We look at only three of labour's brainworkers to illustrate the rapid emergence of an independent perspective and the beginnings of a long challenge to the neoclassical economic analysis of unemployment.

William Collins, a retired machinist in Burlington who had read the works of Adam Smith, David Ricardo, John Stuart Mill, and Herbert Spencer, opened a debate with the dominion royal commissioners investigating the relations of capital and labour in the 1880s. Here in embryo was a debate that would echo through discussions of unemployment for another century at least. 'You see the effect of the introduction of machinery by the manufacturers is to abridge labor and cheapen everything. That must necessarily be against the interests of the man who has his labor to sell, because an unskilled kind of labor can be introduced by the application of mechanism, whereas it is by skill that the skilled artisan lives.'

Against Collins's deskilling argument the commissioners argued that technological change, by expanding total output and productivity, had also expanded employment. Whether they knew it or not, their opinion had a respectable lineage in political economy. They were also echoing the view of contemporary American experts that labour displacement caused by machinery would be offset by the job-creating capacity of new inventions.[49]

Collins answered that employment had increased, but at a slower rate than population growth or technological change.

I think, as regards the employés [sic], that their outlook and possibilities of remaining employed are more precarious, and will continue to be so ...
Q. Have you not thought that a great deal of employment is created by the manufacture of those machines?
A. I believe that is the case. But you see, unfortunately for the employé, that the object of the manufacture of those machines is to reduce manual labor ... There is less demand for labor now than there was twenty years ago. This comes of necessity, because there is a larger quantity of steam power used, and the power of multiplying in the arts or in ordinary mercantile transactions has been enormously increased ... No doubt there are more mechanics employed today, but I hold that they have not kept pace with the rest of the population, that is as mechanics.

William Collins's view reflected the experience of many craft workers.

Q. Has machinery interfered with the making of barrels in late years?
A. Yes. That is the cause of all our grievances.[50]

The coopers readily attributed their joblessness to technological change, since in their trade machinery was rapidly replacing manual labour. Carriage-makers offered the same kind of analysis: 'The over-production of machinery has caused a great many men to be thrown out of work. I know they have one machine in the waggon shop here that takes the place of about twenty men.'[51] As Craig Heron has pointed out, awareness of the labour-displacing effects of machinery was widespread.[52] One disgruntled tailor observed succinctly: 'Between science and progress the working classes are ground as between millstones.'[53]

Like many workers, Collins remained puzzled over the causal relationship between machinofacture and job displacement: 'There is some hocus-pocus about this that I cannot exactly get at the bottom of myself. I feel somehow or other that the employé is run out in this question – he is not considered. He is just a pawn in the game, and there is where the trouble lies, and until the employé awakens he will lie there.' 'There is where the trouble lies': it was not possible to predict whether growth in machines would continue indefinitely to outpace growth in employment, precisely because one could not anticipate the effects of workers' knowledge and action in future. Deskilling did not reduce the intelligence of labour or the dependence of capital on labour: 'With respect to the interest of the manufacturer, I hold that he cannot have any interest without the employé's [sic] labor – labor being the source of profit; but to have labor, do what he will, he must have intelligent labor, whether he will or not.'[54] Since labour was the source of profit, it might interrupt the invidious effects of technology on employment. A young carpenter made a similar point in 1883: 'It is not machinery which is the cause of the trouble – it is the wrong system of distribution – it is monopoly of opportunities.'[55] Machinery was not at fault; the capitalist system was.

When Collins sought to discuss solutions, however, the royal commissioners balked, especially when he mentioned Henry George. In Hamilton, as elsewhere, they wanted no discussion of uncongenial 'theory,' especially the theory of George.[56] The commissioners offer an early example of official evasion. They would hear employers justify unemployment by reference to the theory of supply and demand. They were not equipped, however, to deploy the full intellectual artillery of liberal political economy against Collins, so they quickly terminated an uncomfortable debate.

By 1887 the radical journalist Phillips Thompson had gone some way towards dispelling the 'hocus-pocus' that troubled Collins. Thompson knew that immigration was not the source of the problem: 'No amount of foreign immigration could injure the American working-man, if monopoly did not bar access to the soil and control every avenue of employment.'[57] Unemployment, Thompson argued, was part of the boom-and-bust cycles of capitalism and the major reason for declining standards-of-living.[58] In debating the standards of living question with political economists, Thompson rested his case on a point that many later 'optimists' in this discussion forgot: 'Obviously, any calculation based on the wages paid at particular levels leaves out of account altogether the condition of the unemployed.'[59] He also rejected official U.S. Labor Bureau estimates of the extent of unemployment on the grounds that they counted only a static rate, not the extent or frequency of unemployment. The 'half-employed class' must also be considered part of 'the army of the unemployed.' This army, Thompson thought, was the Achilles' heel of the entire capitalist system: 'Capitalism has created a monster which threatens to destroy the classes, if not the system, that gave it life. The number of men and women who cannot get work on any terms implies a far larger class whose pay has become a mere pittance by reason of competition.'[60]

For so deep-rooted a problem there was no panacea. Thompson argued for the eight-hour day, which might, 'in most industries, secure an opportunity to work for all.'[61] But his answer went beyond there, to envisage an evolutionary process by which capital would become 'socialized' through 'the extension of the powers of government to include the organization of industry.'[62] The means by which the state would be persuaded to act in this way were not fully worked out in a critique of capitalism that was heavily influenced by Spencerian ideas of a gradual social evolution.[63] Thompson's 'new political economy' clearly depended, however, on 'the solidarity of labor.' In working out its own emancipation, labour would 'regenerate the world' and achieve 'the annihilation of capitalism.'[64] Unemployment would play a key role in this process: business cycles, by inflicting poverty and unemployment, would 'teach the absolute inadequacy of private enterprise.'[65]

Here was a direct attack on the liberal view of society and the economist's faith in an 'iron law of wages.' In the 1890s the labourite critique confronted liberal political economy even more directly, in the dialogue between Goldwin Smith and the Nova Scotian working-class intellectual Colin McKay. The exchange followed from the kind of tragedy that compelled even mainstream newspapers to notice unemployment: a young man who could not find work had committed suicide.[66] Many reformers had called on government to provide work. Smith responded with the economist's laws of supply and demand: society could not create that which did not exist; left to operate freely, the economy would create a demand for labour.

McKay went directly to the core of liberal political economy. Supply and demand was not an immutable law independent of human control. There was nothing 'natural' about unemployment. For one thing, state intervention in labour markets, which political economy seemed to disallow, was fully consistent with the interests of both workers and employers: 'If all of the workingmen who are now unemployed and who necessarily consume but a small portion of the products of industry, were given work, there would at once be a demand for commodities of all sorts, and not only these men would be benefitted, but business men in general would benefit by the increased demands for commodities.'

Even if the end were economic growth within a capitalist economy, state intervention would be 'natural,' and so government should intervene to limit the hours of labour. Again McKay went to the heart of the liberal defences: did state intervention infringe on the liberty of the worker or the employer? 'What is liberty? As well say that the Government should not trespass upon the liberty of one man to kill another man. The workingman who does his own work and then steps in and takes the work for which another is starving, is simply murdering his fellow, and it would be just as well to argue that a government has no more right to interfere with a man's liberty to kill his fellow man, as to argue that a government should not interfere with a man's liberty to do another man out of his means of earning a livelihood.'

If McKay had stopped here, he would have framed an answer consistent with much of the labour radicalism of his generation, but still within the premises of liberalism itself. He went further. Where Phillips Thompson realized that curtailing immigration would not solve unemployment, McKay knew that even shorter hours was no panacea. There were simply no easy solutions for a problem that was structural (and here the writer used not only the word 'unemployed' but also 'unemployment'): 'Production would be increased in cost, and consequently there would be a great stimulus to invention. Machinery to supplant human labour would be perfected, and the old army of unemployed would soon appear again. Then it would be necessary to further reduce the working hours, and to keep on doing so. This if kept up indefinitely would be a solution to the problem of the unemployment, but it wouldn't be a solution of the Labour Question at all. The condition of the great wage-earning class would remain practically unchanged.'[67]

Unemployment was structural, but not because there was an inevitable tendency for machinery to displace labour. McKay offered no simple technological explanation for unemployment. He was saying that there was a necessary tendency, within the system, for individual capitalists to reduce production costs. It was this tendency that stimulated invention and the reduction of capital's main variable cost – the cost of labour.

There was no solution to unemployment within liberal political economy: 'Even political economy then sees that the production of a relative surplus population is a necessary accompaniment of modern industry.'[68] And there was no answer within industrial capitalism:

Capital increases its supply of labour more quickly than its demand for labourers. The overwork of the employed part of the working class swells the ranks of the reserve part; while, conversely, the greater pressure that the latter by its competition exerts on the former forces them to submit to overwork and subjugation under the dictates of the employers. Thus the inter-action of the over-employed and the unemployed becomes the means of enriching individual capitalists, and at the same time accelerates the production of an industrial reserve army in an ever-increasing degree.[69]

The solutions lay outside the system, and they must begin with nationalization of production and distribution. Not all people would accept McKay's views, but he suggests how far the discovery of unemployment had advanced in a few decades. In its range and depth, the nineteenth-century working-class analysis of unemployment was complete. What followed in Canada in the twentieth century was a long series of footnotes to the work of those who first struggled with the problem.

Phillips Thompson and Colin McKay were perhaps exceptional, but by the early 1900s the idea that unemployment was endemic within capitalism was increasingly common. The most usual starting point was the thesis that machine production led to overproduction. From there it was a small step to arguing that unemployment fed on itself: lay-offs reduced purchasing power, and this in turn induced further lay-offs: 'Goods cannot be sold, because the volume on hand is greater than the purchasing power of the workers. Every curtailment of production only aggravates the situation, as the purchasing power is still further lessened as workers are thrown out and their wage stops.'[70]

The only way to balance production and consumption, in this analysis, was through collective ownership and control of production. Clearly not all workers accepted the emerging structuralist interpretation of unemployment. The *Western Clarion* vented its frustration over unemployed workers who voted for mainstream political parties. 'The right of men to own shingle mills and other forms of property' and the right of capitalists to 'take advantage of the conditions of the labor market to secure the cheapest labor ... has not been denied by the workingmen ... So long as the workers give their support to a system of property which can only stand by virtue of that right, they should logically accept the consequences of its application.'[71] 'Until they did away with capitalism they would not have solved the unemployed problem.'[72]

Varied as were labour's responses, unemployment had become a leitmotif of labour politics in an age of uncertainty. Canada's social reformers were soon persuaded to respond. Yet they were responding to a problem that scarcely had a name and on which labour leaders had not achieved consensus. Little wonder that reformers dealt with the problem indirectly and subsumed it within other social problems. An early example is the conference held by the Social Problems Association of Toronto in 1893. The organization sent to leading reformers in Toronto a series of questions on the problem of the unemployed worker. Reformers were asked, among other things, to recommend means of providing work and to suggest how cities offering public works could avoid being 'overrun by workers from less favoured communities.'[73] The answers, as summarized by J.G. Hume of the University of Toronto, reveal both the unfocused nature of responses and the way in which the problem provided ammunition for other favoured causes. There was 'a wonderful array of remedies for one disease,' including income taxes, land taxes, free land grants, support for cooperative societies, state management of natural monopolies, reduction of the hours of labour, the Knights of Labor platform, extension of education, abolition of the liquor traffic, higher salaries for members of Parliament, and 'greater care in teaching good habits and instilling moral principles in children.' To these solutions Hume added the wry comment that 'they cannot all be right for some are entirely hostile to each other.'[74] Faced with a similar litany of responses one unemployed worker in Victoria was more to the point: 'We must all live and if some of the "jawsmiths" who like to air their opinions at public meetings would only give us picks instead of palaver things would be better.'[75] Others, such as Phillips Thompson, were more blunt: middle-class reformers were 'so loaded up with capitalist ideals' that 'they haven't the sense to understand the situation.'[76]

Social reformers did not respond to unemployment in precisely the same way as did those philanthropists who addressed the problem of 'tramps' and applied work tests before issuing relief. As James Pitsula has argued, the managers of associated charities and houses of industry assumed that the character defects of the poor, not the unavailability of work, was the central issue.[77] Urban social reformers of the 1890s and early 1900s had no doubts about the need for moral regeneration, but they also knew that municipal relief and charity were by themselves inadequate. Some were prepared to admit even that the unemployed could be without work through 'no fault of their own.' 'It is sad and disheartening to know that there are today hundreds of thousands on both sides of the Atlantic in this pitiable condition, and that too, by no fault of their own.'[78]

Yet the rhetoric of moral culpability, which was so strident in the anti-tramp campaigns, had not disappeared from the language of social reformers. On the contrary, pressure for reform through legislation could coexist with continuing emphasis on individual moral responsibility and with distinctions between the deserving and the undeserving. A good example is the address by Helen Reid on 'The Problem of the Unemployed,' published in the 1890s by the National Council of Women. Reid, who had been influenced by J.A. Hobson, argued that the major cause of unemployment was 'the imperfect organization of the industrial system.' Unemployment resulted from the fact that consumer demand remained artificially depressed; since demand could not keep pace with the power to produce goods, industry fell into depressions and workers were thrown out of work. Seasonality, immigration, and the substitution of machinery for hand labour were all 'secondary' causes.

Yet Reid did not follow her own logic to Hobson's conclusion that consumer demand might be stabilized by a national minimum wage. Though some of her solutions required legislative action, all needed either voluntary action by employers or moral reform on the part of workers. Technical education would 'teach people how to help themselves.' More equal access to schooling would 'abate the dangers of ignorance and destitution.' Employment bureaux and public relief would help the unemployed find useful work. These and other solutions (including shorter hours) were applied only to those for whom joblessness was 'merely temporary.' Those 'permanently without regular employment' were beyond the scope of legislative or collective solutions. They included the casual labourer, 'whose inefficiency together perhaps with mental, moral and physical unfitness for regular work' guaranteed chronic joblessness. They included also the 'vagrant class' who were 'economically worthless' because of 'physical or moral defect.'[79] In the end such analysis reduced a systemic problem to a moral problem. Legislation might help to increase the number of jobs available, but the result was little more than an extension of the work tests applied by houses of industry. Once the short list of reforms had been applied, the large number who remained unemployed would be so of their own volition or through moral defect.

Unemployment became part of 'the synthesis of morality and science, of evangelism and sociology,' in the age of 'light, soap, and water.'[80] It remained subsumed within the moral problem of the city, rather than being a separate cause with its own name and its own organizations. This does not mean that the problem was not significant. Herbert Ames, for instance, had no doubt about the importance of unemployment: for him, the chief cause of poverty was 'insufficient employment.'[81] But for him the solution, like the problem, was both economic and moral. 'Prolonged idleness unfits many a man for steady work.' Moral degeneration was a link in the causal chain: 'Irregularity [of work], demoralization and poverty is the order of descent.'[82] The solution was no longer merely the responsibility of individuals; solutions were both individual and collective, and governments must assist in providing a material basis for the moral transformation of the working class.

Unemployment fell within many loops in the reform discourse. Immigration policies, by admitting the unfit, tended towards racial degeneration; unemployment was part of the loop because poor selection of immigrants left many without work and so put them on the moral slope from idleness to degeneracy. Feeble-mindedness was also related to unemployment, as Dr Helen MacMurchy told the Ontario Commission on Unemployment in 1915.[83] Unemployment therefore was one link in the connections that Mariana Valverde observed among deviant sexuality, feeble-mindedness, immigrants, and national degeneration.[84] Unemployment was also part of the link between intemperance and poverty. It did not matter, said Herbert Ames, whether liquor caused poverty or poverty caused intemperance. Poverty, 'irregularity,' and drink were part of the same chain of degeneration. The social gospeller T. Albert Moore agreed, and he too applied science and morality to the relationship between liquor and work: 'The capital of the working man is labour. His ability to work is his principal resource. Whatever depletes his earning power impairs his working capital. Scientific investigation reveals very clearly how alcohol impairs the ability to labour ...

Intemperance unfits men for their present work and causes permanent inefficiency in all their work.'[85]

The new discourse of moral reform acknowledged a role for the state in the great work of regeneration. Prohibition, immigration controls, vocational education, and public labour bureaux all fell within the responsibility of governments.[86] Social reformers helped to put unemployment into the realm of politics and to spread the view that collective solutions existed. At the same time they narrowed the understanding of unemployment: theirs was a political ideology of moral regeneration that focused on the working class as the targets of policy. This was not a crude victim-blaming ploy. Nevertheless, the social gospel turned attention away from the structural problems that lay beyond moral remedy. Reformers were not acting as servants of either the state or the bourgeoisie; but by suffusing political discourse with the language of moral regeneration, they shaped the Canadian dialogue on unemployment.

Social reformers diverted the debate from other structural solutions and even away from the idea of national insurance. William Beveridge, whose theory of social insurance was a British alternative to socialist solutions, had 'immense' influence on U.S. social reformers but found fewer followers in Canada.[87] The British National Insurance Act of 1911 found little support in Canada. Not until the Ontario Commission on Unemployment during the First World War did an official agency take the idea seriously, and even then all that the commission recommended in its 1916 report was government assistance 'to those voluntary associations of workingmen which undertake to provide unemployment benefits to their members.'[88] Certainly moral concerns and the 'less eligibility' principle contributed to the commission's caution: 'Some men who look forward to receiving unemployment benefit may be willing to shirk work on that account.'[89] In supporting voluntary benefit schemes, the Ontario Commission was agreeing with the position already taken by the Canadian Manufacturers' Association.[90]

The modest influence of British precedents in Canada suggests the need for us to set the Canadian discovery of unemployment in a wider comparative context. A thorough comparative analysis would require another book, and here we can only make a suggestion about the nature of Canada's distinctness. In Canada, unemployment arrived relatively late in politics, and Canada was one of the last Western industrial nations to create a national system of unemployment insurance. A major reason, as James Struthers has argued, was the preoccupation of Canadian reformers and politicians with the land.[91] The obsession with an ever-developing agricultural frontier reflected the economic base of a country in which 40 per cent of the members of the labour force were farmers or farm workers at the turn of the century and 62.5 per cent of the population lived in rural areas.[92] The discovery of unemployment coincided with the numerical preponderance of politicians from rural constituencies and the dominion's ongoing quest for new immigrants. While unemployed immigrants lived in parks and walked city streets in search of work, dominion immigration agents insisted that there were no unemployed in Canada because 'any man who is able and willing to work can find employment.'[93] The idea that Canada consisted of empty land and endless opportunity for the morally fit was fully consistent with the country's economic and political structure.

Back-to-the-land movements gathered support especially in times of severe unemployment: in the 1890s, in 1913–14, in 1919, and again in the 1930s. Labour leaders sometimes accepted the solution, while insisting that it required appropriate state action.[94] Among middle-class reformers the argument about land encompassed an emphasis on moral responsibility, even when the language of moral blame was absent or muffled: if the unemployed only had the moral strength to move, they would find work. In his discussion of unemployment in 1893, William Galbraith, president of the Toronto Social Problems Association, called for 'a movement back to the land.' His refrain would become a commonplace in the discussion of unemployment in Canada: 'The natural resources of the earth were more than sufficient, if properly utilized, to meet all the wants of far more people than now occupy the earth.'[95] The *Victoria Colonist*, while insisting that thousands were unemployed 'by no fault of their own,' put the solution into the hands of the unemployed themselves: 'Let them keep out of the cities.' In the rural frontier they would rediscover the work ethic: 'Would it not be better for the great bulk of the population to depend upon Nature for the means of subsistence than upon an artificial system which is not conducive to the health, physical, moral or intellectual, of the workers, and which periodically breaks down and leaves them in a most pitiable condition?'[96] The back-to-the-land solution was reinforced by a false memory of full employment on the pre-industrial frontier. As one reformer put it, the early pioneers had 'converted the wilderness into a land of civilization. There were many disadvantages; but there was no unemployment.'[97]

The refrain about empty land was not new. In his responses to the Nine Hours movement in 1872, Toronto politician and *Globe* publisher

George Brown shows most clearly how the denial of unemployment was connected to the ideal of the independent yeoman farmer in an empty land:

We all work. We all began with nothing. We have all got by hard work all we own – and the richest among us work on still, and like to do it. ... In very few countries, if in any, are there so large a proportion of the workers who achieve an ample independence. We have no such class as those styled capitalists in other countries. The whole people are the capitalists of Canada. The earnings of our prosperous farmers provide the means to settle their sons on new lands and subdue the forest ... The demand for workmen of all descriptions from every corner of Ontario is constant and urgent – the supply is never equal to the demand.[98]

Forty years later the obsession with land still clouded politicians' responses to unemployment. During the unemployment crisis of 1913–14, opposition critics in Ottawa blamed the dominion government for misinforming immigrants about opportunities in Canada and paused only to blame the newcomers themselves: 'Immigrants from Central and Southern Europe who were formerly almost entirely agricultural and went upon the land, today are apparently not going on the land ... Whether it is because we are getting a different class of people or what may be the reason, the fact is they have been going into the towns rather than on the land and consequently there is congestion in the towns.'[99] The dominion minister of the interior shared the assumption that equated abundant land with individual moral responsibility: 'Many of these people could get employment in the country if they would only go and take it. I understand that many persons in Winnipeg could get situations on the land if they would accept the same, but many of them will not do so.'[100]

A few years later the Ontario Commission on Unemployment rejected the idea of compulsory national insurance but recommended 'a vigorous policy of Community and Assisted Land Settlement,' training schools for agricultural labourers, better transportation to rural areas, and tax reforms to discourage speculation in land. The obsession with land neatly complemented the fascination with individual moral responsibility. While these preoccupations existed in other countries, they remained particularly potent in Canada, and together they help to explain the silence that awaited the ideas of William Beveridge and his followers.

The refrain about empty land maintained its appeal despite the overwhelming evidence that rural demand could not absorb all of the nation's supply of labour and the common knowledge that farm demand was seasonal only. Many workers also knew, from bitter experience, that empty land held disappointment as well as promise. Those who moved to the land, said the *Western Clarion*, found 'that it would require several hundreds of pounds expended on "clearing" it, before a plough could be so much as thought of.' Failures 'are the general rule.'[101]

In 1887, Ontario's assistant commissioner of agriculture had no doubt that 'there is on the whole a superabundance of labor in the country,' but he too knew that agricultural demand could not solve the problem. He knew this because, as secretary of the government's Bureau of Industry, he collected and published information on work duration. His data suggested that Ontario workers were employed 'only some 270 days in the year.' There was no way that agriculture could absorb the surplus. His reaction to the problem was limited but more realistic than utopian dreams about land: nothing could be done to adjust the imperfections of labour markets.

Q. Would it be possible to establish absolute equality between supply and demand in labor?
A. It might be possible, but it would be very difficult, I think.
Q. Practically, would it be possible?
A. No, I do not think that it would be practically possible, that is continuously.[102]

Such answers would not serve politicians very well. A better tactic was to borrow some of the rhetoric of one's critics. Land must be 'properly utilized,' for instance: politicians took a part of the radical reform package, omitted tax reform, and came up with a justification for further growth through private enterprise. 'And with the immense number of undeveloped resources on every side, it is safe to predict that ere long British Columbia will redeem with interest every promise to those within her borders.'[103] The undeveloped frontier held the solution to unemployment, so long as it could attract capital. There were many other ideas that could be safely appropriated: controls on immigration, particularly that of the Chinese; assurances that immigrants would be fit for work; a limited alien-labour law; and a *Labour Gazette* to provide information on labour markets for both workers and employers.

In the early 1900s the dominion government vacillated between denial of the problem and application of limited solutions. In 1912

R.H. Coats, Canada's pre-eminent labour statistician and editor of the *Labour Gazette*, noted that 'the subject of unemployment ... has never been statistically treated in Canada.' While blaming trade unions 'and their reluctance to furnish regular information,' he concluded: 'In any event the problem is not as pressing in Canada as in older countries.'[104] The Department of Labour's view, as late as 1915, was that unemployment was 'a phase of industrial life which had not been previously prominent in Canada.'[105] The *Board of Inquiry Report on the Cost of Living* (1915) stated that 'unemployment long continued or on any extensive scale has been practically non-existent.'[106]

The Department of Labour had other answers, however. One was that jobs followed capital and that interruptions to the flow of investment were a major cause of unemployment. R.H. Coats had a simple explanation for pre-war unemployment when he spoke to the Ontario Commission on Unemployment in 1915: 'Unemployment appeared when the effects of the Balkan Wars began to divert the stream of capital that had been flowing into Canada.'[107] This argument was consistent with the denial of unemployment: when capital did flow, there was a surplus of jobs, not a shortage. It fitted well with the concern of politicians to ensure a stable environment for investors and employers. As Premier Davie of British Columbia said to a 'mass meeting' on unemployment in 1894: 'The employer of labor was the man who should be encouraged, but if he was to be made a target to be shot at he would be driven away, and then where would the rest of us be?'[108]

Politicians had to accept that the economy was subject to cyclical fluctuations, but even business cycles could be used to minimize the problem of unemployment and divert responsibility back to workers themselves. Workers had to learn to save during the peaks of the business cycles. There had been 'a considerable decrease in employment' in the winter of 1907–8, noted the Department of Labour. Nevertheless, 'the remarkable and continued prosperity of industry and especially of manufacturing during the past few years in Canada had enabled employees to provide for the temporary falling-off in activity to a degree which would otherwise have been impossible.'[109] Unemployment was not a problem because work was so widely available in good times that workers had the opportunity to practise thrift, to limit spending on luxuries, and to save enough to see themselves and their families through hard times. The evidence presented in the *Labour Gazette*, to the effect that many industrial employers faced 'a scarcity of labour,' served to confirm the point that work was available and saving was possible.[110]

Ottawa also turned unemployment into a problem of the inefficient distribution of labour. Complaints by farmers of a shortage of labour seemed to confirm that the problem required only more efficient distribution. It was being solved, or so many politicians concluded, by private employment agencies, the new municipal labour bureaux, improved transportation, and job information circulated by trade unions and the *Labour Gazette*. The Department of Labour heard the reform argument that something could be done but applied a modest solution – information – which left the burden of action and responsibility to workers themselves.

The labour department had another response to the associated problems of poverty, unemployment, and wage demands: it often reduced them to a single issue – that of rising prices. Its emphasis on prices and living costs was fully consistent with the denial of unemployment: rising costs of living limited families' ability to save enough to see themselves through economic slumps and unemployment.

The department's conclusion, after fifteen years of work on living costs, was a new version of the social reformers' rural 'work test' ethic, dressed up in the language of liberal political economy. 'The great rise in prices that has taken place in Canada is accordingly found to centre largely in the new distribution problem which has been created by the lessening of local food supply during an era of heavy expenditures on capital account.'[111] In other words, too many workers had been attracted away from agriculture by the prospect of high wages and short hours in industry, mining, and construction. Unemployment was a function of living costs, and the solution was the responsibility of workers: let them go back into farming. 'The scarcity of trained farm labour at a reasonable price has been the despair of the farmer.'[112] How would labour be persuaded to move into agriculture? The 1915 *Report on the Cost of Living* offered only vague remedies: 'The encouragement of food production and the removal of every possible economic weight in the distribution process.'[113]

The more specific remedies fell to workers themselves, as economic analysis dissolved into its initial 'work test' assumption and the moralizing projection of blame onto workers: 'The "gospel of ease," preached from every platform, has permeated the national life of the Anglo-Saxon race and has had its influence in the formation of present conditions. It is beyond question that productive efficiency is essential in the average citizen if he is to be capable of maintaining his economic value in the community, and becoming and continuing socially and industrially a sustaining and helpful unit rather than a burden ... Work is the discipline of life, and when the necessity arises, we should have the energy to respond to its call.'

Even shorter hours, which the labour movement proposed as a solution to unemployment, now served to project blame on its advocates: 'In this Dominion, we are proportionately working fewer hours than ever before, and we have a greater number of the inefficient and the idle in our midst. The result of proportionately fewer men working shorter hours with more valuable land has been an increased cost for which labour-saving devices have not compensated. These are the underlying economic conditions which through the law of supply and demand have contributed to the increased cost of the necessities of life.'[114] The official political economy was a form of specious moralizing in which workers were to blame both for unemployment and for rising prices.

The first major dominion initiative on unemployment followed not from the crisis of 1912–14 but from the First World War. The Employment Service of Canada dominated job-exchange activities in the fiscal year 1919–20 and helped to find jobs for some 329,000 workers in that year. The creation of the service was a response to the problem presented by returning veterans and to the threat of class conflict in the postwar years.[115] The service was consistent, however, with pre-war assumptions: unemployment was a labour-distribution problem, and work was available for the morally fit and deserving.

Workers and their leaders brought the issue of unemployment into Canadian politics and so entered a dialogue with employers and the state. The demands for a living wage and for union recognition were part of the debate. So also was the national state's preoccupation with what it saw as obstacles to labour efficiency and thrift. Foremost among these impediments were time lost through strikes and lockouts and rising prices. The dialogue took place in a country only recently emerging from a predominantly rural and preindustrial past, where the movement of labour into the western agricultural frontier was still held to be the key to economic development and nation building. Canada's twentieth-century debates over unemployment had begun.

9

Conclusion

Unemployment has a long history in Canada. Joblessness was part of working-class experience long before the Depression of the 1930s. Until the late nineteenth century it lacked official recognition and even a name of its own. Yet the problem was pervasive. Unemployment helps to explain inequalities, both within the working class and between classes. It makes sense of the mobility of workers: the migration of young people in Quebec to towns and cities and to the United States, the out-migration from the Maritime provinces, and the movement of thousands every year from city to hinterland and back again. Unemployment deepened the division of labour within households and thereby exacerbated gender distinctions. It was part of the recurring conflict between workers and employers. It helps to explain the opposition to immigration and the virulent hostility towards certain ethnic and racial groups that emerged in the late nineteenth century. Unemployment can help us to understand the growth of urban charities and of social-reform movements in the cities. It left a deep imprint on the politics of the labour movement. By the 1880s and 1890s unemployment was no longer latent; it had become a pervasive condition of class relations in urban Canada.

The unemployed at the turn of the century were not a marginalized 'other' within the Canadian working class. More than one out of every five urban wage earners was without a job at some point during the year. If we include those adults who reported no occupation, then more than one in every three workers experienced joblessness during the year.[1] Nor was unemployment related mainly to one large city. Montreal can no longer be seen as unusual in the extent of its unemployment and poverty.[2] In 1901 there were proportionately more poor families in Halifax, Winnipeg, and Vancouver.

TABLE 9.1
Working-class unemployment frequencies by sector, six cities, 1901

Sector	Men		Women	
	%	No.	%	No.
Clerical	6.1	1,191	8.9	384
Retailing/commercial	5.4	579	16.7	66
Services	13.2	591	11.3	989
Primary industry	28.8	160	–	–
Industrial				
Factory	26.3	2,338	27.4	725
Home	22.2	221	22.0	173
Small shops	32.9	960	31.3	163
Transport	14.5	737	21.4	14
Labouring	38.3	946	24.3	37

Workers in industrial and labouring occupations had most reason to fear unemployment. Table 9.1 is a reminder of its pervasiveness in these sectors, for both men and women. The unemployment frequencies – the proportion of the labour force experiencing this phenomenon at some time during the year – are similar to those in the United States at the turn of the century.[3] In 1891 the national unemployment frequency for U.S. men and women in 'manufacturing and mechanical industries' was 21 per cent; a decade later it was 27 per cent.[4] The comparable figure for industrial production in our six Canadian cities was 27.7 per cent in 1901. In Canada, as in the United States, one did not escape the threat of unemployment by moving from artisanal production to the new factories of the industrial era, for there too more than one of every four workers experienced joblessness during the year.

The risks of being unemployed differed with location, sex, age, type of household, and whether or not one was an immigrant. The risks differed even more dramatically with occupation. The odds of being unemployed are a type of risk factor, and the risks do rise for identifiable groups, such as labourers, recent immigrants, young adults and the elderly, and those living in Vancouver in 1901. Some categories were particularly vulnerable, but the high risk factors of specific groups do not explain unemployment itself. The unemployed were not marginalized people suffering from specific disabilities or specific labour-market disadvantages. If you found an unemployed person in urban Canada in 1901, the chances were very good that you had found a man or a woman of English-Canadian or French-Canadian background who was not an immigrant, one who normally worked in manufacturing or transportation or construction, and one who lived in a dwelling place with other kin.

For one out of every seven urban families, the capitalist labour market at the turn of the century failed to provide employment and earnings adequate for survival. Standards of living can be measured only in the context of family and only when wage earnings are adjusted for the effects of unemployment. Family cycle mattered a great deal, and poverty occurred at the intersection of class with stages in the family cycle. Standards of living fell steeply in the middle stages of the cycle of the working-class family. The poor, in short, were not only young and single, or the elderly living in institutions: the poor included large numbers of middle-aged parents with children.

Unemployment was a family condition, and family was a first line of defence against the joblessness of its members. Unemployment frequencies rose as families matured, and unemployment struck hard at those having young children or other dependants. Given market discrimination against the remunerative employment of women, unemployment struck especially hard at families composed of more women than men. To meet the need for food, clothing, and shelter, families sent their younger members into the labour force: indeed, a major finding reported in this book is the role of children's earnings; for all families with offspring aged fifteen or over, 40 per cent of income was contributed by those children. At the same time as young workers might have been saving to prepare for marriage and the arrival of dependent children, they were faced with the demands of ageing parents, for whom earnings and work duration were falling. Caught between the future and the past, young workers entered a difficult process of negotiation over the division of their earnings. Unemployment was a source of tension within the family. It walked with offspring as they grew up and grew old.

The first defence against poverty was the deployment of new wage earners, but all too often it failed. One of our more striking findings is the high ratio of 'unemployed,' or non-waged time, to wage earning time among adults in the working-class family. Among the poorest fifth of such families, adults spent seven months without paid work for every twelve months with a job (the ratio would be much higher if we included the labouring time of housewives). This 'unemployed' time is in part a measure of the size and role of the informal, non-measured economy of the city. The impact of unemployment intensified, and unemployment became identified as a social problem, as the city placed limits on the informal economy: by the end of the century it was more difficult to keep livestock in the city; the small size of city lots and the elimination of vacant spaces made it more difficult to grow vegetables or keep animals.[5] The informal economy survived none the less: scrounging, bartering, peddling, taking in laundry, renting rooms to boarders, gathering wood or coal cinders for fuel – such was the daily round for many urban women and children. These and many other non-waged activities engaged in especially by women and young children kept families alive and so sustained the labour force on which the economy depended. The growing capitalist economy interacted with and depended on the informal economy. Non-waged and waged work, family space, and factory/shop space interacted: to survive, families had to have compensated for unemployment in one by more intensive employment in the other.

Unemployment became visible when alternatives to waged employment shrank. But the relationship runs deeper. Unemployment was part of wage dependence rather than simply a condition of climate or season. The factories of the first industrial revolution commanded a growing share of the working time of individuals and of the working class as a whole. They offered longer work duration in return for lower average wages and generated unemployment by competing with the smaller but more labour-intensive workshops and gradually replacing them. Capital created some jobs while destroying jobs in other workplaces and in specific regions. This was the beginning of a structural unemployment that the movement of labour between cities could not and did not solve.

The frequency of unemployment varied among cities, but no city was immune to the problem. Unemployment had become a condition of labour markets across the nation. Within most cities the unemployed were not marginalized. Though overrepresented in certain neighbourhoods, they were dispersed in ways that limited collective action. Yet the working class discovered and defined the problem of unemployment, even if it did not speak with a single voice. The quest for labour-market control emerged not so much from the social space of neighbourhood as from the interrelated social space of family and factory. Labourers marched to municipal offices in winter demanding work and wages. Trade unionists struggled to keep immigrants, women, and other competitors out of labour markets. And out of the search for a stable family wage, union leaders constructed a reform platform that demanded a massive reduction of capitalists' power in labour markets.

Responses to unemployment in Canada were delayed and uncertain because of the continuing confusion in people's minds of structural unemployment with seasonal lay-offs. By the late 1890s and early 1900s, however, the dominion government was prepared to use new methods to influence class relations. Limited remedies were possible: 'compulsory conciliation' would stabilize employment by limiting strikes and lock-outs; restrictions on Chinese immigrants would limit the most unwelcome of job competitors; an alien-labour law would answer one of labour's many labour-market grievances; information on job opportunities and on living costs would leave workers better prepared to find jobs and to save in hard times. The shift was subtle, and much less impressive than what occurred in the United States at the same time.[6] Nevertheless, the change in official attitudes was important: government could no longer simply dismiss unemployment as the inevitable and temporary consequence of life in a wintery, resource-based economy. Unemployment had become an issue that necessitated some, albeit cautious and limited, intervention on the government's part in an attempt to promote social stabilization and economic growth.

Slowly and uncertainly, individuals in the dominion state equipped their ideological arsenal in order to respond to labour's challenge. Liberal political economy told officials in the Department of Labour that capital created jobs and that unemployment was the result of barriers to the flow of capital. It argued that unemployment was largely the result of cyclical fluctuations, which would teach people to alter their time horizons and to save money in good times. It insisted that real wages had increased so rapidly in recent decades that saving in good times was easy.[7]

In the early 1900s, Alfred Marshall and his successors developed the argument that unemployment was caused by wage rigidities – the failure of wages to adjust to price changes. Theoretically, it could be eliminated by the lowering of wages so that employers would cut prices, increase output, and hire more workers.[8] These and other elements of emerging neoclassical economics echo through official thinking by the 1910s.[9] These were the distant beginnings of the state's acceptance of a limited role in ameliorating the harsher effects of unemployment, without interfering with the basic structure of capitalist markets.

The distant ideological cross-fire reverberates through the decades into our own time, a reminder that ideology is sometimes as durable as the problem to which it is applied. In returning to the discovery of unemployment in Canada, we rediscover the problem as it exists in our own time. Studies of unemployment by government or its agencies sometimes offer insultingly brief historical preambles. History is a mere preface, unconnected to the analysis that follows, leaving the mislead-ing impression that unemployment is a recent phenomenon, apart from the unfortunate Depression decade long ago. Part of the problem is that the type of data required for econometric analysis does not exist for most of the long history of unemployment: what cannot be measured is therefore ignored. Only by analysing unemployment in its longer dura-tion, however, may we distinguish the structural from the cyclical or the short term. The historical perspective is a necessary reminder that unemployment did not begin in the Depression and resurface only in the recessions of the 1980s and 1990s. It has a long history within which the decades of relatively full employment, the 1940s and 1950s, are anomalous.

In the longer history of unemployment, old arguments reappear in new language. It is commonplace in the 1990s to attribute unemploy-ment to rapid technological change. The unemployed become workers in transit from obsolescent industries to the new opportunities of the information age, with the rate of their redeployment determined by lev-els of skill, education, and willingness to move. Certainly, technological change helps to explain varying rates and locations of unemployment. History tells us, however, that technological change by itself does not explain unemployment, which persists and attains very high levels even where change is slow.

The ideological reduction of unemployment to a problem of labour mobility began a century ago and is with us still in the neoconservative analysis of the 1980s and 1990s. The difference today is that transfer pay-ments, unemployment insurance, and welfare are seen as the villains that impede labour mobility by offering workers reasons not to move.[10] His-tory dissolves the veneer of argument to reveal a hoary untruth. Long before the welfare state existed, workers trekked on foot and by train, within their regions and beyond, in search of work. The high rates of mobility, the widespread willingness to bear the costs of travel and sep-aration from home, did not solve the problem of unemployment. The neoclassical stance simply elevates one direction of cause and effect and misses the other: unemployment was a barrier to labour mobility. There was little point in moving from from Montreal to Vancouver when both places had high unemployment; the jobless were precisely those who could least afford to move and who moved the least; no movement of workers, whatever its volume, would solve the problem.

The hypothesis that workers themselves caused unemployment by bidding up the price of labour is an old one, dressed up anew in the 1980s and 1990s in the patina of econometrics. The solution, of course, is that government must take steps to reduce wage levels by weakening trade unions and eliminating legislated minimum wages and other income supports.[11] Once again the causal interactions are grossly over-simplified: the argument misses the fact that willingness to work for low wages did not reduce one's risk of being unemployed. In fact, the reverse was true: as the evidence in chapter 6 indicates, those who worked in low-wage jobs had the highest risk of being unemployed. The point also applies regionally: as the long history of unemployment in the Atlantic provinces suggests, the presence of a labour surplus did not by itself serve to attract capital and create jobs. The argument also misses the fact that unemployment itself contributed to the pressure for higher wages: as we have seen in chapter 7, some workers were able to bargain successfully for slightly higher wages as compensation for a high risk of unemployment. The need for a living wage adequate to see families through 'idle seasons' also contributed to the rise of trade unions.

Today we tend to dismiss the moralizing of the late Victorians who insisted that the unemployed were lazy, intemperate, or thriftless. Yet the ethics of individual moral responsibility are revived in our own time, in the secular language of workfare, deficit reduction, and free trade. The unemployed are those who choose not to work; the poor 'have behaved in increasingly pathological ways.'[12] Again the thesis, whatever its other flaws, oversimplifies the causal connections by ignor-ing the massive evidence that unemployment is a cause of illness, of increased mortality, and a variety of social pathologies.[13] The claim that some workers choose unemployment is also ahistorical: the lesson of Canadian history is that workers chose work, not unemployment. As Walter Licht discovered in industrializing Philadelphia, 'when jobs are generated and discriminatory barriers are dislodged, people flock to work.'[14] Unemployment was the result of conditions that workers nei-ther chose nor controlled, and they themselves bore the costs of a recur-ring, determined, and thoroughly rational search for work. The quest for jobs was a shared experience that helped to create the Canadian working class.

There are differences between labour markets of today and those of a century ago, of course. One is the smaller effect of seasonal conditions today. Seasonality obscured structural unemployment, as did the cultural images of Canada as a largely empty land where multitudes could wrest a living from the land if they wanted to. At the end of the twentieth century we have seen the invention of newer ways to conceal or distance the unemployed. Unemployment is no longer merely seasonal; it is 'natural,' part of a natural order in market economies, its level determined by a natural rate (or non-accelerating inflation rate), which it is the task of economists to discover. Unemployment is also, from this perspective, necessary and even healthy, in order to limit inflation and to lower the cost of labour throughout the economy. 'The more rigid wages and salaries are ..., the more unemployment is necessary to convince individuals that it is appropriate to accept smaller increases in money incomes.'[15]

The old liberal political economy is here stood on its head: instead of lower wages serving to reduce unemployment, higher unemployment serves to lower wages. Theorists of the late Victorian era had other ways to rationalize the inevitability of unemployment; yet the argument takes us to the foundations of unemployment in the era of its discovery. The labour surplus, then as now, was an efficient means of lowering a significant variable cost, even if some workers tried to use the risk of lay-off as a bargaining lever. Labour had become a commodity, and the laws of supply and demand dictated that a surplus of the commodity would lower its cost. Unemployment was, and remains, a form of work discipline, not only at the level of the firm, but in the national labour market.

History reminds us that the costs of unemployment are beyond precise measurement. The tools of micro- and macroeconomic analysis are of little assistance in measuring the social, familial, and psychological costs of unemployment.[16] Yet the costs are not an insignificant residual, which society can afford to bear in return for other benefits. The costs that lie beyond measurement are the greatest and the most threatening. They are most clearly perceived in our past, before unemployment insurance and the welfare state. They include extensive absolute and relative poverty, high rates of infant mortality, deepening ethnic and racial conflict, worsening divisions between workers and employers, untold levels of conflict within families, and unmeasurable mental and physical hardships.

In 1995 the president of the World Bank reported that there were 100 million unemployed people in the world. Unemployment, he said, is a potent force for political destabilization. Unemployment, says the OECD, 'brings with it unravelling of the social fabric, including a loss of authority of the democratic system, and it risks resulting in the disintegration of the international trading system.'[17] In Canada, unemployment is the most serious and costly of our social and economic problems. As this book has demonstrated, it is far from new: it was as much a part of our first industrial revolution as it is of post-industrial capitalism. A problem with roots so deep is not easily eradicated, for the roots may be as deep as capitalism itself. A century ago the Canadian state failed either to solve the problem or to protect workers from its effects. At the end of the twentieth century we risk returning to a society that has neither solutions for unemployment nor protection for the unemployed and their families. History does not offer panaceas. It does, however, allow us that memory of past experience without which a solution is impossible, a record of workers' own struggles and solutions, and a powerful reminder of how the present echoes the past.

APPENDIX A

The Census as Historical Source

Our samples from the censuses of 1891 and 1901 are randomized, 10 per cent samples by dwelling place. The sampling unit is the dwelling place as numbered by the enumerator in column 1 of each census form; for each dwelling selected, we entered all persons in the dwelling. We stratified the samples by household size. In other words, we listed all dwelling places in four categories: those having between one and three persons; those with four or five persons; those having six to nine persons; and those with ten or more persons. For each census district we entered 10 per cent of dwellings in each category. In this way we ensured that persons living in small or large households are not over- or underrepresented.

The 1891 sample contains 36,221 individuals in 6,434 dwellings in seven cities (in the analysis we grouped New Westminster with Vancouver). The 1901 sample contains 41,081 individuals in 8,010 dwellings from the seven cities. For 1891 we also use a file containing all individuals said to be unemployed and all other individuals in the dwelling places of the unemployed. This latter file contains 30,028 individuals in 4,775 dwellings. Table A8 (p. 208) shows the number of dwellings by city. Since the analysis in this book shifts from dwelling (which in almost all cases is the same as 'household' in the census definition) to individual, it is important for us to show that the sample of individuals obtained by our methods is representative. Tables A9 and A10 (pp. 209, 213) help to confirm the appropriateness of the sampling method, by comparing distributions in our samples with those in the published census volumes.[1]

Given the extensive use of information from the 1891 and 1901 censuses in this book, a discussion of the provenance and of the strengths and weaknesses of those sources is necessary. Since we make greater

196   Appendix A

use of data from the 1901 census in this book, our discussion here focuses on this census. Table A1 (p. 203) sets the context by comparing Canadian, British, and American census categories.

Most of the existing commentary on Canadian censuses deals with pre-1891 censuses. By 1891 and 1901 census taking was a much more sophisticated and well-funded effort.[2] Much of the revisionist literature argues that censuses are problematic documents that tend to construct social reality in the interests of a male-dominated political and economic elite.[3] Our investigation of the 1901 census lends some support to this perspective; yet to view this document as merely an example of an imposed construction of reality would be to miss a large part of the process by which it was created. Put simply, the workforce was constructed by the census and also helped to construct it.[4]

The census was more than a count of population: it was a means by which the state codified and sanctioned certain values, including gender and status divisions of labour. A closer look at the evolution of the census in its definition of workforce confirms these points. The census of 1901 was in part an attempt to count both labour and industrial establishments: the correct means of doing so prompted a lengthy debate in Parliament.[5] The growing concern to expand available information on labour and industry resulted in a census in which the respondent was able to define more precisely her or his niche in the workforce. The state was still engaged in a social and cultural construction of 'work,' but respondents now had a wider range of choices than ever before. The state structured and controlled the information for its own purposes, leaving individuals more leeway to define their own workforce activity.

The census asked no less than fourteen questions about the labour force. These questions break down into four categories (see Table A2). The first category is the general one: 'profession, occupation, trade, or means of living of each person,' which we refer to simply as 'occupation.' The second category relates to employment status and is an elaboration on the simple employer/wage earner dichotomy used in 1891. In 1901 there were five possibilities: 'retired,' 'living on own means,' 'employer,' 'employee,' or 'working on own account.' Instructions to the enumerators did not say that these possibilities were mutually exclusive; thus it was possible for individuals to answer positively in more than one column. It was possible therefore for a person to be both employer and employee (a ship's master, for instance); an individual could be both employer and working on her or his own account (our sample yielded 243 of these).

The third category of information relates to employment duration. The 1901 census provided unemployment data of a different sort than those provided in 1891. The census asked about type of employment and duration of employment within each type. Once again census officials were constructing work into specific categories, but the categories allowed for a more flexible reflection of working experience than ever before. The fourth category relates to earnings from employment – earnings from one's main and from one's secondary occupation. Within this category there is implied recognition of occupational pluralism.

The collection of information in these categories was of course structured in terms desired by the state. The four categories were embedded in a conceptual frame that restricted and channelled the collection process. The historian must recognize the tension between the state's intention and respondents' agency. It is clear that the state had specific aims. For instance, in the enumerators' schedule, and in the instructions to the enumerator, a single heading appeared above all columns relating to employment status and employment duration. That heading read simply: 'Wage Earners.'[6] 'Wage earners,' it will be recalled, was used in direct contrast to 'employers' in 1891. Moreover, the 1901 instructions described earnings as relating to people who were 'employed in any industry or other occupation.' People 'employed' were said to be those 'paid salary, wages or other money allowances.' 'Salary' and 'wages' referred specifically to money received 'which one person employed by another' obtained 'for his service.' In 1901, employers, people self-employed, or even partially self-employed, and those of independent means were distinguished in significant ways from wage earners: the former were encouraged to ignore questions about earnings and months worked; the latter were not allowed to do so.

Within the general preoccupation with wage earners, there is evidence of a new concern for types of wage earner. In 1881 enumerators received only one-third of a page of instruction on how to classify an occupation, and a great deal of imprecision resulted in the reporting of occupations. In 1891, accordingly, six pages of instruction concerned the correct way of providing a 'fully descriptive [occupational] designation.' Most revealing was the distinction made between a 'maker' and an operative factory hand. 'Thirty years ago,' the enumerators were reminded, 'a shoemaker made a whole shoe, and a tailor made a whole suit of clothes; at the present time, owing to the sub-division of labour, few workmen begin and complete any article of manufacture. In every branch of work the specialist has succeeded the general worker, and statistics of occupation at the present day must possess the most specific detail or they will not satisfy the demands of the inquirer.' Thus 'cotton-mill operative' or 'factory hand' would not suffice: 'the actual occupation or kind of labour done, as cotton mill spinner, is what is needed.'[7] These instructions reflected an attempt to define and classify elements of the emerging urban, industrial class. General labels had sufficed for an agricultural and artisanal population: the industrial revolution, however, necessitated more descriptive precision.

To what extent is the reporting of an occupation a useful guide to a respondent's being in the workforce? We know that for those with stated occupations (17,339), all but a mere 684 offered some information under one or more of the columns on employment status, months, and earnings. There is a very high correlation between having an occupation and defining oneself with more specificity about employment status (our second general category – living on own means, employer, employee, and so on – see Table A2). Indeed, 94.3 per cent of the 17,339 with stated occupations provided further information about their employment status. Slightly more than two of every five who did not do so were in our occupational category 'professional,' and one in every five of those who were professionals did not provide information on their employment status.[8] By contrast, while 18.5 per cent of all who failed to provide further information were in the 'industrial, production and transport' categories, they represented only a minuscule 2.4 per cent of all people whose occupations fall within those general categories. This finding is consistent with what one might expect given the enumerators' instructions and the structure of the schedule: if you were in an industrial or transportation occupation, you were much more likely to have your employment status reported. This is consistent with the emphasis on collecting information on wage earners.

An obvious question about underreporting relates to gender. Were men more likely than women to provide information on employment status? In fact, the difference is slight: 7.8 per cent of women with occupations did not provide information on employment status; 5.0 per cent of men with occupations did likewise. The underreporting of women occurred more often in the occupation category than in the employment-status columns.

There are ways in which this complex census can tell us things about women that no previous census did. For example, there were 484 people who had no stated occupations yet did provide information about employment status! Of those 484, 71 per cent were women. Of those women, 92 per cent defined themselves as 'living on own means.' The census, by asking so many questions about labour-force participation, allowed people to say something about their status even when they had no occupation. Within a structured and gendered document, there was nevertheless greater opportunity for self-definition than ever before.

In contrast to information on employment status, we have a much higher proportion of missing information relating to number of months worked: fully 26.8 per cent of individuals with stated occupations did not offer information on duration of work during the year (see Table A3). Once again, the professional category accounts for a disproportionate number of those with no months reported: almost one in four. Just over half of people in professional occupations reported no months. This finding is consistent with the directions in the enumerators' instructions: months are to be reported for wage earners only, and few professionals were wage earners.

Somewhat more difficult to explain, however, a significant number of individuals in the industrial/transport categories gave no information on months worked: 28.5 per cent of all those with months unreported were in the industrial/transport category; and of all the people in those categories, 17.8 per cent reported no months. Regrouping those with no months reported into wage earners and employers or self-employed goes far towards explaining this seeming anomaly. Thirty per cent of those in the industrial/transport categories who provided no information on months worked identified themselves as employers and/or self-employed. A further 7 per cent did not provide any information on employment status, and another 10 per cent were retired. Thus just under 50 per cent of the people in industrial/transport occupations who did not provide details on months worked were non–wage earners. When one divides all of those missing duration-of-work information into wage earners and employer/self-employed, 40 per cent were employers or self-employed, though such people represented only 17.5 per cent of the workforce. A further 17 per cent provided no information on employment status. Of those 772 individuals who did not detail work duration or employment status, close to 50 per cent were students over eighteen years of age, ministers, nuns, or hospital patients. In other words, the document contains less underreporting than one might think. Thus we can explain most of those cases where information on months worked is missing other than by positing mere laziness on the part of the enumerator or a failure in communication between enumerators and respondents.[9]

Of the 17,339 who reported an occupation, 81.9 per cent reported their earnings in column 26 (see Table A4). The reason for missing information on earnings is identical to the reason for the absence of figures on 'months worked': those who did not report earnings tended to be people of least immediate concern to enumerators – employers, people working on their own account, or people 'living on own means.' Only 7 per cent of those with stated occupations who defined themselves as employees failed to state their earnings. By contrast, 52 per cent of non-employees (employers and those working on their own account) did not report earnings.

How valid are the earnings data?[10] Tests for such validity are difficult to devise. In 1907 the dominion government published a summary of earnings by occupations drawn from the 1901 personal census returns. The introduction to that bulletin compared those earnings with income figures generated from the 1901 manufacturing schedule. The author concluded that 'the individual records of wage-earnings taken by enumerators were not only short as regards the number of employees, but also that employees of the better classes were recorded probably in undue proportion' (see Table A5).[11]

These conclusions may look persuasive. Personal censuses, after all, are notorious for their underreporting of economically and socially disadvantaged individuals. Moreover, the manufacturing schedules deliberately ignored most workplaces that employed fewer than five people. It is true that on average those employed in the 'factory system of manufacture' received lower wages than those traditional craft-workers employed in hand trades in small shops.

There are, however, other realities that are ignored in the above analysis that may account for the seeming disparity in employee numbers and average earnings reported in the manufacturing schedule as compared to the personal schedule. In fact, the disjuncture may be more apparent than real. The data generated for the manufacturing schedule differed not only in units of analysis but also in the manner of collection. The enumerators who compiled the manufacturing schedules contacted only the owners of workshops that employed five or more individuals. Individual workers were not contacted. Owners provided information on total annual wages and on the total number of people who worked for them over the course of the year.[12] The compilers of the Postal Census of Manufactures in 1916 recognized one problem with this procedure. After careful analysis they concluded that asking employers to state the total number of employees during the year 'tended to increase somewhat the number of employees recorded, as manufacturers ... tended to make their returns for the period of full activity.' Asking for number of employees during each month of the year corrected for this bias, which postal census compilers estimated at about 12 per cent.[13]

One must of course set against this overestimate provided by the manufacturers the fact that employees in most shops with fewer than five workers were not included in the manufacturing schedules and were at least potentially enumerated in the personal schedule. In 1891 those employed in small workshops represented 26.4 per cent of all manufacturing employees; in 1916, under 7 per cent.[14] Our six-city sample suggests that 24.5 per cent of industrial-production employees worked in small workshops.

Before concluding that the personal schedules did indeed undercount employees in the manufacturing sector we must consider one further and very significant point. Employers provided an estimate of workers who laboured for them, but in 1901 occupational pluralism was common. Turnover rates in factories were high; workers sought and found other jobs when laid off from their primary trade. Our analysis of work duration indicates that many respondents with a clearly seasonal occupation reported working a full twelve months in the year. We therefore infer that they found work supplementary to that of their primary occupation. Very probably manufacturing-schedule returns suffer from some degree of double counting.

This last point also has particular relevance to the apparent discrepancy in average income rates as reported in the two schedules. The manufacturing schedule reported average rates for employment in a particular factory. Yet, given high turnover rates and occupational pluralism, those averages would tend to understate the real income of many workers. The personal schedule, which reported the individual worker's total income, is not subject to the same problem and is therefore a more adequate measurement of yearly earnings.

It is, however, true that workers in small handicraft establishments tended to earn more than did workers who toiled in shops of five or more employees. In our six-city census sample, in the manufacturing sector employees who worked in factories averaged $379 per year and those who worked elsewhere averaged $461. This suggests that the erosion of the traditional artisan did come at a high cost to such workers and their families. It also hints that wage rates in the personal and in the manufacturing censuses are not usefully comparable. Comparing the incomes of only factory workers to income figures provided in the manufacturing schedules, and then breaking them down by city, offer a better comparison (see Table A6).

Our census sample yields a higher proportion of women than do the data calculated from the manufacturing returns and thus helps lower the overall average income.[15] Yet the data in Table A6 surely confirm the substance of our argument thus far. The difference in wage rates between the men can be comfortably attributed to the problem inherent in the manufacturing enumeration. Total earnings were underestimated even as total wage earners were overestimated.

There is then no compelling reason to suspect significant undercounting of manufacturing employees in the personal census relative to the manufacturing census. There is good reason to believe that the income information is more satisfactory in the former than in the latter. Moreover, the manufacturing-schedule data are available only in an aggregated form, most often expressed as averages. They are thus in a form not suitable for answering the questions many would wish to ask. The disaggregated information provided in the nominal-level (personal) census returns can meet our analytical demands. Viewed from a wider perspective, it is certainly the case that the personal census enumerators missed many more workers in the lower than in the higher income cohorts. Nothing we have stated here contradicts that reality. What we have argued is that the personal schedules provide the best available data on work and income for the period under review.

Table A7 offers the headings printed on the population schedule of the 1901 census. Table A8 indicates the number of dwellings sampled for each of our six cities in 1891 and 1901. Tables A9 and A10 compare distributions in our samples with those published by census officials.

In some significant cases, the 1901 census provides more than a static portrait of a moment frozen in time. Unlike the 1891 census, it asks many questions relating to work and wages covering a year's lived experience. No single historical source or combination of sources can provide an exact replica of past behaviour. Nevertheless, we feel confident in stating that the 1901 nominal-level census returns, when used carefully with other qualitative and routinely generated sources, can provide more satisfactory answers to questions on the employment, income, and living standards of urban Canadians at that time than any other source or combination of sources known to us.

TABLE A1

International comparison of workforce characteristics: Canadian, British, and American censuses, 1880–1901

Characteristic	1880–1	1890–1	1900–1
Occupation	A,B,C*	A,B,C	A,B,C
Unemployed	A,B	A,C	A†
Employer	‡	B,C	B,C
Wage earner	‡	B,C	B,C
Working on own account	B§	B,C	–
Retired	–	–	C
Living on own means	–	–	C
Working at home	–	–	B,C
Working in factory	–	–	C
Working in both factory and home	–	–	C
Months employed at trade in factory	–	–	C
Months employed at trade in home	–	–	C
Months employed in other occupation than trade in factory or home	–	–	C
Earnings from occupation or trade	–	–	C
Extra earnings from other than chief occupation or trade	–	–	C

*A = American, B = British, C = Canadian.

†The Canadian census did ask questions concerning months worked, and from those one can estimate unemployment.

‡The United Kingdom did provide for collection of employer and wage-earner information before 1891, but the question was asked only of the employer and the placement of the question on the back of the forms led most respondents to ignore it. The 1891 census was the first time the question was put to the general populace.

§If the Canadian respondent had an occupation, was not unemployed, and left the employer and wage-earner questions blank, then one can infer that the respondent was self-employed or working on her or his own account.

TABLE A2
Employment status of persons with stated occupations, Canada, 1901

Employment status	Number	% of total
1 Total with occupations	17,339	100
2 Retired	(274)*	
3 Living on own means	341	2.0
4 Employer	575	3.3
5 Employee	13,484	77.8
6 Working on own account	1,611	9.3
7 Employers and 3 and/or 6 above	289	1.7
8 Employees and 3 and/or 6 above	53	0.3
9 No information	986	5.7

*Enumerators were directed to enter 'r' in column 17 (occupation) where people were retired. Some of the 274 have stated occupations; others do not. We do not include the retired in the employment status percentages.

TABLE A3
Number of persons with occupations who reported months worked in three workplace categories,* 1901

Occupation	No. of persons
Total with occupations	17,339
'Months employed at trade in factory'	4,725
'Months employed at trade in home'	1,385
'Months employed in other occupation than trade in factory or home'	6,642
Missing	4,649

*There were sixty-three people who reported months worked in more than one category.

TABLE A4
Number of persons with occupations who report earnings,* 1901

Source of earnings		No. of persons
Occupations		17,339
'Earnings from occupation or trade'		14,194
'Extra earnings from other than chief occupation or trade'	279	
Missing		3,145

*Note that 14,194 and 3,145 add up to 17,339. Note also that 168 people with no stated occupation did report earnings! These 168 are not included in this table.

TABLE A5
Census estimates of average wages in the manufacturing sector, 1901

	Manufacturing census schedule		Personal census schedule	
	Number	Average income ($)	Number	Average income ($)
Male	241,976	365	226,001	403
Female	66,371	180	49,662	193
Total	308,347	324	275,663	365

Source: Census and Statistics Office, *Bulletin I: Wage-Earners by Occupation* (Ottawa, 1907), xxviii.

TABLE A6
Average annual income from manufacturing census and five-city sample, 1901

	Manufacturing schedule*		Five-city sample†	
	Number	Average income ($)	Number	Average income ($)
Male	39,533	403	3,172	429
Female	10,662	212	1,061	224
Total	50,195	362	4,233	378

*City figures for male and female were calculated from the manufacturing-census information in the following way. We assumed that the proportion of male and female workers in the city was the same as that published in the returns for that city's province.
†These figures represent all employees who said that they worked in factories and were thus not in our professional- or managerial-occupation categories. Wage income for total workers was available in the published returns for only five of the six cities in our sample: Victoria, Winnipeg, Hamilton, Montreal, and Halifax. See 1901 Census of Canada, Vol. 3, 160–1, 168–71, 184–7, and 232–7.

TABLE A7
Headings on the population schedule of the 1901 Canadian census

Personal Description

Name of each person in family or household on 31st March 1901	Sex	Colour	Relationship to head of family or household	Single married widowed or divorced	Month and date of birth	Year of birth	Age at last birthday

Citizenship, Nationality and Religion

Country or place of birth (If in Canada specify province or territory, and add "r" for rural or urban, as the case may be)	Year of immigration to Canada	Year of naturalization	Racial or tribal origin	Nationality	Religion

Principal Profession or Trade

Profession, occupation, trade or means of living of each person. (If person has retired from profession or trade, add "r" for retired)	Living on own means	Employer	Employee	Working on own account

TABLE A7 (concluded)

Wage Earner

Working at trade in factory or in home (Specify by "f" for factory and "h" for home, or both, as the case may be)	Months employed at trade in factory	Months employed at trade in home	Months employed in other occupations than trade in factory or home	Earnings from occupation of trade $	Extra earnings. (From other than chief occupation or trade) $

Education and Language of each person five years of age and over

Months at school in year	Can read	Can write	Can speak English	Can speak French	Mother tongue (If spoken)

TABLE A8
Number of dwellings sampled, by city, 1891 and 1901

City	1891 random sample	1891 unemployed sample	1901 random sample
Vancouver/ New Westminster	373	375	677
Victoria	338	218	416
Winnipeg	480	158	799
Hamilton	968	848	1,185
Montreal	3,722	2,788	4,175
Halifax	553	388	758
Total	6,434	4,775	8,010

TABLE A9

Comparisons of selected variables between 1891 random sample and published census aggregates, five cities

Variable	Census		Sample	
	Number	%	Number	%
Victoria				
Age of male and female				
1–14	N/A	N/A	425	24.7
15–19			142	8.3
20–29			506	29.4
30–39			306	17.8
40–49			167	9.7
50–59			110	6.4
60–64			31	1.8
65+			33	1.9
Total			1,720	100.0
Gender				
Male	10,653	63.3	1,081	63
Female	6,188	36.7	635	37
Total	16,841	100.0	1,716	100
Marital status				
Married	5,031	91.3	545	91.4
Widow	480	8.7	51	8.6
Total	5,511	100.0	596	100.0
Major religions				
Roman Catholic	1,782	14.0	202	15.7
Church of England	5,364	41.7	494	38.4
Presbyterian	2,981	23.2	299	23.3
Methodist	2,113	16.4	218	17.0
Baptist	621	4.8	73	5.7
Total	12,861	100.1	1,286	100.1
Winnipeg				
Age of male and female				
1–14	8,688	34.0	919	32.9
15–19	2,335	9.1	237	8.5
20–29	6,115	24.0	701	25.1
30–39	4,452	17.4	528	18.9
40–49	2,322	9.1	249	8.9
50–59	1,075	4.1	92	3.3
60–64	301	1.2	36	1.3
65+	305	1.2	31	1.1
Total	25,593	100.1	2,793	100.0

(*continued*)

TABLE A9 (*continued*)

Variable	Census		Sample	
	Number	%	Number	%
Gender				
Male	13,406	52.3	1,490	53.3
Female	12,233	47.7	1,302	46.7
Total	25,639	100.0	2,792	100.0
Marital status				
Married	8,640	91.9	936	91.5
Widow	764	8.1	87	8.5
Total	9,404	100.0	1,023	100.0
Major religions				
Roman Catholic	2,470	12.0	242	10.6
Church of England	6,854	33.2	791	34.7
Presbyterian	5,952	28.8	650	28.5
Methodist	4,310	20.9	429	18.8
Baptist	1,046	5.1	166	7.3
Total	20,632	100.0	2,278	99.9
Hamilton				
Age of male and female				
1–14	15,722	33.3	1,555	31.9
15–19	5,088	10.8	570	11.7
20–29	9,516	20.2	1,043	21.4
30–39	6,459	13.7	624	12.8
40–49	4,579	9.7	468	9.6
50–59	3,096	6.6	332	6.8
60–64	1,138	2.4	127	2.6
65+	1,596	3.4	156	3.2
Total	47,194	100.1	4,875	100.0
Gender				
Male	22,726	48	2,300	47.2
Female	24,579	52	2,574	52.8
Total	47,305	100	4,874	100.0
Marital status				
Married	16,013	87.1	1,665	88.4
Widow	2,379	12.9	219	11.6
Total	18,392	100.0	1,884	100.0
Major religions				
Roman Catholic	8,557	19.2	922	20.0
Church of England	11,821	26.6	1,216	26.4
Presbyterian	10,190	22.9	1,051	22.8
Methodist	12,037	27.0	1,201	26.1
Baptist	1,912	4.3	218	4.7
Total	44,517	100.0	4,608	100.0

TABLE A9 (*continued*)

Variable	Census		Sample	
	Number	%	Number	%
Montreal				
Age of male and female				
1–14	56,604	31.0	6,211	31.9
15–19	18,693	10.3	1,927	9.9
20–29	39,892	21.9	4,323	22.2
30–39	26,616	14.6	2,804	14.4
40–49	18,750	10.3	1,986	10.2
50–59	11,452	6.3	1,207	6.2
60–64	4,228	2.3	409	2.1
65+	6,194	3.4	604	3.1
Total	182,429	100.1	19,471	100.0
Gender				
Male	86,186	47.2	9,184	47.2
Female	96,509	52.8	10,275	52.8
Total	182,695	100.0	19,459	100.0
Marital status				
Married	61,957	86.8	6,711	86.6
Widow	9,436	13.2	1,043	13.4
Total	71,393	100.0	7,754	100.0
Major religions				
Roman Catholic	131,420	75.4	14,077	74.9
Church of England	19,684	11.3	2,200	11.7
Presbyterian	14,851	8.5	1,602	8.5
Methodist	6,802	3.9	754	4.0
Baptist	1,525	0.9	156	0.8
Total	174,282	100.0	18,789	99.9
Halifax				
Age of male & female				
1–14	12,708	33.1	1,682	33.2
15–19	4,365	11.4	534	10.5
20–29	7,674	19.9	1,001	19.7
30–39	4,830	12.6	701	13.8
40–49	3,890	10.1	498	9.8
50–59	2,455	6.4	315	6.2
60–64	876	2.3	117	2.3
65+	1,642	4.3	229	4.5
Total	38,440	100.1	5,077	100.0
Gender				
Male	18,202	47.3	2,423	47.7
Female	20,293	52.7	2,658	52.3
Total	38,495	100.0	5,081	100.0

(*continued*)

TABLE A9 (*concluded*)

Variable	Census		Sample	
	Number	%	Number	%
Marital status				
Married	11,886	84.5	1,621	84.6
Widow	2,179	15.5	295	15.4
Total	14,065	100.0	1,916	100.0
Major religions				
Roman Catholic	15,658	41.9	2,316	46.4
Church of England	9,964	26.7	1,275	25.6
Presbyterian	4,877	13.1	556	11.2
Methodist	3,995	10.7	472	9.5
Baptist	2,854	7.6	369	7.4
Total	37,348	100.0	4,988	100.1

TABLE A10
Comparisons of selected variables between our sample of 1901 census and published census aggregates, six cities

Variable	Census Number	%	Sample Number	%
Victoria				
Age of male and female				
1–14	N/A	N/A	532	27.7
15–19			177	9.2
20–29			370	19.3
30–39			386	20.1
40–49			244	12.7
50–59			119	6.2
60–64			38	2.0
65+			54	2.8
Total			1,920	100.0
Gender				
Male	12,618	60.3	1,131	58.9
Female	8,301	39.7	788	41.1
Total	20,919	100.0	1,919	100.0
Marital status				
Married	7,576	90.2	721	90.7
Widow	821	9.8	74	9.3
Total	8,397	100.0	795	100.0
Major religions				
Roman Catholic	2,179	11.9	195	13.5
Church of England	7,895	42.9	619	42.7
Presbyterian	4,056	22.1	293	20.2
Methodist	3,252	17.7	241	16.6
Baptist	1,007	5.5	102	7.0
Total	18,389	100.1	1,450	100.0
Vancouver				
Age of male and female				
1–14	N/A	N/A	742	28.0
15–19			239	9.0
20–29			567	21.4
30–39			517	19.5
40–49			323	12.2
50–59			156	5.9
60–64			53	2.0
65+			53	2.0
Total			2,650	100.0

(*continued*)

TABLE A10 (*continued*)

Variable	Census		Sample	
	Number	%	Number	%
Gender				
Male	15,978	59.2	1,517	57.2
Female	11,032	40.8	1,134	42.8
Total	27,010	100.0	2,651	100.0
Marital status				
Married	8,825	92.5	940	91.1
Widow	718	7.5	92	8.9
Total	9,543	100.0	1,032	100.0
Major religions				
Roman Catholic	3,064	13.9	246	11.5
Church of England	7,063	32.1	776	36.1
Presbyterian	6,505	29.6	593	27.6
Methodist	3,785	17.2	395	18.4
Baptist	1,556	7.1	138	6.4
Total	21,973	99.9	2,148	100.0
Winnipeg				
Age of male and female				
1–14	13,999	33.2	1,438	34.4
15–19	4,127	9.8	398	9.5
20–29	9,180	21.8	847	20.2
30–39	6,653	15.8	704	16.8
40–49	4,614	10.9	436	10.4
50–59	2,209	5.2	214	5.1
60–64	521	1.2	67	1.6
65+	871	2.1	84	2.0
Total	42,174	100.0	4,188	100.1
Gender				
Male	21,940	51.8	2,140	51.0
Female	20,400	48.2	2,050	49.0
Total	42,340	100.0	4,190	100.0
Marital status				
Married	14,555	91.7	1,459	92.3
Widow	1,326	8.3	121	7.7
Total	15,881	100.0	1,580	100.0
Major religions				
Roman Catholic	5,143	15.0	448	13.3
Church of England	10,175	29.7	1,090	32.5
Presbyterian	10,172	29.7	896	26.7
Methodist	6,741	19.7	675	20.1
Baptist	2,055	6.0	249	7.4
Total	34,286	100.1	3,358	100.0

TABLE A10 (*continued*)

Variable	Census		Sample	
	Number	%	Number	%
Hamilton				
Age of male and female				
1–14	14,918	28.4	1,676	28.7
15–19	5,516	10.5	666	11.4
20–29	10,494	20.0	1,162	19.9
30–39	7,867	15.0	852	14.6
40–49	6,016	11.4	648	11.1
50–59	3,882	7.4	444	7.6
60–64	1,393	2.7	146	2.5
65+	2,479	4.7	245	4.2
Total	52,565	100.1	5,839	99.9
Gender				
Male	24,925	47.4	2,769	47.5
Female	27,709	52.6	3,066	52.5
Total	52,634	100.0	5,835	100.0
Marital status				
Married	18,791	86.7	2,012	86.8
Widow	2,878	13.3	306	13.2
Total	21,669	100.0	2,318	100.0
Major religions				
Roman Catholic	8,872	18.0	1,025	18.7
Church of England	12,443	25.2	1,399	25.6
Presbyterian	11,542	23.4	1,294	23.7
Methodist	13,737	27.8	1,443	26.4
Baptist	2,814	5.7	309	5.7
Total	49,408	100.1	5,470	100.1
Montreal				
Age of male and female				
1–14	57,026	28.5	6,846	31.0
15–19	19,666	9.8	2,319	10.5
20–29	43,576	21.8	4,550	20.6
30–39	29,977	15.0	3,158	14.3
40–49	22,057	11.0	2,363	10.7
50–59	14,806	7.4	1,590	7.2
60–64	4,890	2.5	486	2.2
65+	8,009	4.0	773	3.5
Total	200,007	100.0	22,085	100.0

(*continued*)

TABLE A10 (*concluded*)

Variable	Census		Sample	
	Number	%	Number	%
Gender				
Male	96,037	47.3	10,696	48.4
Female	107,041	52.7	11,383	51.6
Total	203,078	100.0	22,079	100.0
Marital status				
Married	67,819	86.2	7,373	87.3
Widow	10,886	13.8	1,069	12.7
Total	78,705	100.0	8,442	100.0
Major religions				
Roman Catholic	148,063	77.1	15,521	75.0
Church of England	20,471	10.7	2,431	11.8
Presbyterian	15,637	8.1	1,834	8.9
Methodist	6,378	3.3	692	3.4
Baptist	1,530	0.8	185	0.9
Total	192,079	100.0	20,663	100.0
Halifax				
Age of male & female				
1–14	N/A	N/A	1,233	32.5
15–19			383	10.1
20–29			729	19.2
30–39			489	12.9
40–49			421	11.1
50–59			269	7.1
60–64			106	2.8
65+			164	4.3
Total			3,794	100.0
Gender				
Male	19,529	47.8	1,728	45.6
Female	21,303	52.2	2,065	54.4
Total	40,832	100.0	3,793	100.0
Marital status				
Married	13,141	85.8	1,256	87.9
Widow	2,177	14.2	173	12.1
Total	15,318	100.0	1,429	100.0
Major religions				
Roman Catholic	16,693	41.7	1,529	41.4
Church of England	10,877	27.2	972	26.3
Presbyterian	4,864	12.2	348	9.4
Methodist	4,507	11.2	511	13.8
Baptist	3,103	7.8	335	9.1
Total	40,044	100.1	3,695	100.0

APPENDIX B

Estimates of Cost of Living

Costs of Daily Diet

Table B1 (p. 221) estimates the cost of the daily diet of an adult male in our six cities in 1900. In estimating food needs of other family members we use the following weights, which approximate those in Bettina Bradbury, *Working Families: Age, Gender and Daily Survival in Industrializing Montreal* (Toronto, 1993): women fifteen and over = .80; boys aged fifteen to nineteen = .85; children fourteen and under = .55. These weights were applied to all families by city, so that food costs would reflect the varying sizes of families and ages of family members. Note that we allow small amounts of meat a week, in order to adjust Rowntree's diet to North American consumption patterns. *Report of the Board of Inquiry into the Cost of Living*, 2 vols. (Ottawa, 1915), allowed no less than nine pounds of meat (not including bacon) a week for a 'fairly typical' family of five (vol. 1, 137). We allocate only eight ounces of mutton or beef to an adult male per week, or 1.9 pounds for a family of five per week. Our estimates may be compared with the 'Family Budgets' in *Board of Inquiry*, vol. 2, 1018. The same report (vol. 1, 142) gives the 'Cost of Food Budget' for a family of five in 1900.

Table B2 (p. 223) shows that our food estimates are significantly lower for each city than those in the report. We assume that the family of five consisted of husband, wife, a son over fourteen, and two younger children. Our food allocations are significantly lower than those of the 'typical' working class family.

Annual Housing Costs

Family of One

Our source is the *Labour Gazette* (Nov. 1900), 100: 'Schedule Showing Rates Paid for Board and Lodging by Workingmen.' For each city we assume that 60 per cent of the cost was for board; the other 40 per cent is for lodging. BC city figures in this table are clearly inflated, so we take instead two-thirds of the cost of renting a tenement flat of four rooms. This method yields the following estimate of housing costs for a person living by himself or herself: Victoria, $68; Vancouver, $76; Winnipeg, $83; Hamilton, $62; Montreal, $73; Halifax, $62. To these figures we add one-fifth of the cost of 'additions' (furnishings, soap, travel to work, water – items that we regard as essential) and one-fifth of the cost of fuel from Table B3 below. The estimated total costs of housing, fuel, and 'additions' for the single person is: Victoria, $80.90; Vancouver, $88.90; Winnipeg, $100.70; Hamilton, $76.70; Montreal, $88.70; Halifax, $77.70.

Family of Two, Three, or Four

We begin with an estimate for a family of four persons. Rental costs are taken from two places: *Labour Gazette* (Nov. 1900), 100, and (Nov. 1901), 280 (we deduct 2 per cent for inflation from figures taken from the latter). From the former we take rents of houses of four rooms for each of our cities; from the latter we take rents of four-room 'flats' in tenements. Where both figures are available, we take the average of the two. Note that our people-per-room ratio is one. The estimated annual rentals are: Victoria, $101; Vancouver, $120; Winnipeg, $108; Hamilton, $89; Montreal, $89; Halifax, $95. To these we add two-fifths of the cost of 'additions' and two-fifths of the costs of fuel from Table B3 below, to yield the following figures for rent, fuel, and sundries for a family of four: Victoria, $127; Vancouver, $146; Winnipeg, $143; Hamilton, $118; Montreal, $120; Halifax, $126. For a family of three we take the mid-point between the costs for a family of four and a family of one; for a family of two we take the mid-point between costs for a family of three and a family of one.

Family of Five or More

For all families of five and more people we use the same estimates for housing, fuel, and miscellaneous additions. The results allow for overcrowding. We use, wherever possible, not one but two sources for rental costs: *Labour Gazette* (Nov. 1900), 100, gives monthly rental costs of houses of six rooms; *Board of Inquiry*, vol. 1, 474–8, gives the rental cost of a six–room dwelling without sanitary conveniences in a working-class neighbourhood. For all cities but Victoria we take the average of the lowest figures for such housing from these two sources. The rationale for this procedure is that a large proportion of dwellings in working-class neighbourhoods had no sewage connections; averaging the two takes into account the variation in the two sources and the generally lower figures for dwellings 'without sanitary conveniences.' For Victoria we take the average of the lowest values in Table A (*Board of Inquiry*, vol. 1, p. 474) and Table B (dwellings without sanitary conveniences, vol. 1, p. 476). Table B3 reports the annual rental costs in line 1, followed by the miscellaneous additions (light, furnishings, soap, travel to work, and water) for a family of five and the estimated fuel costs for such a dwelling place.

Annual Cost of Fuel

Board of Inquiry, vol. 2, 1018, gives thirteen family budgets for Winnipeg from the early 1900s. The average family size was 5.15. The average monthly fuel cost was $7.88, or 22.5 per cent of the average family food budget. The price of stove coal in Winnipeg was $9.50 per ton in 1900. This means that the family was using ten tons in the year. Labourer Thomas Gratorex argued that if great care was taken an average house in Montreal could be heated over the winter with four tons of coal, and this is what Bradbury uses (Bradbury, *Working Families*, 97). *Board of Inquiry*, vol. 2, 75: 'Table III: Weekly Expenditures on Staple Foods, Fuel and Lighting for a Family of Five, 1900–1913,' assumes 1/16th ton of coal per week = 0.06 ton. This is close to Gratorex's estimate for Montreal (four tons per year = 0.08 ton per week).

Method 1, by volume and cost of fuel, uses prices from *Labour Gazette* (Nov. 1900), 99. (See Table B4). To check these figures, we looked at the ratio of food to fuel costs in other sources. Fuel as a proportion of food budget is somewhere between 19 per cent and 22 per cent in most cities outside British Columbia. Bertram and Percy have four groups with food weighted at 43.8, fuel and light at 8.7, rent at 22.5, and clothing at 25.0; Gordon W. Bertram, 'Real Wage Trends in Canada 1900–26: Some Provisional Estimates,' *Canadian Journal of Economics*, 12, no. 2 (1979), 310–12. Thus fuel plus light makes up 19.9 per cent of food. Bartlett has fuel and light at 13 per cent of food for Vancouver; Eleanor Bartlett, 'Real Wages and the Standard of Living in Vancouver, 1901–1939,' *BC Studies* 51 (autumn 1981), 3–62. The Department of Labour has coal plus wood at 22 per cent of food; *Board of Inquiry*, vol. 2, 75.

Table B5 presents the annual fuel costs which we have used, together with fuel as a percentage of our annual food budget for a family of five.

Annual Cost of Clothing

Bradbury, following Rowntree, puts annual clothing expenditures at 14 per cent of food costs (Bradbury, *Working Families*, 98). This estimate may be too low, since the thirteen Winnipeg family budgets (*Board of Inquiry*, vol. 2, 1018) estimate clothing at $11.35 monthly, or $136.2 per year, or 32.6 per cent of cost of food per year. This figure is certainly too high. In Bertram and Percy the food group weight is 52.5; clothing group, 18.0, or 34 per cent of food. The Eaton's catalogues c. 1900 suggest that one complete man's outfit (consisting of one coat, one denim overalls, one pair pants, two wool underwear, two work shirts, one pair of gloves, one cap, one pair of boots, one pair of shoes, and one night robe) would cost $16.00. We assume that such an outfit would have to be replaced every two years, and so we allow $8 for clothing. We allow the same amount in all cities because clothing would be more expensive in Vancouver and Victoria, but, given the climate, less would be required. The ratio of clothing to food budget for an adult male ranges from 12 per cent to 16.6 per cent. Clothing costs of adult women are weighted at .8, teenagers at .7, and children aged 5–13 at .5.

Weights of Cost-of-Living Components

Applying the above estimates to a family of five in each city yields weights for each item in the minimum-living-cost total (Table B6). Note again that we are trying to estimate not average spending by working-class families, but rather a minimum budget. It follows that the weights will differ from those based on typical or average family budgets. The weights for Victoria are very close to Vancouver's and so are not reported separately below.

TABLE B1
Price (cents) of daily adult male diet, by city, 1900

	Victoria	Vancouver	Winnipeg	Hamilton	Montreal	Halifax
Sunday						
*Bread 16 oz	4.5	4.5	2.5	2.5	2.3	2.5
*Margarine: sub						
Butter 1 oz	1.8	1.8	1.6	1.6	1.5	1.5
*Tea 1 oz	2.6	2.6	2.2	2.5	1.8	1.2
*Bacon 3 oz	3.3	3.3	2.6	2.8	2.8	2.4
*Pease pudding						
beans, 6 oz	1.8	1.8	1.8	1.5	1.5	1.6
Coffee 1 oz	2.2	2.2	2.2	1.6	1.4	2.2
Total	16.2	16.2	12.9	12.5	11.3	11.4
Monday						
*Bread 16 oz	4.5	4.5	2.5	2.5	2.3	2.5
*Porridge						
Oatmeal 4 oz	1.1	1.1	0.7	0.7	0.7	0.7
Milk 1/4 quart	1.8	1.8	1.8	1.2	1.8	1.5
*Potato 16 oz	1.3	1.3	1.0	0.5	0.7	0.6
*Cheese 4 oz	4.2	4.2	3.7	3.7	3.3	3.7
*Veg. broth	0.6	0.6	0.6	0.5	0.5	0.5
veg. 2 oz						
Tea 1 oz	2.6	2.6	2.2	2.5	1.8	1.2
Butter 1 oz	1.8	1.8	1.6	1.6	1.5	1.5
Sugar 2 oz	0.8	0.8	0.8	0.7	0.6	0.7
Total	18.7	18.7	14.9	13.9	13.2	12.9
Tuesday						
*Bread 8 oz	2.3	2.3	1.3	1.3	1.2	1.3
*Porridge						
Oatmeal/milk	2.9	2.9	2.5	1.9	2.5	2.2
*Veg. broth	0.6	0.6	0.6	0.5	0.5	0.5
2 oz veg						
*Cheese 4 oz	4.2	4.2	3.7	3.7	3.3	3.7
*Dumpling	1.4	1.4	0.8	0.8	0.7	0.8
5 oz bread						
Coffee 1 oz	2.2	2.2	2.2	1.6	1.4	2.2
Sugar 1 oz	0.4	0.4	0.4	0.4	0.4	0.4
Total	14.0	13.7	11.5	10.2	10.0	11.1
Wednesday						
*Bread 8 oz	2.3	2.3	1.3	1.3	1.2	1.3
*Porridge	3.6	3.6	3.3	3.3	3.1	3.6
sub. 2 eggs						
*Treacle	0.8	0.8	0.8	0.7	0.6	0.7
2 oz sugar						
*Bacon 3 oz	3.3	3.3	2.6	2.8	2.8	2.4
*Potato 16 oz	1.3	1.3	1.0	0.5	0.7	0.6
*Milk 1/4 quart	1.8	1.8	1.8	1.2	1.8	1.5
Tea 1 oz	2.6	2.6	2.2	2.5	1.8	1.2
Cheese 2 oz	2.1	2.1	1.9	1.9	1.7	1.9
Total	17.2	17.2	14.9	14.2	13.7	13.2

(*continued*)

TABLE B1 (*concluded*)

	Victoria	Vancouver	Winnipeg	Hamilton	Montreal	Halifax
Thursday						
*Bread 16 oz	4.5	4.5	2.5	2.5	2.3	2.5
*Porridge as for Mon.	2.9	2.9	2.5	1.9	2.5	2.2
*Milk 1/4 quart	1.8	1.8	1.8	1.2	1.8	1.5
*Coffee	2.2	2.2	2.2	1.6	1.4	2.2
*Cheese 4 oz	4.2	4.2	3.7	3.7	3.3	3.7
*Veg. broth mutton 4 oz	3.8	4.5	3.4	2.0	3.3	2.5
Total	19.4	20.1	16.1	12.9	14.6	14.6
Friday						
*Bread 12 oz	3.4	3.4	1.9	1.9	1.7	1.9
*Porridge 1 lb flour	3.0	3.0	2.0	1.8	2.4	2.4
*Treacle sugar 2 oz	0.8	0.8	0.8	0.8	0.8	0.8
*Bacon fish (Halifax)						2.5
beef (Other cities)	3.5	3.5	3.7	2.5	2.3	
*Potato 16 oz	1.3	1.3	1.0	0.5	0.7	0.6
*Gruel beans 6 oz	1.8	1.8	1.8	1.5	1.5	1.6
Tea 1 oz	2.6	2.6	2.2	2.5	1.8	1.2
Total	16.4	16.4	13.4	11.5	11.2	11.0
Saturday						
*Bread 16 oz	4.5	4.5	2.5	2.5	2.3	2.5
*Porridge oatmeal 4 oz	1.1	1.1	0.7	0.7	0.7	0.7
*Milk 1/4 quart	1.8	1.8	1.8	1.2	1.8	1.5
*Veg. broth						
Apple 4 oz	2.5	1.2	3.7	2.3	2.5	2.5
Veg. 2 oz	0.6	0.6	0.6	0.5	0.5	0.5
*Cheese 4 oz	4.2	4.2	3.7	3.7	3.3	3.7
*Suet pudding						
Sugar 2 oz	0.8	0.8	0.8	0.8	0.8	0.8
Tea 1 oz	2.6	2.6	2.2	2.5	1.8	1.2
Butter 1 oz	1.8	1.8	1.6	1.6	1.5	1.5
Lard 4 oz	2.5	3.0	3.0	2.6	3.7	3.0
Total	22.4	21.6	20.6	18.4	18.9	17.9
Weekly total	124.3	123.9	104.3	93.6	92.9	92.1

Sources: *Labour Gazette*, Nov. 1900; Bettina Bradbury, *Working Families*; B. Seebohm Rowntree, *Poverty: A Study of Town Life* (London, n.d.). The asterisks indicate items in Rowntree, with some substitutes such as beans for pease pudding and bread for dumpling.

TABLE B2
Weekly food-cost estimates, by city, 1900

	Board of Inquiry estimate (expenditures) ($)	Our estimate (minimum costs) ($)
Halifax	5.41	3.45
Montreal	6.01	3.48
Hamilton	4.88	3.51
Winnipeg	5.83	3.91
Vancouver	6.41	4.64
Victoria	7.23	4.66

TABLE B3
Annual rental and miscellaneous living costs, by city, 1900

	Victoria	Vancouver	Winnipeg	Hamilton	Montreal	Halifax
Rental	132	156	156	102	114	120
Additions						
Light	12	12	12	12	12	12
Furnishings*	8.4	8.4	8.4	8.4	8.4	8.4
Soap†	9	9	9	9	9	9
Travel to work‡	9	9	9	9	9	9
Water§	5	5	5	5	5	5
Sum of the additions	43.4	43.4	43.4	43.4	43.4	43.4
Sum	175.4	199.4	199.4	145.4	157.4	163.4
Add fuel from Table B5	21	21	45	30	35	35
Sum	196.4	220.4	244.4	175.4	192.4	198.4

Note: This leaves nothing at all for medical care, schooling, laundry, lodge or church dues, newspapers, and recreation.

*One complete outfit of a small house including one kitchen table, four chairs, four beds, bedroom suite, four blankets, one ice refrigerator, one coal-oil stove, four pots, plates, knives, forks, pail, brooms, and a few chairs would cost $84. Prices from Eaton's catalogues and Board of Inquiry, vol. 1. We assume that 10 per cent has to be replaced every year.

†In Winnipeg it was $1.43 per month for a family of five, or $17.16 a year (Board of Inquiry, vol. 2, 1018). In Eaton's it was three cakes for twenty-five cents. Assume nine to ten cakes (eight cents each) a month for a family of five = $9.00 a year (roughly half as much soap as used by the Winnipeg family of five).

‡In Winnipeg it was $1.12 per month for a family of five. Assume two 2.5-cent rides per day or thirty cents per week, for fifty-two weeks and one person in family only: $15.60 per year. We take a lower figure – seventy-five cents a month, or $9 a year – on the grounds that a large proportion walked to work.

§Rates vary. For Winnipeg families (Board of Inquiry, vol. 2, 1018) it was sixty-nine cents a month; Hamilton: flat rate of seventy-five cents per quarter on property assessed at $800 and additions for w.c.; Montreal: 7.5 per cent of assessed rental, which would be about $9 per year.

TABLE B4
Annual fuel costs, by city (method 1)

City	Annual consumption	Total ($)
Victoria	As for Vancouver	
Vancouver	5 cords wood @ $3.50	17.50
	6 cords wood @ $3.50	21.00
Winnipeg	10 cords wood @ $5.00	50.00
	8 tons coal @ $9.50	76.00
Hamilton	5 tons coal @ $6.00	30.00
Montreal	5 tons coal @ $7.00	35.00
Halifax	5 tons coal @ $7.00	35.00

Sources: Prices from *Labour Gazette* (Nov. 1900), 99.

TABLE B5
Annual fuel costs, by city (method 2)

City	Annual food budget per family of five	Fuel as % of food budget	Annual fuel cost ($)
Victoria	242	8.7	21
Vancouver	242	8.7	21
Winnipeg	203	22.2	45
Montreal	181	19.3	35
Hamilton	183	16.4	30
Halifax	179	19.5	35

TABLE B6

Weights of cost-of-living components, by city, 1901

	Cost ($)	Weight (%)
Vancouver		
Food	242	49.4
Rent	156	31.8
Fuel and light	33	6.7
Clothing	28	5.7
Additions	31	6.3
Winnipeg		
Food	203	42.7
Rent	156	32.8
Fuel and light	57	12.0
Clothing	28	5.9
Additions	31	6.5
Hamilton		
Food	183	47.4
Rent	102	26.4
Fuel and light	42	10.9
Clothing	28	7.3
Additions	31	8.0
Montreal		
Food	181	45.1
Rent	114	28.4
Fuel and light	47	11.7
Clothing	28	7.0
Additions	31	7.7
Halifax		
Food	179	44.2
Rent	120	29.6
Fuel and light	47	11.6
Clothing	28	6.9
Additions	31	7.7

Notes

1: Introduction

1 James Struthers, *No Fault of Their Own: Unemployment and the Canadian Welfare State, 1914–1941* (Toronto, 1983), 3.

2 On the early uses of 'unemployment' see John A. Garraty, *Unemployment in History: Economic Thought and Public Policy* (New York, 1978), especially chap. 6. See also Alexander Keyssar, *Out of Work: The First Century of Unemployment in Massachusetts* (New York, 1986), 1–8; John Burnett, *Idle Hands: The Experience of Unemployment, 1790–1990* (London, 1994), especially chap. 5.

3 *Palladium of Labor*, 6 Nov. 1886; Victoria *Colonist*, 18 March 1893; Toronto *Globe*, 17 Feb. 1894.

4 Daniel Scott Smith, 'Inheritance and the Social History of Early American Women,' in R. Hoffman and P.J. Albert, eds., *Women in the Age of the American Revolution* (Charlottesville, Va., 1989), 45–66; Chad Gaffield, 'The New Regional History: Rethinking the History of the Outaouais,' *Journal of Canadian Studies*, 26 (1991–2), 5–17.

5 Data for New Westminster are also part of our files; in most of the analysis that follows for 1891 and 1901, census data for New Westminster are included within the data for Vancouver, since the two adjacent cities exhibited only minor differences.

6 'The Unemployed Problem,' *Western Clarion*, 25 March 1905.

7 We have analysed people with occupations in selected rural or small-town census subdivisions in the 1891 nominal-census returns: district 9 (Sifton, Man.); district 71 (the township of Nelson in Halton District, Ont.); district 174 (Ste Eulalie, Que.); and district 32 (Cape Canso, NS). Of 2,006 people with occupations, only sixty-one stated that they were unemployed in the week

prior to the taking of the census. Of the sixty-one no less than fifty-seven were in Cape Canso, and unemployment there was clearly related to seasonal occupations (shipbuilding, fishing, and coastal trades).

8 The census asked whether occupied people were employers or wage earners (most of those lacking positive responses in these categories were likely to be self-employed). In the rural subdivisions that we sampled, only 21 per cent of all persons with occupations were said to be 'wage earners.'

9 We are indebted to Christine Godfrey for making available to us her database from the 1891 census for the Kootenay districts of British Columbia. Of 3,206 people with occupations in the Kootenays in 1891, 4.4 per cent stated that they were unemployed. The majority of the unemployed were either miners or railway labourers. Wage labour already dominated: 59 per cent of those with occupations were wage earners. See Christine Godfrey, 'Winds of Change: A Re-Examination of Some Factors Influencing the Development of Nelson and Its Commercial Relations, 1891–1901' (MA thesis, University of Victoria, 1994). In the small industrial town of Desoronto, Ont., 12.6 per cent of those with occupations were said to be unemployed in 1891 (census district 73). Most of the unemployed were general labourers or sawmill workers. Here the wage earners were 87 per cent of all persons with occupations. For the extent of unemployment in the cities focused on in this book, see the chapters that follow.

10 Manufacturing accounted for 22.4 per cent of gross domestic product (GDP) in 1870, 22.2 per cent in 1900, and 22.5 per cent in 1910: Kenneth Norrie and Douglas Owram, A History of the Canadian Economy (Toronto, 1991), 376. For a recent discussion of industrialization in Ontario see Craig Heron, 'Factory Workers,' in Paul Craven, ed., Labouring Lives: Work and Workers in Nineteenth-Century Ontario (Toronto, 1995), 479–590.

11 For a sampling of this debate within Canadian history see Michael Bliss, 'Privatizing the Mind: The Sundering of Canadian History, the Sundering of Canada,' Journal of Canadian Studies, 26 (winter 1991–2), 5–17; and G.S. Kealey, 'Class in English-Canadian Historical Writing: Neither Privatizing, Nor Sundering,' Journal of Canadian Studies, 27 (1992), 123–8. For the debate within American historiography see Bernard Bailyn, 'The Challenge of Modern Historiography,' American Historical Review, 87a (1982), 1–24; Thomas Bender, 'Wholes and Parts: The Need for Synthesis in American History,' Journal of American History, 73 (1986), 120–36; Eric H. Monkkonen, 'The Dangers of Synthesis,' American Historical Review, 91 (1986), 1146–57.

12 Bliss, 'Privatizing the Mind,' 17.

13 Lynn Hunt, 'Introduction: History, Culture, and Text,' in Lynn Hunt, ed., The New Cultural History (Berkeley, Calif., 1989), 12; Raphael Samuel, 'Reading

the Signs,' *History Workshop Journal*, 32 (autumn 1991), 88–109, and 33 (spring 1992), 220–51.

14 *Globe and Mail*, 28 Dec. 1996, 1.

15 'One of the reasons I shy away from the cultural is that I have seen in cultural studies too many vast generalizations drawn from scattered and isolated quotes and artifacts.' Walter Licht, 'Symposium on Getting Work,' *Labor History*, 35 no. 1 (1994), 105; Licht, 'Cultural History/Social History: A Review Essay,' *Historical Methods*, 25 (winter 1992), 37–41.

16 An early exception is the *Report of the Ontario Commission on Unemployment* (Toronto, 1916).

17 Work by historians on early Canadian unemployment include Udo Sautter, 'Measuring Unemployment in Canada: Federal Efforts before World War Two,' *Histoire sociale/Social History*, 15 (1982), 475–89, and 'The Origins of the Employment Service of Canada, 1900–1920,' *Labour/Le Travail*, 6 (1980), 89–112; Robin John Anderson, 'Sharks and Red Herrings: Vancouver's Male Employment Agencies, 1889–1915,' *BC Studies*, 98 (summer 1993), 43–84; Mary MacKinnon, 'Relief not Insurance: Canadian Unemployment Relief in the 1930s,' *Explorations in Economic History*, 27 (1990), 46–83; Struthers, *No Fault of Their Own*. These studies emphasize state policy and focus on a later period than that considered in this book. We have published two articles dealing with aspects of unemployment in 1891: 'The First National Unemployment Survey: Unemployment and the Canadian Census of 1891,' *Labour/ Le Travail*, 23 (1989), 171–78, and 'Locating the Unemployed in Urban British Columbia: Evidence from the 1891 Census,' *Journal of Canadian Studies*, 25 (1990), 38–54.

   Among the many studies of unemployment and public policy in Canada are Noah Meltz, *Economic Analysis of Labour Shortages: The Case of the Tool and Die Makers in Ontario* (Toronto, 1982); F.T. Denton et al., eds., *Unemployment and the Labour Force Behaviour of Young People* (Toronto, 1980); M. Gunderson, *Unemployment among Young People and Government Policy in Ontario* (Toronto, 1981); S. Gera, *Canadian Unemployment: Lessons from the 80s and Challenges for the 90s* (Ottawa, 1991); Stephen McBride, *Not Working: State, Unemployment, and Neoconservatism in Canada* (Toronto, 1992); Brian K. MacLean and Lars Osberg, eds., *The Unemployment Crisis: All for Nought?* (Montreal, 1996). Recent work that examines unemployment in the United States and Britain at the turn of the century includes Keyssar, *Out of Work*; Paul T. Ringenbach, *Tramps and Reformers, 1873–1916: The Discovery of Unemployment in New York* (London, 1973); Peter Seixas, *Shifting Sands beneath the State: Unemployment, the Labor Market, and the Local Community, 1893–1922* (New York, 1993); Walter Licht, *Getting Work: Philadelphia, 1840–1950* (Cambridge, Mass., 1992);

T.J. Hatton and J.G. Williamson, 'Unemployment, Employment Contracts and Compensating Wage Differentials: Michigan in the 1890s,' *Journal of Economic History*, 51 (1991), 605–32; Ester Fano, 'A "Wastage of Men": Technological Progress and Unemployment in the United States: Evidence from Connecticut Manufacturing,' *Technology and Culture*, 32 (1991), 264–92; E. Aerts and B. Eichenberg, eds., *Proceedings of the Tenth International Economic History Conference* (Leuven, 1990); Gareth Stedman Jones, *Outcast London: A Study in the Relationship between Classes in Victorian Society* (Oxford, 1971); G. Phillips and N. Whiteside, *Casual Labour: The Unemployment Question in the Port Transport Industry, 1880–1970* (Oxford, 1985); Richard Flanagan, *'Parish-Fed Bastards': A History of the Politics of the Unemployed in Britain, 1884–1939* (New York, 1991); Krishan Kumar, 'Unemployment as a Problem in the Development of Industrial Societies: The English Experience,' *Sociological Review*, (1984), 185–233; Burnett, *Idle Hands*; and *Social Research*, 54 (1987), for a special issue dealing with unemployment.

18 Ruth Roach Pierson, 'Gender and the Unemployment Insurance Debates in Canada, 1934–1940,' *Labour/Le Travail*, 25 (spring 1990), 77–103; Ann Porter, 'Women and Income Security in the Post-war Period: The Case of Unemployment Insurance, 1945–1962,' *Labour/Le Travail*, 31 (spring 1993), 111–44.

19 Much of Canada's social and fiscal policy making in the 1980s and 1990s has tended to assume that 'the determinants of unemployment lie primarily on the supply side of labour markets – in the job-search decisions and skills training of individual workers.' Brian K. MacLean and Lars Osberg, 'Introduction,' in MacLean and Osberg, eds., *The Unemployment Crisis: All for Nought?* (Montreal, 1996), xiv.

20 Charles Booth, *Life and Labour of the People of London* (London, 1902), vol. 1, 149–52.

21 *Report ... on Unemployment*, 11.

22 Ibid., 83, 86.

23 Michael Katz, *Improving Poor People: The Welfare State, the 'Underclass,' and Urban Schools as History* (Princeton, NJ, 1995). The emphasis on the personal in today's workfare programs is nicely caught in the following quote from André Lemay, head of Sudbury's workfare advisory committee: 'No organization is interested in a pair of hands attached to an unwilling heart.' The statement ranked as the *Globe and Mail*'s quote of the day, on 28 December 1996.

24 H.A. Kennedy, *The Unemployed in Canada: Causes of the Trouble* (London, 1908), 13–14.

25 Struthers, *No Fault of Their Own*, 6–11 and passim. For the National Anti-Poverty comments, see Victoria *Times Colonist*, 30 July 1995, a5.

26 Keyssar, *Out of Work*; T.J. Hatton and J.G. Williamson, 'Unemployment, Employment Contracts'; Robert A. Margo, 'Unemployment in 1910: Some Preliminary Findings,' in E. Aerts and B. Eichenberg, eds., *Proceedings of the Tenth International Economic History Conference* (Leuven, 1990), 51–60; Susan Carter and Richard Sutch, 'The Labor Market in the 1890s: Evidence from Connecticut Manufacturing,' in Aerts and Eichenberg, eds., *Proceedings of the Tenth*, 15–24. Mark Thomas takes up this issue in the British context, 'Unemployment in Edwardian Britain: A New Perspective,' in Aerts and Eichenberg, eds., *Proceedings of the Tenth*, 36–50.

27 *Proceedings of the Sixth Session of the Trades and Labor Congress of the Dominion of Canada*, 2–5 Sept. 1890, 20; National Archives of Canada (hereafter NA), RG 2, vol. 5190, file 2569, G.W. Dower to J.A. Chapleau, 10 Nov. 1890. We offer an appraisal of this question's utility in 'The First National Unemployment Survey,' 171–5.

28 See Baskerville and Sager, 'Finding the Workforce,' 55, and see Appendix A to this volume.

29 In Appendix A we provide various measures of the representativeness of our samples for each year.

30 See P. Baskerville and E. Sager, 'Finding the Workforce in the 1901 Census of Canada,' *Histoire sociale/Social History*, 56 (Nov. 1995), 521–40.

31 In the 1890s the Ontario Bureau of Industries collected and published data on wages earned and days worked in the year. The data were gathered by special agents across the province, and much of the detail on wages and work duration came from employers. The published results are likely to oversample stable industries, craft or skilled workers, and workplaces willing to supply information. See, for instance, *Annual Report of the Bureau of Industries for the Province of Ontario, 1889* (Toronto, 1891), Part IV, 1.

32 Keyssar, *Out of Work*, especially 155–66.

33 See also Eric W. Sager, 'Employment Contracts in Merchant Shipping: An Argument for Social Science History,' in Franca Iacovetta and Wendy Mitchinson, eds., *On the Case* (Toronto, forthcoming).

34 Smith, 'Inheritance and the Social History,' 50.

35 An example of a study that is especially sensitive to standard deviations is Gordon Darroch,'Occupational Structure, Assessed Wealth and Homeowning during Toronto's Early Industrialization, 1861–1899,' *Histoire sociale/Social History*, 16 (1983), 381–410.

36 Some representative examples from that literature are Larry D. McCann, 'Class, Ethnicity and Residential Differentiation in Mid-Victorian Halifax,' in R. Preston and B. Mitchell, eds., *Reflections and Visions: Twenty-five Years of Geography at Waterloo* (Waterloo, Ont., 1990); Robert Lewis, 'The Segregated

City: Class, Residential Patterns and the Development of Industrial Districts in Montreal, 1861 and 1901,' *Journal of Urban History*, 17 (1991), 123–52; Daniel Hiebert, 'Class, Ethnicity and Residential Structure: The Social Geography of Winnipeg, 1901–1921,' *Journal of Historical Geography*, 17 (1991), 56–86, and 'The Social Geography of Toronto in 1931: A Study of Residential Differentiation and Social Structure,' *Journal of Historical Geography*, 21 (1995), 55–74; Sherry Olson, 'Occupations and Residential Spaces in Nineteenth Century Montreal,' *Historical Methods*, 22 (1989), 81–96; Richard Harris, 'Residential Segregation and Class Formation in Canadian Cities: A Critical Review,' *Canadian Geographer*, 28 (1984), 186–96.

37 Michael Katz, 'Occupational Classification in History,' *Journal of Interdisciplinary History*, 3 (1972), 63–88; Ira Katznelson, 'Working Class Formation: Constructing Cases and Comparisons,' in Ira Katznelson and A.R. Zolberg, ed., *Working Class Formation: Nineteenth-Century Patterns in Western Europe and the United States* (Princeton, N.J., 1985); Gordon Darroch, 'Occupation, Property and Family in Central Ontario, 1861–1871: Steps toward Understanding a Society of Scanty Fortunes,' paper given at the Canadian Historical Association meetings, Montreal, 1995.

38 In addition to the growing Canadian literature, see Ira Katznelson, *Marxism and the City* (Oxford, 1992); Olivier Zunz, *The Changing Face of Inequality: Urbanization, Industrial Development and Immigrants in Detroit, 1880–1920* (Chicago, 1982); Yda Schreuder, 'Labor Segmentation, Ethnic Division of Labor and Residential Segregation in American Cities in the Early Twentieth Century,' *Professional Geographer*, 41 (1989), 131–43.

39 For a perceptive review that argues for the need to situate Canada's workers within the context of their families as well as their workplaces see Chad Gaffield, 'The Character and Circumstance of Canada's Industrialization,' *Labour/Le Travail*, 24 (fall 1989), 219–30.

40 Bettina Bradbury, ed., *Canadian Family History: Selected Readings* (Toronto, 1992); Cynthia R. Comacchio, 'Beneath the "Sentimental Veil": Families and Family History in Canada,' *Labour/Le Travail*, 33 (spring 1994), 279–302.

41 Bettina Bradbury, *Working Families: Age, Gender, and Daily Survival in Industrializing Montreal* (Toronto, 1993).

42 Terry Copp, *The Anatomy of Poverty: The Condition of the Working Class in Montreal, 1897–1929* (Toronto, 1974); Michael J. Piva, *The Condition of the Working Class in Toronto, 1900–1921* (Ottawa, 1979); J.G. Snell, 'The Cost of Living in Canada in 1870,' *Histoire sociale/Social History*, 12 (1979), 186–91; G.W. Bertram and M.B. Percy, 'Real Wage Trends in Canada, 1900–1926: Some Provisional Estimates,' *Canadian Journal of Economics*, 12 (1979), 299–312; Eleanor A. Bartlett, 'Real Wages and the Standard of Living in Vancouver, 1901–1929,'

BC Studies, 51 (1981), 3–62; Edward J. Chambers, 'New Evidence on the Living Standards of Toronto Blue Collar Workers in the Pre-1914 Era,' *Histoire sociale/ Social History* 18 (1985), 285–314; Trevor J.O. Dick, 'Consumer Behaviour in the Nineteenth Century and Ontario Workers, 1885–1889,' *Journal of Economic History*, 46 (1986), 477–88; and David Gagan and Rosemary Gagan, 'Working Class Standards of Living in Late Victorian Urban Ontario: A Review of the Miscellaneous Evidence on the Quality of Material Life,' *Journal of the Canadian Historical Association*, 1 (1990), 171–94.

43 Michael R. Haines, 'Industrial Work and the Family Life Cycle, 1889/1890,' in Paul Uselding, ed., *Research in Economic History*, 4 (1979), 298–301; Patricia Van den Eeckout, 'Family Income of Ghent Working Class Families, ca. 1900,' *Journal of Family History* 18 (1993), 87–110; Robert V. Robinson, 'Economic Necessity and the Life Cycle in the Family Economy of Nineteenth-Century Indianapolis,' *American Journal of Sociology*, 99 (1993), 49–74; Claudia Goldin, 'Family Strategies and the Family Economy in the Late Nineteenth Century: The Role of Secondary Workers,' in T. Hershberg, ed., *Work, Space, Family, and Group Experience in Nineteenth-Century Philadelphia* (Oxford, 1981); Cheryl Elman, 'Turn of the Century Dependence and Interdependence: Roles of Teens in the Family Economy of the Aged,' *Journal of Family History*, 18 (1993), 65–85; Peter Shergold, *Working-Class Life: The 'American Standard' in Comparative Perspective, 1899–1913* (Pittsburgh, 1982).

44 Appendix B to this volume provides a detailed breakdown of our cost-of-living calculations for each city.

45 In his useful, edited version of the evidence, Greg Kealey does not mention the issue; G. Kealey, ed., *Canada Investigates Industrialism* (Toronto, 1973). G. Kealey and B. Palmer, in their detailed study of the Knights of Labor, give no explicit recognition to the unemployment situation: *Dreaming of What Might Be: The Knights of Labor in Ontario, 1880–1900* (Cambridge, 1982). For comments on unemployment see Bryan Palmer, *Working-Class Experience: Rethinking the History of Canadian Labour, 1800–1991* (Toronto, 1992), 116, 164–5, 187, 196, and *A Culture in Conflict: Skilled Workers and Industrial Capitalism in Hamilton, Ontario, 1860–1914* (Montreal, 1979), 232–3. The issue appears briefly in the encyclopeadic treatment by Eugene Forsey, *Trade Unions in Canada, 1812–1902* (Toronto, 1982), 400, 428, where Forsey notes the efforts of local trades and labour councils in Vancouver and Montreal to find work for the unemployed in the 1890s.

46 An excellent introduction to this system is Larry McCann, ed., *Heartland and Hinterland: A Geography of Canada* (Scarborough, 1987). See also R.E. Preston, 'The Evolution of Urban Canada: The Post-1867 Period,' in R.M. Irving, ed., *Readings in Canadian Geography* (Toronto, 1978), 19–46.

47 P. Baskerville, *Beyond the Island: Victoria, An Illustrated History* (Burlington, Ont., 1986), and 'Deindustrializing the Island: Vancouver Island and the Industrial World, 1881–1901,' unpublished paper, Islands 86 Conference, Victoria, 1986; John Lutz, 'Losing Steam: The Boiler and Engine Industry as an Index of British Columbia's Deindustrialization, 1880–1915,' in Canadian Historical Association, *Historical Papers* (1988), 168–208.

48 Patricia E. Roy, 'Vancouver: "The Mecca of the Unemployed," 1907–1929,' in Alan F.J. Artibise, ed., *Town and City* (Regina, 1981), 393–413.

49 Lutz, 'Losing Steam,' 169; Sager and Baskerville, 'Locating the Unemployed.'

50 Larry McCann, 'Urban Growth in a Staple Economy: The Emergence of Vancouver as a Regional Metropolis, 1886–1914,' in L.J. Evenden, ed., *Vancouver: Western Metropolis* (Victoria, 1978); Pat Roy, *Vancouver: An Illustrated History* (Toronto, 1981); Robert A.J. McDonald, *Making Vancouver: Class, Status, and Social Boundaries, 1863–1913* (Vancouver, 1996).

51 Alan F.J. Artibise, *Winnipeg: A Social History of Urban Growth, 1874–1914* (Montreal, 1975).

52 *Census of Canada*, 1901, 1, Table 17; Daniel Hiebert, 'Class, Ethnicity and Residential Structure,' 68.

53 Artibise, *Winnipeg*, chap. 11; Gerald Tulchinsky, *Taking Root: The Origins of the Canadian Jewish Community* (Toronto, 1992), 153; *Winnipeg Tribune*, 10 March 1891.

54 Hiebert, 'Class, Ethnicity and Residential Structure,' 56–9.

55 Larry McCann, 'Staples and the New Industrialism in the Growth of Post-Confederation Halifax,' *Acadiensis*, 8 (1979), 47–79.

56 R.L. Gentilcore, ed., *Historical Atlas of Canada*, vol. 2 (Toronto, 1993), Plate 48; D. Kerr and D.W. Holdsworth, eds., *Historical Atlas of Canada*, vol. 3 (Toronto, 1990), Plate 24.

57 McCann, 'Staples and the New Industrialism,' Table 9, 76.

58 *Suburban*, 13 Jan. 1906, cited in McCann, 'Staples and the New Industrialism,' 77. Figures on immigrants are drawn from our 10 per cent sample of the city's population in 1901.

59 Significant immigration from eastern Europe commenced only after 1901: see John Weaver, *Hamilton: An Illustrated History* (Toronto, 1982), 93. Figures on immigrants are from *Census of Canada*, 1901, Table 17.

60 John C. Weaver, 'The Location of Manufacturing Enterprises: The Case of Hamilton's Attraction of Foundries, 1830–1890,' in R.A. Jarrell and A.E. Roos, eds., *Critical Issues in the History of Canadian Science Technology and Medicine* (Ottawa, 1983); D.J. Middleton and D.F. Walker, 'Manufacturers and Industrial Development Policy in Hamilton, 1890–1910,' *Urban History Review*, 8 (1980), 20–46. Calculated from data in *Census of Canada*, 1901, 3, Table 13.

61 McCann, 'Staples and the New Industrialism,' Table 3, 62.
62 Gentilcore, *Historical Atlas of Canada*, vol. 2, Plates 47 and 49; Kerr and Holdsworth, eds., *Historical Atlas of Canada*, vol. 3, Plates 14 and 30.
63 Patricia A. Thornton and Sherry Olson, 'The Tidal Wave of Irish Immigration to Montreal and Its Demographic Consequences,' *Shared Spaces/Partage de l'éspace*, 13 (Montreal, 1993); *Census of Canada*, 1901, Table 13.
64 This is a common claim. See Lewis, 'The Segregated City,' 136. Copp, *The Anatomy of Poverty*, 140–8.
65 Our conclusions are closer to those reported by Michael Piva, 'Urban Working Class Incomes and Real Incomes in 1921: A Comparative Analysis,' *Histoire sociale/Social History*, 16 (1983), 145–68.
66 McCann, 'Staples and the New Industrialism,' Table 9, 76.
67 Herbert Brown Ames, *The City below the Hill*, with an introduction by P.F.W. Rutherford (Toronto, 1972).

2: The Discovery of a Social Problem

1 *Acadian Recorder*, 21 Dec. 1816, cited in Judith Fingard, 'The Poor in Winter: Seasonality and Society in Pre-Industrial Canada,' in Michael S. Cross and Gregory S. Kealey, *Pre-Industrial Canada, 1760–1849* (Toronto, 1982), 71.
2 Jim Phillips, 'Poverty, Unemployment, and the Administration of the Criminal Law: Vagrancy Laws in Halifax, 1864–1890,' in Philip Girard and Jim Phillips, eds., *Essays in the History of Canadian Law*, Vol. 3, *Nova Scotia* (Toronto, 1990), 128–62.
3 *Free Press*, 21 Oct. 1817, cited in Judith Fingard, 'The Relief of the Unemployed: The Poor in Saint John, Halifax, and St John's, 1815–1860,' in Gilbert A. Stelter and Alan F.J. Artibise, eds., *The Canadian City: Essays in Urban History* (Toronto, 1979), 344–5.
4 William N.T. Wylie, 'Poverty, Distress, and Disease: Labour and the Construction of the Rideau Canal, 1826–1832,' *Labour/Le Travail*, 11 (spring 1982), 7–30.
5 H. Clare Pentland, *Labour and Capital in Canada, 1650–1860* (Toronto, 1981), 117.
6 William Evans, 16 March 1843, cited in Peter Way, *Common Labour: Workers and the Digging of North American Canals, 1780–1860* (New York, 1993), 238. Even in summer the number of days worked depended on the weather, and workers averaged about twenty days a month: H. Clare Pentland, 'The Lachine Strike of 1843,' *Canadian Historical Review*, 29 no. 3 (Sept. 1948), 267.
7 *St. Catherines Journal*, 16 February 1844, cited in Ruth Bleasdale, 'Class Con-

flict on the Canals of Upper Canada in the 1840s,' *Labour/Le Travail*, 7 (spring 1981), 13.

8 Bleasdale, 'Class Conflict,' 11, 32.

9 Way, *Common Labour*, 236–9.

10 Ibid., 267.

11 Quebec *Mercury*, 17 Nov., 1857; Toronto *Globe*, 20 Nov. 1857.

12 Quebec *Mercury*, 17 Nov., 19 Nov., 3 Dec. 1857.

13 *Documents de la Session du Québec*, 1869, vol. 1, doc. 4, cited in Bruno Ramirez, *On the Move: French-Canadian and Italian Migrants in the North Atlantic Economy, 1860–1914* (Toronto, 1991), 79; cf. Terry Crowley, 'Rural Labour,' in Paul Craven, ed., *Labouring Lives: Work and Workers in Nineteenth-Century Ontario* (Toronto, 1995), 27–8.

14 *L'Avenir* (Quebec), 22 Dec. 1857 (article entitled 'Les causes de l'appauvrissement de notre population').

15 Ibid.

16 'Annual Report of the Emigration Agent,' Toronto *Globe*, 20 Nov. 1857.

17 Terry Crowley, 'Rural Labour,' 46.

18 *Iron Molders Journal* (March 1864), cited in Gregory S. Kealey, *Toronto Workers Respond to Industrial Capitalism, 1867–1892* (Toronto, 1980), 69; *Cooper's Ritual* (Cleveland, 1870), 6, cited in Kealey, *Toronto Workers*, 55.

19 *Cooper's Ritual*, cited in Kealey, *Toronto Workers*, 57.

20 Toronto Typographical Society (TTS), minutes, 2 July 1845, cited in Steven Langdon, *The Emergence of the Canadian Working-Class Movement* (Toronto, 1975), 7.

21 Kealey, *Toronto Workers*, 92, 96–7.

22 Richard Price, *Masters, Unions, and Men: Work Control in Building and the Rise of Labour, 1830–1914* (Cambridge, 1980), 52ff.

23 *Ontario Workman*, 9 May 1872.

24 John Hewitt, Toronto *Globe*, 15 Feb. 1872; Langdon, *Emergence*, 18.

25 *Ontario Workman*, 25 April 1872. Fourteen years later, in Victoria, the *Industrial News* was careful to avoid the logical problem: 'What reasonable objection can they have to a reduction of the hours of labor? It is true that production might be less (although that is an open question), but if so the number of workers would be increased, thereby increasing the number of consumers; it would relieve the labor market, already overstocked.' *Industrial News*, 2 Jan. 1886.

26 B. Rosamund, *House of Commons Journals*, 1876, App. 3, 200; cited in Langdon, *Emergence*, 25.

27 'Convict Labor,' *Ontario Workman*, 17 April 1873. On 13 February 1873 the *Ontario Workman* reported a meeting in Toronto's St Lawrence Hall that

passed a motion against convict labour being used in competition with 'free labor.' It alleged that the Ontario government was offering prison labour to the Canada Car Company.

28 'Emigration,' *Ontario Workman*, 5 June 1873. Speakers at the 1873 Congress of the Canadian Labor Union also deplored 'the great amount of wrong information given to the workingmen of the old country.' Leslie E. Wismer, ed., *Proceedings of the Canadian Labor Union Congresses; 1973–77* (Montreal: Trades and Labor Congress, 1951), 26.

29 *Ontario Workman*, 24 April 1873.

30 'Chinese Labor,' *Ontario Workman*, 22 Jan. 1874.

31 'Number and Condition of the Unemployed,' ibid., 18 Dec. 1873; 'The Unemployed,' ibid., 5 Feb. 1874.

32 'Labor and Leisure,' ibid., 26 Feb. 1874. 'The supply in the market is greater than the demand, and therefore capitalists rejoice, while labour perishes,' said the tailor A.F. Jury to a *Globe* reporter: 'Labourers' Living,' Toronto *Globe*, 3 Feb. 1883.

33 'Labor Statistics,' *Ontario Workman*, 22 May 1873.

34 'The Unemployed,' ibid., 5 Feb. 1874.

35 Kealey, *Toronto Workers*, 158.

36 Fourth Congress of the Canadian Labor Union; Wismer, ed., *Proceedings*, 67.

37 Report of the Canadian Labor Union Committee on Immigration, 1875, cited in Wismer, ed., *Proceedings*, 55.

38 Fifth Canadian Labor Union Congress (1877), cited in ibid., 81.

39 Third Canadian Labor Union Congress (1875), cited in ibid., 56.

40 Ibid., 167.

41 Michael Bliss, *A Living Profit: Studies in the Social History of Canadian Business, 1883–1911* (Toronto, 1974), 102.

42 Ottawa *Daily Citizen*, 5 April 1877. For the references to Ottawa demonstrations we are indebted to Debi Wells, '"The Hardest Lines of the Sternest School": Working-Class Ottawa in the Depression of the 1870s' (MA thesis, Carleton University, 1982).

43 Ottawa *Daily Citizen*, 6 April 1877.

44 Ibid.

45 Ibid., 5 April 1877.

46 Petition of the unemployed to Ottawa City Coucil, Ottawa *Daily Citizen*, 26 Feb. 1880.

47 John A. Macdonald addressing 'the workingmen' of Ottawa: Ottawa *Daily Citizen*, 12 Dec. 1878.

48 Ibid., 6 March 1880.

49 Ibid., 23 Feb. 1880; Wells, 'The Hardest Lines,' 93.

50 Ottawa *Daily Citizen*, 6 March 1880; Ottawa *Free Press*, 1, 6 March 1880; Wells, 'The Hardest Lines,' 98.
51 *Trades Journal* (Nova Scotia), 30 May 1883, cited in F.W. Watt, 'The National Policy, the Workingman, and Proletarian Ideas in Victorian Canada,' *Canadian Historical Review*, 40 (1959), 9.
52 'Political Falsehoods,' *Palladium of Labor*, 2 Feb. 1884. On disillusionment with the National Policy see also in *Palladium of Labor*, 'Hard Times,' 15 Dec. 1883, 'Out of Work,' 2 Feb. 1884, 'Boom and Finance,' 1 March 1884, and 'Industrial Slavery,' 2 Aug. 1884. Many of the articles were written by Phillips Thompson.
53 Ottawa *Free Press*, 27 Feb. 1880; Wells, 'The Hardest Lines,' 95.
54 Ottawa *Free Press*, 23 Feb. 1880, cited in Wells, 'The Hardest Lines,' 92.
55 Toronto *Globe*, 8 April 1880.
56 Richard Keys, interviewed by Ottawa *Free Press*, 13 Jan. 1880.
57 The case of the *Queen v. Israel Beaume*, 1878, cited in Bettina Bradbury, *Working Families: Age, Gender, and Daily Survival in Industrializing Montreal* (Toronto, 1993), 80. The unemployed were 'driven to do a thousand and one things against which every worthy instinct of manhood rises up in fierce rebellion.' 'The Unemployed Problem,' *Western Clarion*, 25 March 1905.
58 'The Holiday Season,' *Palladium of Labor*, 29 Dec. 1883. On the ritualization of Christmas see John Gillis, 'Making Time for the Family: The Invention of Family Time(s) and the Reinvention of Family History,' *Journal of Family History*, 21 no. 1 (Jan. 1996), 12–13.
59 'Manliness,' *Ontario Workman*, 12 March 1874.
60 'The Modern Hell,' *Industrial Banner* (London, Ont.), April 1899.
61 James M. Pitsula, 'The Relief of Poverty in Toronto, 1880–1930' (PhD thesis, York University, 1979), 89–107.
62 Letter from 'Felix,' *Palladium of Labor*, 26 Jan. 1884. Referring to the 'black flag' parade in Toronto in February 1891, the *Globe* reported: 'Mechanics were there in plenty who have not worked for months and see but little prospect of doing so.' 12 Feb. 1891.
63 British Columbia Archives and Record Services (BCARS), N/D/B77, British Columbia Benevolent Society, *Annual Report*, 1894; *Globe*, 20 Feb. 1894.
64 Desmond Morton, 'Taking on the Grand Trunk: The Locomotive Engineers Strike of 1876–7,' *Labour/Le Travail*, 2 (1977), 12.
65 In this analysis we focus on interviews in Halifax, Hamilton, and Montreal only. People not interviewed about working conditions specifically (politicians, managers of houses of industry, experts on schooling, and the like) are not included. Of 436 workers, employers, supervisors, overseers, and foremen interviewed in the three cities, 165 answered a question or volunteered

information about constancy of employment or work duration over the year. Questions about constancy of employment were asked in Halifax and Hamilton more often than in Montreal.

66 Susan Trofimenkoff, 'One Hundred and Two Muffled Voices: Canada's Industrial Women in the 1880s,' *Atlantis*, 3 no. 1 (fall, 1977), 66–83.

67 These figures include responses of employers, workers, and a separate category of supervisors, overseers, and foremen. The percentages are not much different if we include only the ninety-six who were workers: 13.5 per cent said that work was constant or full time over the year; 20 per cent that it was available but hours were cut in the slack season; 23 per cent, that time was lost, but they did not specify weeks or months; another 27 per cent, that they lost three months or more in the year. Our tabulation treats each response singly, though often the respondent was estimating an average employment for workers in his or her occupation.

68 *Report of the Royal Commission on the Relations of Capital and Labor in Canada*, 5 vols. (Ottawa, 1889), vol. 3, 531–2.

69 Ira Ferguson, newspaper compositor, Halifax, in ibid., vol. 2, 148.

70 V. Belanger, in ibid., vol. 3, 247.

71 Hector Leblanc, Halifax, in ibid., vol. 2, 224.

72 W. Hobden, Hamilton, in ibid., 808. D. Cashion, moulder in the Grand Trunk shops, said that the men usually had holidays in June and December, but 'they would prefer working the year through.' Ibid., 784.

73 'Clearing Decks for Action,' *Western Clarion*, 18 June 1904.

74 Edward Finnegan, stone cutter, Halifax, in *Report* (1889), vol. 2, 211; see also H.R. Ives, Montreal iron founder, in ibid., vol. 3, 254.

75 F. Walter, Hamilton, in ibid., vol. 2, 794.

76 Olivier Benoit, boot and shoe maker, Montreal, in ibid., vol. 3, 369.

77 *Eighth Report of the Bureau of Labor for 1907* (Toronto, 1908), 169ff.

78 *Second Report of the Bureau of Labor of the Province of Ontario* (Toronto, 1902), 39.

79 F. Thiviegre, moulder, Montreal, in *Report* (1889), vol. 3, 313.

80 J. O'Flaherty, Montreal, in ibid., 464–5.

81 W. Borland, supervisor, North American Glass Co., Montreal, in ibid., 589.

82 'The New Unionism,' *Labor Advocate*, 11 Sept. 1891, quoting an article from the *New Nation*.

83 Craig Heron, 'Factory Workers,' in Paul Craven, ed., *Labouring Lives: Work and Workers in Nineteenth Century Ontario* (Toronto, 1995), 505–6. 'The fact of the wage question is labor saving machinery has supplanted labor to the extent that about one fifth of the wage workers are idle all the time,' claimed an article entitled 'Wages Will Not Go Down,' *Industrial News*, 13 Feb. 1886.

'The cause in this case is so clear as to be unmistakable, and is due entirely to the invention of improved labor-saving machinery without a corresponding reduction in the hours of toil,' argued the *Industrial Banner* (London, Ont.), Dec. 1898. See also the article on 'Labor-Saving Machines,' *Labor Advocate*, 17 April 1891.

84 This argument was also heard in British Columbia: 'The Sin of Cheapness,' *Industrial News*, 26 Dec. 1885.

85 *Globe*, 13 Feb. 1891. See also *Labor Advocate*, 20 and 27 Feb. 1891. Similar public protests took place in Vancouver in the spring of 1891: see Robert A.J. McDonald, *Making Vancouver: Class, Status, and Social Boundaries, 1863–1913* (Vancouver, 1996), 65.

86 'Work or Bread,' Toronto *Globe*, 12 Feb. 1891.

87 Ibid.

88 Ibid., 21 Feb. 1891.

89 Ibid., 12 Feb. 1891. See also the articles in the *Globe*, 26, 27, and 28 Feb. 1894.

90 *Palladium of Labor*, 6 Nov. 1886. See also 'Enjolras' (Phillips Thompson), in *Palladium of Labor*, 21 Feb. 1885, cited in Bryan Palmer, *A Culture in Conflict: Skilled Workers and Industrial Capitalism in Hamilton, Ontario, 1860–1914* (Montreal, 1979), 127; *Labor Advocate*, 27 Feb. 1891.

91 Toronto ITU local 99, minute book, 1894, cited in Charles Lipton, *The Trade Union Movement of Canada, 1827–1959* (Toronto, 1973), 90.

92 'Toronto on the Shady Side,' Toronto *Globe*, 21 Feb. 1891. See also *Globe*, 17 Feb. and 10 March 1894, and Victoria *Colonist*, 24 Jan. 1894. It was 'very evident' that the men marching behind the flag 'belonged to other classes than the day laborers.' *Globe*, 12 Feb. 1891. In December 1907, 550 men applied for work in clearing land in Point Grey, near Vancouver, a provincial relief project. Applicants were 'men of all trades from accountants to common laborers:' Vancouver *Province*, 14 Dec. 1907.

93 Toronto *Globe*, 21 Feb. 1891. See also Burnett, *Idle Hands*, 149.

3: A Profile of the Urban Unemployed

1 Alexander Keyssar, *Out of Work: The First Century of Unemployment in Massachusetts* (New York, 1986), 109.

2 See Appendix A for a more detailed discussion of our sample.

3 The current definition of 'labour force' used by Statistics Canada divides those aged fifteen and over into three categories, the first two of which constitute the labour force: the employed (those who did any work at all, excluding housework, maintenance around the home, and volunteer work); the unemployed (those without work who had actively looked for work in the

past four weeks, as well as those who had been on lay-off and expected to
return to their jobs and those who had definite arrangements to start new
jobs in four weeks or less); and those not in the labour force (those persons
who, in the week prior to enumeration, were unwilling or unable to offer or
supply their labour services under conditions existing in the labour market).
Statistics Canada, *Labour Force Survey Economic Regions, 1986 Census: Labour
Analytic Report No. 5* (Ottawa, 1989), xxvii, xxxi, xxxvi.
4 See Michael B. Katz, Michael J. Doucett, and Mark J. Stern, *The Social Organization of Early Capitalism* (Cambridge, Mass., 1982), 69.
5 For useful discussions of the British and American censuses in this period
see Richard Lawton, ed., *The Census and Social Structure: An Interpretative
Guide to Nineteenth Century Censuses for England and Wales* (London, 1978);
Office of Population Censuses and Surveys, General Register Office, *Guide to
Census Reports: Great Britain, 1801–1966* (Edinburgh, 1978); Edward Higgs,
'The Struggle for the Occupational Census, 1841–1911,' in R. MacLeod, ed.,
Government and Expertise (Cambridge, 1988), 73–86; Simon R.S. Szreter, 'The
Genesis of the Registrar General's Social Classification of Occupations,' *Brit-
ish Journal of Sociology*, 35 no. 4 (1984), 522–46; Catherine Hakim, 'Census
Reports as Documentary Evidence: The Census Commentaries, 1801–1951,'
Sociological Review, 28 no. 3 (1980), 551–80; Margo Conk, 'Labor Statistics in
the American and English Census: Making Some Invidious Comparisons,'
Journal of Social History, 10 (1982–3), 83–102; M. Conk, 'Occupational Classification in the United States Census: 1870–1940,' *Journal of Interdisciplinary History*, 9 no. 1 (1978), 111–30; Steven Ruggles and Russell Menard, 'A Public
Use Sample of the 1880 U.S. Census of Population,' *Historical Methods*, 23 no.
3 (1990), 104–15; Steven Ruggles, 'Comparability of the Public Use Samples
of the U.S. Census of Population, 1880–1980,' *Social Science History*, 15 no. 1
(1991), 123–59.
6 Higgs, 'Struggle,' 82–3; Office of Population Censuses, *Guide to Census
Reports*, 51; Department of Agriculture, *The Instructions to Officers Employed in
the Taking of the Census of Canada*, (1891), 18; John R. Moen, 'From Gainful
Employment to Labor Force: Definitions and a New Estimate of Work
Rates of American Males, 1860 to 1980,' *Historical Methods*, 21 no. 4 (1988),
149.
7 Office of Population Censuses, *Guide to Census Reports*, 38–9; Conk, 'Occupational Classification,' 113.
8 Higgs, 'Struggle,' 82; Bryan D. Palmer, 'Labour Protest and Organization in
Nineteenth-Century Canada, 1820–1890,' *Labour/Le Travail*, 20 (1987), 69, 73;
*Proceedings of the Sixth Session of the Trades and Labor Congress of the Dominion
of Canada*, 2–5 Sept. 1890, 20; NA, RG 2, vol. 5190, file 2569, G.W. Dower to

J.A. Chapleau, 10 Nov. 1890; for a more detailed discussion of the 1891 census see Baskerville and Sager, 'The First National Unemployment Survey.'
9 J.A. Chapleau, Canadian House of Commons, *Debates* (1890), vol. 2, 4843, 4398.
10 *Proceedings of the Annual Convention of the Trades and Labor Congress* (1899), 9, reporting on a meeting of the executive committee with Sir Wilfrid Laurier. See also *Proceedings of the Annual Convention of the Trades and Labor Congress* (1898), for a motion on statistics.
11 Jeremy Webber, 'Compelling Compromise: Canada Chooses Conciliation over Arbitration, 1900–1907,' *Labour/Le Travail*, 28 (1991), 15–57; Douglas Cruikshank and Greg Kealey, 'Canadian Strike Statistics, 1891–1950,' *Labour/Le Travail*, 20 (1987), calculated from Table B, 134.
12 William Mulock, Canada House of Commons, *Debates* (1901), 3, 8399.
13 Barry Ferguson, *Remaking Liberalism: The Intellectual Legacy of Adam Shortt, O.D. Skelton, W.C. Clark, and William A. Mackintosh, 1890–1925* (Montreal, 1993); Ken Cruikshank, 'Policy Entrepreneurs and Regulatory Innovation: Simon James McLean, William Lyon Mackenzie King and Business Government Relations in the Age of Laurier,' in Peter Baskerville, ed., *Canadian Papers in Business History*, 2 (Victoria, 1993), 103–24; Ken Cruikshank, *Close Ties: Railways, Government, and the Board of Railway Commissioners, 1851–1933* (Montreal, 1991); Marlene Shore, *The Science of Social Redemption: McGill, the Chicago School, and the Origins of Social Research in Canada* (Toronto, 1987).
14 Such an objective was central to the operation of Victorian science in Canada. 'The basis of science as it was practised in Canada during the Victorian Age,' Suzanne Zeller has demonstrated, 'was inventory, systematic surveys of the land and its resources with the ultimate goal of assessing its material potential.' Zeller, *Inventing Canada: Early Victorian Science and the Idea of a Transcontinental Nation* (Toronto, 1987), 269.
15 Sidney Fisher, House of Commons, *Debates* (1905) 7, 645, 637.
16 One recent and balanced treatment is Richard H. Steckel, 'The Quality of Census Data for Historical Inquiry: A Research Agenda,' *Social Science History*, 15 (1991), 579–99; see also the articles by Steven Ruggles, Russell Menard, and others on the Minnesota Historical Census Projects in *Historical Methods*, 28 no. 1 (winter 1995). For women, see N. Folbre and M. Abel, 'Women's Work and Women's Households: Gender Biases in the U.S. Census,' *Social Research*, 56 (1989), 545–70. Bruce Curtis, 'On the Local Construction of Statistical Knowledge: Making up the 1861 Census of the Canadas,' *Journal of Historical Sociology*, 7 (1994), 416–34, presents a critique of one mid-nineteenth-century Canadian census. For an appraisal of underenumeration in U.S. censuses, see Miriam L. King and Diana L. Magnuson, 'Perspectives

on Historical U.S. Census Undercounts,' *Social Science History*, 19 (winter 1995), 455–66. See also the very useful collection of papers on 'Use of Census Manuscript Data for Historical Research,' Kris Inwood and Richard Reid, eds., *Histoire sociale/Social History*, 28 (Nov. 1995).

17 In Montreal, the figures were much higher: the Protestant House of Refuge and Industry provided overnight lodging to 23,305 men in 1899, and 23,567 in 1900. *Montreal Star*, 25 April 1901.

18 Richard Anderson, '"The Irrepressible Stampede": Tramps in Ontario, 1870–1880,' *Ontario History*, 84 (1992), 33–56; and James M. Pitsula, 'The Treatment of Tramps in Late Nineteenth Toronto,' Canadian Historical Association, *Historical Papers* (1980), 116–32. Jim Phillips, 'Poverty, Unemployment and the Administration of the Criminal Law: Vagrancy Laws in Halifax, 1864–1890,' in Phillip Girard and J. Phillips, eds., *Essays in the History of Canadian Law*, vol. 3 (Toronto, 1994), 128–62; David Bright, 'Loafers Are Not Going to Subsist upon Public Credulence: Vagrancy and the Law in Calgary, 1900–1914,' *Labour/Le Travail*, 36 (fall 1995), 37–58. For the situation in an American border city, see S.L. Harring, 'Class Conflict and the Suppression of Tramps in Buffalo, 1892–1894,' *Law and Society Review*, 11 (1976–7), 873–911. See also Daniel Hiebert's comments on a similar group in Winnipeg at the turn of the century, 'Class, Ethnicity, and Residential Structure: The Social Geography of Winnipeg, 1901–1921,' *Journal of Historical Geography*, 17 (1991), 56–9. For British Columbia, see *Victoria Colonist*, 23 Feb. 1893. For a pioneering discussion of women as part of the 'vagrant' population, see Tamara Myers and Mary Anne Poutanen, 'Tales of Women's Lives on the Street: Urban Space, Women, and the Policing of Vagrancy in Montreal, 1810–1842 and 1890–1930,' paper presented to the Canadian Historical Association, Calgary, 1994.

19 Folbre and Abel, 'Women's Work'; Edward Higgs, 'Women, Occupations and Work in the Nineteenth-Century Censuses,' *History Workshop Journal*, 23 (1987), 59–80; P. Baskerville, '"She Has Already Hinted at Board": Enterprising Urban Women in British Columbia, 1863–1896,' *Histoire sociale/Social History*, 26 (1993), 205–28.

20 Keyssar, *Out of Work*, 50, 356–8, 375.

21 In 1891, employers represented 9.2 per cent of the workforce.

22 Cross-tabulating sex with the unemployed/not unemployed variable in our 10 per cent random file yields a contingency coefficient of only 0.06; lambda with sex dependent is .0000. Ellen Jordan argues that in England enumeration practices masked female unemployment and that, given sex segmentation of work, female unemployment was built into the occupational structure. Jordan, 'Female Unemployment in England and Wales, 1851–1911:

An Examination of the Census Figures for 15–19 Year Olds,' *Social History*, 13 no. 2 (May 1988), 175–90.

23 'The Unemployed,' Toronto *Globe*, 7 March 1894. The speaker is identified as 'Mrs. Kellogg.'

24 'The Unemployed Problem,' *Western Clarion*, 25 March 1905.

25 Keyssar, *Out of Work*, 95.

26 Persons in the workforce are defined as those aged fifteen through sixty-five, excluding those for whom the occupation column is blank, unless those people are also said to be unemployed.

27 The present analysis qualifies our earlier conclusion: see Sager and Baskerville, 'Locating the Unemployed in Urban British Columbia: Evidence from the 1891 Census,' *Journal of Canadian Studies*, 25 no. 3 (autumn 1990), 44.

28 Aggregating ages into six cohorts for people aged fifteen through sixty-five and cross-tabulating with unemployed/not unemployed yields a chi square of 23.8 with 5 degrees of freedom, but the contingency coefficient is an uninteresting .04. This finding contrasts with Mark Thomas's findings for England in 1913. Thomas found that unemployment rates for people over fifty were lower than those for younger people but that unemployment rates by age resembled a U (high rates among the young and the old). See Thomas, 'Unemployment in Edwardian Britain,' in E. Aerts and B. Eichenberg, eds., *Proceedings of the Tenth International Economic History Conference* (Leuven, 1990), 36–50, and Robert A. Margo, 'The Microeconomics of Depression Unemployment,' *Journal of Economic History*, 51 (1991), 334–5.

29 J.J. McCook, 'A Tramp Census and Its Revelations,' *Forum*, 15 (1893), 760.

30 'Instructions to Officers Employed in the Taking of the Census,' Department of Agriculture (1891), 18.

31 This observation corresponds to Keyssar's comment that after age fifty 'the prospect of long term joblessness began to loom larger on the horizon.' *Out of Work*, 96.

32 A more sensitive analysis, aggregating occupations into fourteen categories, yields a similar conclusion. While the chi square is significant, the contingency coefficient is .04.

33 The Chinese born were 2.5 per cent of the unemployed in our six cities; they were 2.3 per cent of the not-unemployed adults; the Irish were 8.6 per cent of the unemployed and 6.5 per cent of the not unemployed; Ontario born made up 13.8 per cent of the unemployed and 15.0 per cent of the not unemployed, for instance.

34 Keyssar, *Out of Work*, 79ff.

35 Grouping relationship to head into six categories (head, wife, children of head, lodgers, subhead's family, and others) and cross-tabulating with

unemployed/not unemployed yields a significant chi square but a contingency coefficient of only .06. By comparison, the proportions among the adult 'not unemployed' in the workforce were as follows: heads, 35.8 per cent; children of heads, 14.2 per cent; lodgers, 20.8 per cent; and sub-heads' families, 9.5 per cent.

36 *Census of Canada*, 1891, district 10, subdivision 5, ward 4A, page 84, lines 9–16.

37 Daniel Scott Smith, 'A Mean and Random Past: The Implications of Variance for History,' *Historical Methods*, 17 no. 3 (summer 1984), 142.

38 See, for instance, Cheryl Elman, 'Turn-of-the-Century Dependence and Interdependence: Roles of Teens in Family Economies of the Aged,' *Journal of Family History*, 18 no. 1 (1993), 65–85; and Gordon Darroch and Lee Soltow, *Property and Inequality in Victorian Ontario: Structural Patterns and Cultural Communities in the 1871 Census* (Toronto, 1994). One must take care with certain procedures, such as probit, when a dichotomous dependent variable has few responses in one category. See Carole Shammas, 'Dealing with Dichotomous Dependent Variables,' *Historical Methods*, 14 no. 1 (winter 1981), 47–51; Michael D. Ornstein, 'Discrete Multivariate Analysis: An Example from the 1871 Canadian Census,' *Historical Methods* 16 no. 3 (summer 1983), 101–8.

39 SPSS-X prints goodness of fit statistics: when the goodness-of-fit chi square and its degrees of freedom approach parity, then the observed significance level of the chi square is high, which indicates that the model being used does not differ significantly from a 'perfect' model (i.e., it possesses significant explanatory power).

40 In the backward elimination we used the likelihood-ratio statistic as the criterion for deletion of variables. At each stage the program removes the variable for which the significance level of the log-likelihood ratio is greater than .05.

41 In most cities, lodgers were not more at risk of unemployment than other household members, though they were often perceived to be at the margins of labour markets in the late nineteenth century. Only in Vancouver and Montreal were they overrepresented among the unemployed, i.e., their distribution among the unemployed was greater than their distribution among the not unemployed.

42 The procedure was repeated with age squared and with age as a categorical variable. Using age squared resulted in a lower significance and the exp(B) indicated a very flat relationship between age and the odds of being unemployed. The coefficients for other variables remained almost the same as those in Table 3.3. We ran age as a categorical variable using four categories: 15 through 29, 30 through 44, 45 through 54, and 55 through 65. The oldest

group was our reference category. From the youngest to the oldest the exp(B) statistic was: .51, .62, and .73. Only the first two were significant at below the .05 level. The overall significance level of age as a categorical variable was .00. There was no significant change in the coefficients for the other variables. This procedure confirms the analysis presented in the text: the odds of being unemployed increased with age.

43 Darroch and Soltow, *Property and Inequality*, 59–60.

44 More formally, the chi-square and related statistics in a cross-tabulation of religions with unemployed/not unemployed cannot be used because too many cells have an expected frequency of less than 5.

45 Almost two-thirds of French Canadians in the workforce (62.2 per cent) were in transport, industrial production, or general labour. Just over two-fifths (42.9 per cent) of non-French Canadians in the workforce were in the same categories.

46 Keyssar, *Out of Work*, 80.

47 In this procedure we omitted religion because of its overlap with birthplace and ethnicity. The magnitude of each variable's contribution is here measured by −2 times the log of the likelihood ratio. For a similar use of the technique see Darroch and Soltow, *Property and Inequality*, 87–8. We are indebted to Gordon Darroch and to Arthur Sweetman, Department of Economics, University of Victoria, for their assistance with this procedure.

48 *Manitoba Free Press*, 4 April 1901.

49 Employees were 83 per cent of the workforce as we define it – all persons aged fifteen through sixty-five with stated occupations. Information on months worked is entered for 85 per cent of these employees. See also Appendix A.

50 These estimates of unemployment frequency remain uncertain because of the 15 per cent of employees (and the 23.3 per cent of the workforce) for whom 'months employed' columns are blank (there were three such columns in the census – for months worked in a factory, at home, and in an occupation other than work in factory and home). The 17.8 per cent estimate is the proportion of all persons for whom employment status (columns 17 to 21) is employee, whose total months employed (columns 23 to 25) is less than twelve. The 20.8 per cent estimate is the number of those employees working twelve months as a proportion of all employees for whom months-employed information is given. This latter estimate is acceptable if we assume that the blanks in columns 23–25 mean simply 'unknown,' and that the pattern of work for the 'unknowns' was the same as for all other employees. We think that these assumptions can be accepted.

Of the 1,971 employees for whom 'months employed' columns are blank, 63.4 per cent were in either Halifax or one Montreal district (number 175). In these districts a few enumerators consistently failed to enter employment and earnings information. The only other clear pattern among the 1,971 is that we find them overrepresented in households containing multiple and extended families and among people in the secondary family unit in a household (the family of a subhead). This finding suggests that enumerators may have had difficulty obtaining information about employment duration of individuals in large and complicated households. Since we are reasonably confident that a blank under 'months employed' indicates 'unknown' rather than zero, and since we see no other patterns, we may analyse the other 85 per cent of employees on the assumption that they are representative of all employees.

51 Sharon Myers, '"Not to Be Ranked as Women": Female Industrial Workers in Turn-of-the-Century Halifax,' in Veronica Strong-Boag and Anita Clair Fellman, eds., *Rethinking Canada: The Promise of Women's History* (Toronto, 1997), 222.

52 In entering information on occupation in our computer files, we gave an occupation – housewife – to adult women who were said to be married. There were 6,321 of these in an adult population of 28,372 (persons aged fifteen and above). There were 27,590 people aged fifteen to sixty-nine inclusive.

53 Those without stated occupations, but having some stated earnings, were certainly unknowns – but they numbered only 233 out of 4,787. Similarly, only 538 of the 4,787 had an entry under employment status (columns 18 to 21 of the census). Three-quarters of adults without occupations were women; 41 per cent were daughters of the head of a household; 38.7 per cent were aged nineteen or under.

54 Toronto *Globe*, 3 Feb. 1883.

55 James Pitsula, 'The Relief of Poverty in Toronto 1880–1930' (PhD thesis, York University, 1979), 102–12. Pitsula also notes that a further 25.5 per cent of applicants exhibited two or more of the key conditions – unemployment, poor health, old age.

56 James C. Riley, 'Working Health Time: A Comparison of Pre-Industrial, Industrial, and Post-Industrial Experience in Life and Health,' *Explorations in Economic History*, 28 (1991), Table 1, 175.

57 Cross-tabulating city with two categories of unemployed (less than nine months and more than nine months) yields a contingency coefficient of .13, but the lambda is .0000. If one knows only the city in which a person lived, that gives one no help in predicting whether they were unemployed or not.

58 We applied the same procedure that we used for the 1891 data. In the backward elimination the likelihood-ratio statistic served as the criterion for the

elimination of variables. At each stage the program removed the variable for which the significance level of the log-likelihood ratio is greater than .05.

59 The rate is simply the proportion of women aged fifteen to sixty-five who reported an occupation. If a married woman had no stated occupation, and therefore no place in the measured labour force, we assigned her the occupation housewife. Housewives made up 47.8 per cent of all women aged fifteen to sixty-five in 1891, and 44.7 per cent in 1901. The change could result not from a higher rate of marriage but from an increased tendency on the part of enumerators to assign an occupation to married women. This could in turn be a product of the need to ask the questions about how many months the individual worked in the labour force: since enumerators had this latter question, they may have been more likely to enter a labour-force occupation for women in 1901 than in 1891.

60 *Census of Canada*, Montreal district 178A, subdivision 43, page 13, lines 39–42.

61 As we did with the 1891 data, we repeated the procedure both with age squared and with age as a categorical variable. Once again the results confirmed that older people experienced greater odds of being unemployed.

62 Controlling only for men increases the chances of being unemployed: 5.6 per cent of men 50–54 who were in the workforce lacked employment, as did 6 per cent of the 55–59s, 6.2 per cent of the 60–64s, and 8.6 per cent of those over 65.

63 The quote is from Abraham Epstein, *Facing Old Age* (New York, 1972, orig. 1922), cited in N. Sue Weiler, 'Industrial Scrap Heap: Employment Patterns and Change for the Aged in the 1920s,' *Social Science History*, 13 (1989), 65; for the debate on labour participation and age, see Brian Gratton, *Urban Elders: Family Work and Welfare among Boston's Aged, 1890–1950* (Philadelphia, 1986); Carole Haber and B. Gratton, *Old Age and the Search for Security: An American Social History* (Bloomington, Ind., 1994). R.L. Ransom and R. Sutch, 'The Labor of Older Americans: Retirement of Men on and off the Job, 1870–1937,' *Journal of Economic History*, 46 (1986), 1–30; Jon Moen, 'The Labor of Older Men: A Comment,' *Journal of Economic History*, 47 (1987), 761–6; Ransom and Sutch, 'The Trend in the Rate of Labor Force Participation of Older Men: 1870–1930: A Reply to Moen,' *Journal of Economic History*, 49 (1989), 170–83; Jon R. Moen, 'The Unemployment and Retirement of Older Men: Further Evidence from the 1890 and 1910 Censuses,' *Historical Methods*, 27 (1994), 40–6; special issue on ageing, *Journal of Economic History*, 56 (1996). Jane Synge, 'Work and Family Support Patterns of the Aged in the Early Twentieth Century,' in V.W. Marshall, ed., *Aging in Canada: Social Perspectives* (Toronto, 1980), 135–44; Edgar-André Montigny, 'A Historiography of Destitution: Canadian Historians and the History of Old Age,' paper presented to the Canadian Historical Association, Brock University, June 1996.

64 'The proper occupation of old people is one of the problems of the age. The army of the unemployed is largely recruited from men past their meridian.' Toronto *Daily Mail*, 28 Jan. 1892.

65 BCARS, GR 684, Box 4, file 21, Diary of John Isaac Staples, p. 101.

66 Much of the most recent literature on ageing and industrialization focuses on the United States. For recent reviews of this literature see the issue of the *Journal of Economic History*, 56 (March 1996), especially the articles by Susan B. Carter and Richard Sutch and by Brian Gratton. Carter, Sutch, and Gratton argue for a more optimistic view than we have presented here, partly because of the existence of pensions for Civil War veterans; there was nothing comparable for Canadians. They find also that the American working class at the turn of the century was able to amass significant savings for retirement. As chapter 6 indicates, we have found extreme income differentials within the working class; those in the lowest income quintiles had very limited opportunities to save. Among blue-collar workers in our six cities (those in primary industry, industrial production, transportation, or general labouring) the average annual earnings of those aged under sixty-five was $425; the average earnings for older people was $381.

67 Donald H. Avery, *Reluctant Host: Canada's Response to Immigrant Workers, 1896–1984* (Toronto, 1995), 41, 7.

68 M.C. Urquhart, *Historical Statistics of Canada*, 2nd ed. (Ottawa, 1983), Series A297–326.

69 Of all recent-immigrant wage earners, 18.7 per cent were in general labour; only 7.2 per cent of non-immigrants held jobs in the same category.

70 A contributing possibility is that the census takers' questions in 1901 tended to yield more answers about labour-force participation. Immigrants were probably more likely to respond to a question about the number of months worked than to the blunt question 'Are you unemployed?' Contemporaries often associated unemployment with immigrants. 'The newcomers form a very large proportion, and probably a majority, of the unemployed who are also destitute': H.A. Kennedy, *The Unemployed in Canada: Causes of the Trouble* (London, 1908), 9. See also *Report of the Royal Commission on the Alleged Employment of Aliens* (Ottawa, 1905) and *Report of the Royal Commission to Inquire into the Immigration of Italian Labourers to Montreal* (Ottawa, 1905).

71 Non-immigrants made up 69.5 per cent of the sample in Table 3.11 (wage earners aged fifteen through sixty-five). Of all those working less than twelve months in the year, 65 per cent were non-immigrants.

72 In 1901, 85 per cent of wage earners in Montreal reported working twelve months in the year; the overall proportion for the other cities was 72.9 per cent. There was no significant movement of French Canadians through occupation categories between 1891 and 1901: in both years they were overrepre-

sented in industrial production and general labour and underrepresented in white-collar jobs. Proportionally more French Canadians (83.1 per cent) were unemployed during the year than were non–French Canadians (87.2 per cent).

73 For instance, in Vancouver and Victoria we find a substantial overrepresentation of Confucians and other non-Christians among those working eight months or less; most were born in Asia. The cross-tabulation of religion aggregated into Catholic, Anglican, Presbyterian, Methodist, other Protestant, Confucian, and other) with birthplace (Canada, British Isles, Europe, Asia, and other) yields a significant chi square and a large contingency coefficient, though 19 per cent of Asians were said to be Protestants; European born appeared in every religious category except Confucian.

74 An example of the procedure is as follows: we selected Hamilton-resident males born in Canada, aged twenty to forty-nine, whose 'racial or tribal origin' was English, Scots, or Welsh; from this subset we selected only wage earners in industrial production or transport. We then cross-tabulated religion (Catholic, Anglican, Presbyterian, Methodist, and other) with months worked. If religious groups are seen to be over- or underrepresented among the underemployed, then we can suspect that this result has to do with religion rather than other characteristics. If the significance level of chi square was at .1 or above we accepted the null hypothesis of no association between the variables. In this example the significance was .26.

Only two of twenty-five subsets indicated that religion might have an independent effect. One was Winnipeg-resident English-Scots-Welsh males aged twenty to forty-nine in industrial production or transport; here Anglicans and other religions are slightly overrepresented among those working nine months or less; Presbyterians and Methodists are underrepresented among those working nine months or less. The only other subset that turned up a significant chi square was Asian-origin males aged twenty to forty-nine in Vancouver or Victoria, working in services, primary industry, industrial production, transport, or general labour (there were three religious categories: Confucian; Muslim, Hindu, or Buddhist; and other, mainly Protestant); here the middle group was strongly overrepresented among those working nine months or less, but the result may relate not simply to religion but to overrepresentation in a vulnerable occupation among the occupational categories selected.

Some adjustments were required to ensure sufficient cases in each cell, but other subsets yielding no significant associations between religion and work duration include Hamilton English-Scots-Welsh male wage-earners born outside Canada aged 20–49 in industrial production or transport; Montreal

English-Scots-Welsh-Irish male wage earners born in Canada aged 20–49
working in industrial production or transport (and the same omitting born in
Canada); Halifax male wage-earners aged 20–55 in industrial production or
transport; Winnipeg English-Scots-Welsh and Irish male wage earners aged
20–49 in industrial production or transport (as noted above, omitting the
Irish yields a significant chi square!); Winnipeg European male wage earners
aged 20–54 in industrial production or transport (religions: Jewish, Catholic,
Orthodox, Lutheran, other); Winnipeg English-Scots-Welsh-Irish males aged
20–54 in white-collar occupations; Vancouver or Victoria males born in Canada of English-Scots-Welsh-Irish origin aged 20–49 in industrial production
or transport (and the same adding general labour); all cities, males of
English-Scots-Welsh-Irish origin, born in Canada, aged 20–49, in industrial
production; the previous, but changing occupation to general labour; the
previous, but changing occupation to clerical, sales, or service; all cities,
males of English-Scots-Welsh-Irish origin born outside Canada aged 20–49 in
industrial production; all cities, European-origin males aged 20–49 in industrial production (religions: Catholic, Orthodox, Lutheran, other).
75 Because of problems of collinearity we omit religion and immigrant status.
76 Keyssar, *Out of Work*, 54.
77 Susan Carter and Richard Sutch, 'The Labor Market in the 1890s: Evidence
from Connecticut Manufacturing,' in E. Aerts and B. Eichenberg, eds., *Proceedings of the Tenth International Economic History Conference* (Leuven, 1990),
15–24; see also Craig Heron, 'Factory Workers,' in Paul Craven, ed., *Labouring Lives: Work and Workers in Nineteenth Century Ontario* (Toronto, 1995),
532–3.
78 We should not assume, however, that literacy was as basic to work routines
as it is today. In 1891 the illiterate were twice as likely to be unemployed as
the literate: 8.8 per cent of those who could neither read nor write were
unemployed. This variable was not entered into the procedure for Table 3.3
because the number of illiterates was very small. In 1901 between 4.1 and 4.8
per cent of 'employees' were said to be illiterate, and the probability of working less than nine months is 1.8 times higher for illiterates. The measure of
illiteracy is crude, however, and it prompts questions rather than answers
about education, skill, and employment. The 1901 census also asked about
people's infirmities (were people deaf, blind, or of 'unsound mind'?). The
probability of working less than nine months was high among those reporting a disability, but the numbers are very small (only thirteen people among
those classified as employees aged fifteen through sixty-five).
79 It is no surprise to find some relationship between people's race and the likelihood of their being unemployed. The 1901 census had two questions relat-

ing to race. The first was about 'colour,' in which enumerators were to indicate either white ('the Caucasian race'), red ('the American Indian'), black ('the African or negro'), or yellow ('the Mongolian,' meaning 'Japanese or Chinese'). The children of marriages between whites and other races were to be classed not as white but as red, black, or yellow. Among people described as 'employees,' non-whites were more than twice as likely to be seriously underemployed (working less than nine months) than one would expect, given their share of the workforce. Whatever BC labour leaders and politicians may have said about the effect of Asians on labour markets, it is clear that Asians were much more vulnerable to job loss than were any other racial group except Blacks. The vulnerability of Asians was also a BC fact: our sample contains eighty-two Asian employees living elsewhere in Canada, and all said that they worked for twelve months (chi square was 204.4 at 6 d.f. and contingency coefficient = .13). Aggregating races into two categories – white and non-white – yields a very similar result, and the probability of non-whites being in the under-nine-month category is 2.54.

4: Seasonality, Occupations, and Labour Markets

1 Quits were especially high in larger bureaucratic companies such as the Canadian Pacific Railway. Barton Hamilton and Mary MacKinnon, 'Quits and Layoffs in Early Twentieth Century Labor Markets,' *Explorations in Economic History*, 33 (1996), 346–66. On high turnover and quitting in iron and steel, see Craig Heron, *Working in Steel: The Early Years in Canada, 1883–1935* (Toronto, 1988), 78–9, 82–3, 113–8. For examples of workers quitting and moving on as a form of protest and wage bargaining, see Richard A. Rajala, 'Bill and the Boss: Labor Protest, Technological Change, and the Transformation of the West Coast Lumbering Camp, 1890–1930,' *Journal of Forest History*, 33 no. 4 (Oct. 1989), 168–79, and Eric Sager, *Seafaring Labour: The Merchant Marine of Atlantic Canada 1820–1914* (Montreal, 1989), 186–98.
2 Sanford Jacoby, *Employing Bureaucracy: Managers, Unions and the Transformation of Work in American Industry, 1900–1945* (New York, 1985) 1–38, quote from 34. See also Sanford M. Jacoby and Sunil Sharma, 'Employment Duration and Industrial Labor Mobility in the United States, 1880–1980,' *Journal of Economic History*, 52 (1992), 161–79; Susan B. Carter and Elizabeth Savoca, 'Labor Mobility and Lengthy Jobs in Nineteenth-Century America,' *Journal of Economic History*, 50 no. 1 (March 1990), 1–16. John A. James, 'Job Tenure in the Gilded Age,' in George Grantham and Mary MacKinnon, eds., *Labour Market Evolution* (London, 1994), 185–203, argues that there may be more similarities in job duration between the late nineteenth century and the late

twentieth century than others have suggested. Yet even James concludes (200): 'In the Gilded Age, the labor market was in fact much more fluid and employment relationships more tenuous than today.' Walter Licht also emphasizes high turnover and the irregularity of employment in *Getting Work: Philadelphia, 1840–1950* (Cambridge, Mass. 1992).

3 Bruno Ramirez, 'Migration and Regional Class Labour Markets, 1870–1915: The Quebec Case,' in D.R. Hopkin and G.S. Kealey, eds., *Class, Community and the Labour Movement: Wales and Canada 1850–1930* (St John's, 1989), 128, and 'Brief Encounters: Italian Immigrant Workers and the CPR, 1900–1939,' *Labour/Le Travail*, 17 (spring 1986), 9–27. See also his *On the Move: French-Canadian and Italian Immigrants in the North Atlantic Economy, 1860–1914* (Toronto, 1991).

4 Barton Hamilton and Mary MacKinnon, 'Long-Term Employment Relationships in the Early Twentieth Century: Evidence from Personnel Data,' *Labour Economics*, 3 (1996), 379. They also suggest, cautiously, that 'it is unlikely that long-term spells would be found more often in smaller firms.' Elsewhere MacKinnon argues that the employment duration of Italian immigrants working for the CPR was 'only a little shorter than average': MacKinnon, 'The Great War and the Canadian Labour Market: Railway Workers 1903–39,' in Grantham and MacKinnon, eds., *Labour Market Evolution*, 205–24. See also Craig Heron, 'Factory Workers,' in Paul Craven, ed., *Labouring Lives: Work and Workers in Nineteenth Century Ontario* (Toronto, 1994), 511; Heron, *Working in Steel: The Early Years in Canada, 1883–1935* (Toronto, 1988), passim.

5 Peter Bischoff, '"Travelling the Country Round": migrations et syndicalisme chez les mouleurs de l'Ontario et du Québec membres de l'Iron Molders Union of North America, 1860 à 1892,' *Journal of the Canadian Historical Association* (Ottawa, 1990), 37–71. See Burnett, *Idle Hands*, 161–4.

6 BCARS, RG 684, box 1, vol. 3, file 8.

7 Most studies of transiency extrapolate from rates of persistence calculated from data linkages across several censuses for one area. We do not rely on frail record linkages and focus instead on those who moved as determined from various measures reported in the 1901 census. For an excellent discussion of transiency in this period and of the difficulties in measuring it, see Michael B. Katz, Michael J. Doucet, and Mark J. Stern, *The Social Organization of Early Industrial Capitalism* (Cambridge, Mass., 1982), 102–30.

8 In 1871, 2.3 per cent of all Canadian born lived in provinces other than that of their birth; by 1901 the proportion had risen to 6.4 per cent. Calculated from *Historical Statistics of Canada* ed., M.C. Urquhart and K.A.H. Buckley (Ottawa, 1983), Series A327–338.

9 In Vancouver 93 per cent of the Canadian-born working class had been born outside British Columbia. By contrast, only 2.4 per cent of Hamilton's Canadian-born workers had been born outside Ontario.

10 This percentage remains an underestimate, since the volume of intraprovincial urban migration is not known. The figures are as follows: 2,791 rural-born workers worked in a city in the province of their birth; 1,522 wage earners worked in a city outside the province of their birth; and 4,434 urban workers had been born outside Canada. There were 13,600 wage earners in our six-city sample.

11 We grouped occupations into three categories: professional, managerial, clerical, sales, and service; primary, craft, and industrial production and transportation; and general labourer. 24.1 per cent of those in the first group, 14.9 per cent of the second, and 13 per cent of the third lived outside the province of their birth.

12 Stephan Thernstrom, *The Other Bostonians: Poverty and Progress in the American Metropolis, 1880–1970* (Cambridge, Mass., 1973), 42.

13 McCook, 'A Tramp Census,' 754, 760. There is no reason to assume that Canadian tramps exhibited a profile different from that of the Americans. In fact, for tramps the border would seem to have been quite permeable. In 1891 the Toronto *Globe* interviewed one American tramp who said he came to Canada because 'There's no shooting or anything of that kind.' Cited in Pitsula, 'The Treatment of Tramps,' 121. The border 'is only an imaginary line,' Charles Cassidy of the Stonecutters union informed the Royal Commission on Labour in British Columbia in January 1912; BCARS, GR 684, vol. 1, file 2.

14 Pitsula, 'The Treatment of Tramps,' 122–3.

15 *Western Clarion*, 16 July 1904.

16 Anderson, 'The Irrepressible Stampede,' 52. For examples of skilled workers who 'tramped,' see Bischoff, 'Travelling the Country Round,' 37–71; Gordon Darroch, 'Migrants in the Nineteenth Century: Fugitive or Families in Motion?' *Journal of Family History*, 6 (1981), 257–77. See also 'Vagrancy,' in *Report of the Ontario Commission on Unemployment* (Toronto, 1916), 101–12. Eric Hobsbawm argued that tramping was a normal way of dealing with unemployment among artisans: Hobsbawm, 'The Tramping Artisan,' in his *Labouring Men: Studies in the History of Labour* (London, 1964), 42, 44.

17 'Modern Leg-Iron Civilization,' *Western Clarion*, 20 Aug. 1904.

18 Daniel Rodgers, 'Tradition, Modernity and the American Industrial Worker,' *Journal of Interdisciplinary History*, 7 (1977), 666–7.

19 Jacoby and Sharma, 'Employment Duration,' 161–79.

20 BCARS, GR 684, Royal Commission on Labour, 1912–14, box 1, vol. 1, 156.

21 *Labour Gazette*, 1 (1901), 146.

22 'Seasonality' is sometimes loosely applied to the shutting down of plants in certain seasons because of the decline in demand for a product or because of the manufacturers' desire to avoid overproduction. This is not what we mean by 'seasonality.' Cf. Craig Heron, 'Factory Workers,' 494–7.

23 BCARS, GR 684, vol. 1, file 8, p. 119, re British Columbia Royal Commission on Labour, 1912.

24 Seasonal occupations also include ship stewards, ship firemen, farmers, farm hands, grain inspectors, gardeners, lumbermen, wood cutters, fishermen, seal hunters, wharf foremen, harbour foremen, miners, quarrymen, sawmill workers, shingle makers, cannery workers, tobacco workers (but not cigar makers), stone cutters, can makers (since they served canneries), plumbers, tinsmiths, brick makers, painters, roofers, carpenters, joiners, bridge carpenters, caulkers, longshoremen, able seamen, tugboat deckhands, and canal lockmen. Obviously many other occupations may have been affected indirectly by seasonal effects on markets; but it is unlikely that we have underestimated the direct effects of seasonality as we define it.

25 It is difficult to know what to do with the 217 general labourers (for whom industry or trade is not specified). The 29 per cent figure assumes that general labour was non-seasonal; the 38 per cent figure results from including half of the general labourers among seasonal occupations.

26 *Census of Canada*, 1901, Victoria, subdistrict 12, page 1, line 37.

27 *Report of the Royal Commission on the Relations of Capital and Labour* (Ottawa, 1889), vol. 5, 116.

28 Toronto *Globe*, 3 Feb. 1883. For an extended discussion of technology and unemployment in the United States see Ester Fano, 'A "Wastage of Men": Technological Progress and Unemployment in the United States,' *Technology and Culture*, 32 no. 2 (1991), 264–92.

29 It is not always possible to identify those in injured trades, but our list includes sealing captains, miners, moulders, nail makers, weavers, rope makers, cigarmakers, tobacco stuffers, tailors, dressmakers, milliners, sailmakers, seamstresses, shoemakers, bootmakers, carriage builders, coopers, blacksmiths, glass blowers, printers, bookbinders, spar makers, ship carpenters, shipbuilders, riggers, and sailors. These occupations account for about 18 per cent of all employees who worked less than twelve months. We have also isolated the occupations subject to severe underemployment – those where more than 10 per cent of people worked less than nine months. The injured trades account for about 14 per cent of people in such occupations. See Bettina Bradbury, *Working Families: Age, Gender, and Daily Survival in Industrializing Montreal* (Toronto, 1993), 84–6; *Montreal Star*, 30 April and 1, 2 May 1901, for a discussion of technological change in cigarmaking.

30 *Census of Canada*, 1901, Victoria, subdistrict 12, page 27, line 40.
31 In 1996, the annual unemployment rates for the six cities were Halifax, 8.6 per cent; Montreal, 11.9; Hamilton, 7.4; Winnipeg, 8.4; Vancouver, 8.1; and Victoria, 8.9. For purposes of comparing variations we take the mean of these rates and the standard deviation (1.57). The coefficient of variation is the standard deviation as a percentage of the mean: for these six cities it is 17.6. The comparable coefficient for unemployment rates for the six cities in 1891 was 25.0 (all cases) or 30.0 (men only), which confirms that the variation was greater in 1891.
32 We have analysed several distinct occupations across six cities, where numbers are sufficient to allow comparisons. For carpenters, for instance, average monthly wages (not adjusted for cost of living) were $60.51 in Vancouver, $78.89 in Victoria, $55.11 in Winnipeg, $36.40 in Halifax, $39.66 in Hamilton, and $39.25 in Montreal. We have adjusted these nominal wages by cost of living in the following way: we divide nominal wages by the cost of living for a single male adult in each city and multiply by the average living costs for all six cities. We then find the coefficient of variation for the adjusted average monthly wage rates. These coefficients are for carpenters, 26.6; dressmakers, 29.7; painters, 20.5; machinists, 17.2; tailors, 16.7; printers, 16.1; shoemakers, 12.9; and general labourers, 12.8. These results indicate considerable variations in wage rates among cities, independent of differences in cost of living.
33 The other rates were: Victoria, 1 of every 5.6 employees; Winnipeg, 1 of 7.5; Halifax, 1 of 9; and Hamilton, 1 of 7.
34 John Lutz, 'Losing Steam: The Boiler and Engine Industry as an Index of British Columbia's Deindustrialization, 1880–1915,' Canadian Historical Association, *Historical Papers* (Ottawa, 1988), 168–208.
35 In 1891 the proportion of employees in industrial production in Victoria was 43.1 per cent; in Vancouver, 34.6 per cent; in Winnipeg, 28.1 per cent; in Hamilton, 49.3 per cent; in Montreal, 40.5 per cent; and in Halifax, 31.7 per cent.
36 For 85.5 per cent of all employees aged fifteen through sixty-five there is information in one or more of these three columns.
37 *Census of Canada*, 1901, Manufactures (Ottawa, 1905), lxv; *Postal Census of Manufactures of Canada 1916* (Ottawa, 1917), xi.
38 In Winnipeg between 1891 and 1901 per-capita output in manufacturing showed a marginal increase (see Table 1.2). Between 1901 and 1915 per-capita output increased by 56 per cent – a figure calculated from Alan Artibise, *Winnipeg: A Social History of Urban Growth* (Montreal, 1975), Table Five, 123.
39 Looking at specific occupations within the industrial production/manufacturing sector yields the following:

Occupation	Factory		Non-factory	
	Annual earnings ($)	No.	Annual earnings ($)	No.
Iron moulder/iron foundry	488	105	632	11
Tobacco/cigarmaker	337	147	355	11
Tailor/dressmaker	286	304	288	110
Shoemaker	338	178	432	8
Cooper	451	24	560	5
Blacksmith	488	65	574	28
Other metal worker	467	191	584	34
Printer	433	75	570	46
Brickmason/stonemason	465	24	486	49

The difference in food and beverages and in cotton spinning was, however, in favour of factory workers (though in cotton the number of non-factory workers was so small that the comparison is meaningless).

40 In the non-factory workplace 14.5 per cent of workers were women; 85.5 per cent were men. In the 'home' 43.9 per cent were women; 56.1 per cent were men. The difference in mean ages in the three workplaces was significant. The average age of factory workers was 30.7 years; of non-factory workers, 32.8 years. This analysis applies only to workers in our broad industrial production/manufacturing category.

41 In industrial production in Vancouver, average months worked for those in factories was 9.98 and for those in 'other' 9.45. Average annual earnings were $549 (factories) and $490 (other). In Montreal the difference in months worked was insignificant: 11.32 (factories) compared to 11.20 (other). Non-factory workers in Montreal enjoyed a significant earnings advantage: $436 (other) compared to $381 (factories).

42 In 1889, some agricultural-implement factories in Ontario were shut down for eight months; the Grand Trunk Railway shops in London worked 'short time' for six months; CPR shops in Perth ran with a small staff for four months; machinists in Toronto averaged only 268 days' work in the year. *Annual Report of the Bureau of Industries for the Province of Ontario* (Toronto, 1891), 15, 50.

43 There were 110 occupations in which 10 per cent or more reported working less than nine months; these occupations accounted for 64 per cent of all employees who worked less than nine months.

44 These 421 occupations were held by 1,113 people. We are still concentrating on people who said that they were 'employees'; people working 'on their own account' or 'living on own means' are excluded here, and so we are still looking at the working class of six cities.

45 Of 166 employees whose occupations include the words 'manager,' 'inspector,' 'supervisor' or 'superintendent,' only six said that they worked less than twelve months. The probability of being unemployed was higher for foremen, who are not included among the 166.

46 Census and Statistics Office, *Bulletin I: Wage Earners by Occupation* (Ottawa, 1907). Table II clearly refers to 'employees,' and there are two totals: 'aggregate wage earners by occupation' and aggregate wage-earners 'at occupation.' The latter total is used as the denominator in calculating average months worked and average earnings. Employees 'at occupation' are those workers who reported months worked as well as total earnings: *Bulletin*, xiii, states that 'full statistics are compiled for 661,485 males and 153,445 females,' and these are the national totals under 'at occupation.'

47 The average annual earnings for the supervisory elite in manufacturing was $845.61, compared to $403.14 for all men in manufacturing.

48 There were 193,786 men and 873 women in such occupations; they were 23.9 per cent of the 814,930 male and female employees 'at occupation' in Census Office, *Bulletin I*, Table II.

49 There were 242 occupations where the average months worked was less than ten for either men or women; 186 of the occupations were in the bulletin's occupational category manufacturing.

50 Included in the seasonal occupations were farm workers, gardeners, fishermen, seal hunters, foresters, lumbermen, raftsmen, wood choppers, wood labourers, wood yard workers, brick and tile makers, caulkers, cement workers, cider makers, fence builders, fish canners, fruit and vegetable canners, lathers, plasterers, marble and stone cutters, masons, pavers, pile drivers, riggers, sawmill employees, sawyers, shipwrights, snowshoe makers, stucco workers, tobacco factory employees, veneer factory employees, all miners, quarry workers, baseball players, timber surveyors, dock labourers, longshoremen, lightermen, steamboat employees, half of the seamen, and half of the general labourers.

5: Dimensions of Space and Community

1 See, for example, Surenda Gera, *Canadian Unemployment: Lessons from the Eighties and Challenges for the Nineties* (Ottawa, 1991), 6.

2 Richard Harris, 'Residential Segregation and Class Formation in Canadian Cities: A Critical Review,' *Canadian Geographer*, 28 (1984), 186–96.

3 Jason Gilliland and Sherry Olson, 'Claims on Housing Space in Nineteenth Century Montreal,' *Shared Spaces/Partage de l'éspace*, 14 (Montreal, 1993), 1. See also M. Doucet and John Weaver, *Housing the North American City* (Montreal, 1991); M.J. Daunton, 'Cities of Homes and Cities of Tenements: British and American Comparisons, 1870–1914,' *Journal of Urban History*, 14 (1988), 283–319; R. Harris and Chris Hamnett, 'The Myth of the Promised Land: The Social Differences of Home Ownership in Britain and North America,'

Annals of the Association of American Geographers, 77 (1987), 173–90; R.L. Lawrence, 'Integrating Architectural Social and Housing History,' *Urban History,* 19 part 1 (1992), 39–63.

4 On average the difference was about $186. This assumes that the cost of a frame house was $1,021 and that of a brick house $2,000. See Doucet and Weaver, *Housing,* 105. This calculation does not include the value of the land.

5 Data for floors were not reported for 1901, but only one-third of families headed by a severely unemployed person (one employed for less than nine months) lived in brick dwellings, whereas one-half of families whose head worked nine or more months lived in brick houses.

6 In order to calculate housing conditions and rates of ownership from the 1901 census, one must link personal data from schedule 1 to housing data found on schedule 2. At this point we have been able to do this only for Victoria and Hamilton. For non-waged time, see 124–5, below.

7 Gilliland and Olson, 'Claims on Housing Space,' 7–10; Daniel Luria presents a similar argument for American cities in 'Wealth, Capital and Power: The Social Meaning of Home Ownership,' *Journal of Interdisciplinary History,* 7 (1976), 268–9.

8 See, for example, G. Darroch, 'Early Industrialization'; R. Harris, G. Levine, and B. Osborne, 'Housing Tenure and Social Classes in Kingston, Ontario, 1881–1901,' *Journal of Historical Geography,* 7 (1981), 271–90; Doucet and Weaver, *Housing;* Richard Bushman, 'Family Security in the Transition from Farm to City, 1750–1850,' *Journal of Family History,* 6 (1981), 238–56, and, for Victoria, P. Baskerville, 'Property, Class and Gender: Some Preliminary Observations on Two Canadian Cities, 1881–1901,' unpublished paper, Canadian Historical Association, Montreal, August 1995.

9 From a large body of writing we note the following. For Montreal, Sherry Olson, 'Occupations and Residential Spaces in Nineteenth Century Montreal,' *Historical Methods,* 22 (1989), 81–96; Robert Lewis, 'The Segregated City: Class, Residential Patterns, and the Development of Industrial Districts in Montreal, 1861 and 1901,' *Journal of Urban History,* 17 (1991), 123–52. For Winnipeg, Daniel Hiebert, 'Class, Ethnicity and Residential Structure: The Social Geography of Winnipeg, 1901–1921,' *Journal of Historical Geography,* 17 (1991), 56–86. For Halifax, Larry D. McCann, 'Class, Ethnicity and Residential Differentiation in Mid-Victorian Halifax,' in Richard Preston and B. Mitchell, eds., *Reflections and Visions: Twenty-Five Years of Geography at Waterloo* (Waterloo, 1990), 239–65. For Vancouver, Donna McCririck and Graeme Wynn, 'Building "Self-Respect and Hopefulness": The Development of Blue Collar Suburbs in Early Vancouver,' in Graeme Wynn, ed., *People, Places, Patterns, Processes: Geographical Perspectives on the Canadian Past* (Toronto, 1990), 267–

84; R.M. Galois, 'Social Structure in Space: The Making of Vancouver' (PhD
dissertation, Simon Fraser University, 1979). For Hamilton, Michael J. Dou-
cet, 'Working-Class Housing in a Small Nineteenth Century Canadian City:
Hamilton, Ontario, 1852–1881,' in Gregory S. Kealey and Peter Warrian, eds.,
Essays in Canadian Working-Class History (Toronto, 1976), 83–105; John C.
Weaver, *Hamilton: An Illustrated History* (Toronto, 1982); and, of course, the
pioneering work of Michael B. Katz, Michael J. Doucet, and Mark J. Stern,
The Social Organization of Early Industrial Capitalism (Cambridge, Mass., 1982).
Also very useful is Daniel Hiebert, 'The Social Geography of Toronto in 1931:
A Study of Residential Differentiation and Social Structure,' *Journal of Histor-
ical Geography*, 21 (1995), 55–74.

10 The number and size of subdistricts for each city are as follows. A few subdistricts in Winnipeg and Montreal were very small, so we combined them
with adjacent subdistricts in our analysis. The result was to reduce the number of subdistricts in Winnipeg from seventy to fifty, and in Montreal from
144 to 141.

City	No. of subdistricts	Average no. of people per subdistrict in our 10% sample
Victoria	20	96
Vancouver	31	86
Winnipeg	50	84
Hamilton	64	91
Montreal	141	156
Halifax	39	97

11 For an instructive use of the index see Douglas S. Massey and Nancy A. Denton, *American Apartheid: Segregation and the Making of the Underclass* (Cambridge, Mass., 1993), 20 and passim. An overview of traditional segregation
indices can be found in Theodore Hershberg, Alan N. Bustein, and Susan
Drobis, 'The Historical Study of Urban Space,' *Historical Methods Newsletter*, 9
(1976), 99–136; see also Nathan Kantrowitz, 'The Index of Dissimilarity: A
Measurement of Residential Segregation for Historical Analysis,' *Historical
Methods Newsletter*, 7 (1974), 285–9.

12 Daniel Hiebert, 'Class, Ethnicity, and Residential Structure,' 82 n 21; Massey
and Denton, *American Apartheid*, 20.

13 Some might argue that the inclusion of housewives limits the opportunity
for meaningful comparisons with the work of historical geographers, whose
indices are calculated with reference only to adult males in the workforce or

to household heads. For comparative purposes we recalculated the weighted indices for class and work duration for Hamilton and Victoria, excluding housewives and adults with no occupation. The revised indices for Hamilton were only slightly higher (21.5, compared to 18.6, for class; 19.8, compared to 17.0, for work duration). The revised indices for Victoria fell slightly with housewives and persons of no occupation omitted (from 19.0 to 18.1 for class; from 20.6 to 18.6 for work duration).

14 Once housewives are included, as they should be, in the analysis of segregation by birthplace, ethnicity, occupation, and immigrant status, they must be included in the analysis of other variables in order that comparisons can be made across variables and across cities.

15 Weaver, *Hamilton*, 96–7, 103.

16 As well, industrial employees who laboured in smaller workshops were overrepresented in four of seven wards.

17 Lewis, 'The Segregated City,' 127.

18 Hiebert, 'The Social Geography of Toronto in 1931,' 68–71.

19 Concentration elsewhere was as follows: in Hamilton, 66 per cent of the unemployed clustered in 30 per cent of all subdistricts, which had 29 per cent of their workforce severely unemployed; in Victoria, 61 per cent, in 30 per cent of subdistricts, with 26 per cent severely unemployed; in Halifax, 85 per cent, in 28 per cent of subdistricts, with 18 per cent severely unemployed; in Winnipeg, 78 per cent, in 41 per cent of subdistricts, with 27 per cent severely unemployed.

20 See Olson, 'Occupations and Residential Spaces.'

21 Harris, 'Residential Segregation and Class Formation,' 192.

22 Ibid., and Hiebert, 'Class, Ethnicity, and Residential Structure,' 85–6.

23 The seven 'unemployed' subdistricts were those where the location quotient for unemployed (those working less than nine months) was 1.5 or higher.

24 Robert A.J. McDonald, *Making Vancouver: Class, Status and Social Boundaries, 1863–1913* (Vancouver, 1996), 201–29.

25 Kay J. Anderson, *Vancouver's Chinatown: Racial Discourse in Canada, 1870–1980* (Montreal, 1991), especially 51, 62, 65.

26 'Chinese Destitution,' *Industrial News*, 9 Jan. 1886. See also 'Poverty in Chinatown,' Ibid., 16 Jan. 1886; 'Public Meeting,' Ibid., 6 Feb. 1886.

27 'The Chinese Question,' Ibid., 26 Dec. 1885. Anti-Chinese speakers also made clear that not only white male workers, but white families, were in peril. We must refuse to 'submit to have our families brought up in competition with slave labour,' said John Duval. 'They rob not only us, but our children.' Ibid., 6 Feb. 1886.

28 In 1905 the *Western Clarion* argued that 'the curse of the coolies' was really 'the curse of slavery'; Chinese immigrants were also victims of capitalism. 'The Curse of the Coolies,' ibid., 14 Oct. 1905.

29 'The Chinese Question,' *Industrial News*, 2 Jan. 1886.

30 The occupations from which trade-union leadership and VTLC leaders were most likely to come included the following: railway running trades, carpenters, plasterers, printers, typesetters, longshoremen, masons, bricklayers, stonecutters, machinists, painters, engineers, sheet metal workers, tailors, cigarmakers, electricians, cabinetmakers, moulders, brass finishers, shoemakers, and plumbers. For a discussion of Vancouver's labour leadership see Mark Leier, *Red Flags and Red Tape: The Making of a Labour Bureaucracy* (Toronto, 1995); and McDonald, *Making Vancouver*, 175–200.

31 'The Chinese Question,' *Industrial News*, 9 Jan. 1886; emphasis added.

32 James C. Scott, *Domination and the Arts of Resistance: Hidden Transcripts* (New Haven, Conn., 1990), ix–xiii.

33 For a sensitive discussion of such contested terrain in a different context, see Evelyn Brooks Higginbotham, 'African-American Women's History and the Metalanguage of Race,' *Signs: Journal of Women in Culture and Society*, 17 (1992), 251–74, especially 272–4.

34 Pat Roy, *A White Man's Province: British Columbia Politicians and Chinese and Japanese Immigrants, 1858–1914* (Vancouver, 1989); Rennie Warburton, 'Race and Class in British Columbia: A Comment,' *BC Studies*, 49 (1981), 79–85. Peter Ward, *White Canada Forever: Popular Attitudes and Public Policy toward Orientals in British Columbia* (Montreal, 1978).

35 We selected high-unemployment subdistricts by the same criteria as for Vancouver.

36 Per-person income in the family averaged $149 in the unemployed subdistricts and $205 in the fully employed subdistricts; average head's earnings were $446 and $653, respectively.

37 'Toronto on the Shady Side,' Toronto *Globe*, 21 Feb. 1891.

38 In Hamilton 17.8 per cent of those in the 'elite' occupations worked less than nine months in the year; a further 26.4 per cent, between nine and eleven months; and 55.9 per cent, for twelve months. In Vancouver, 71.5 per cent of those in the same occupations worked for twelve months.

39 The occupations of the labour elite are those listed above in note 30.

40 James D. Anderson, 'The Municipal Government Reform Movement in Western Canada, 1880–1920,' in Alan Artibise and Gilbert Stelter, eds., *The Useable Urban Past: Planning and Politics in the Modern Canadian City* (Toronto, 1979), 73–111; John C. Weaver, '"Toronto's Metropolis" Revisited: A Critical Assessment of Urban Reform in Canada, 1890–1920,' in Gilbert Stelter and

Alan Artibise, eds., *The Canadian City: Essays in Urban and Social History* (Ottawa, 1984), 473.

6: Family, Work, and Income in 1901

1 'The Unemployed,' Toronto *Globe*, 26 Feb. 1894.
2 Michael Piva, *The Condition of the Working Class in Toronto, 1900–1921* (Ottawa, 1979), 63. A noteworthy exception is Claudia Goldin, 'Family Strategies and the Family Economy in the Late Nineteenth Century: The Role of Secondary Workers,' in T. Hershberg, ed., *Work, Space, Family and Group Experience in Nineteenth Century Philadelphia* (Oxford, 1981), 277–310.
3 Michael R. Haines, 'Industrial Work and the Family Life Cycle, 1889/1890,' in Paul Uselding, ed., *Research in Economic History*, 4 (1979), 298–301.
4 Patricia Van den Eeckhout, 'Family Income of Ghent Working Class Families, ca. 1900,' *Journal of Family History*, 18 no. 2 (1993), 88.
5 David Gagan and Rosemary Gagan, 'Working-Class Standards of Living in Late-Victorian Urban Ontario: A Review of the Miscellaneous Evidence on the Quality of Material Life,' *Journal of the Canadian Historical Association* (Ottawa, 1990), 178.
6 Bettina Bradbury, *Working Families: Age, Gender and Daily Survival in Industrializing Montreal* (Toronto, 1993), 250 n 8.
7 *Montreal Star*, 2, 10, and 16 April 1901.
8 See, for example, *Manitoba Free Press*, 3 April 1901: the census enumerators have encountered 'little or no difficulty' in obtaining information.
9 For a more detailed discussion of the 1901 census in this context, see Peter Baskerville and Eric Sager, 'Finding the Workforce in the 1901 Census of Canada,' *Histoire sociale/Social History*, 28 (1995), 521–40. See also Appendix A of this volume.
10 Between age cohorts of 30–39 and 40–49, the average annual earnings of Canadian heads increased by 1.8 per cent, whereas average earnings for their U.S. counterparts declined by 10.4 per cent. Between ages 40–49 and 50–59, Canadian heads' earnings fell by 7.3 per cent; U.S. heads' by 11.8 per cent. Between 50–59 and 60 and over, Canadian heads' earnings fell by 14.3 per cent; U.S. heads', by 29.5 per cent. U.S. calculations from Haines, 'Industrial Work,' Table A3, 326.
11 For two analyses that, from different perspectives, provide support for this assumption, see Jane Synge, 'The Transition From School to Work: Growing Up Working-Class in 20th Century Hamilton, Ontario,' in K. Ishwaran, ed., *Childhood and Adolescence in Canada* (Toronto, 1979), 249–70; Donald O. Parsons and Claudia Goldin, 'Parental Altruism and Self-Interest: Child Labor

among Late Nineteenth-Century American Families,' *Economic Inquiry*, 27 (1989), 636–52.

12 Bradbury, *Working Families*, 16 and passim; Haines, 'Industrial Work and the Family Life Cycle,' 295–6; Nancy Folbre, 'Hearts and Spades: Paradigms of Household Economics,' *World Development*, 14 (1986), 245–55.

13 In Birmingham, according to Shergold, the ratio of earnings by all immediate nuclear-family members (head, wife, children) to head's earnings was 1.428 at the turn of the century; the comparable ratio in Pittsburgh was 1.255. For our six-city sample, omitting 'others,' the ratio was 1.24. Peter Shergold, *Working-Class Life: The 'American Standard' in Comparative Perspective, 1899–1913* (Pittsburgh, 1982), 84. We can also compare our findings with those of Haines, who found that U.S. heads contributed 79.5 per cent of family income in 1889–90, and European heads, 72.8 per cent (our recalculation, omitting boarders, of Haines's data in his Table A.3): Haines, 'Industrial Work,' 326. Another example of the contrast between the North American pattern and families in certain European cities is given by Van den Eeckhout, who found that husbands' earnings ranged from a low of 59.3 per cent of family income for linen workers' families in Ghent to a high of 76.7 per cent for Ghent artisans' families (Van den Eeckhout, 'Family Income,' 91).

14 Toronto *Globe*, 3 Feb. 1883.

15 In the case of *Talbot v. Canada Coloured Cotton Mills Company*, 1896, Elizabeth Talbot, a married woman, was injured on the job. A jury of her peers awarded her $1,200 to help compensate for lost income to her and her family. Provincial Archives of Ontario, Chancery Records RG 22, vol. 381.

16 See, for instance, Edward Higgs, 'Women, Occupations and Work in the Nineteenth Century Censuses,' *History Workshop Journal*, 23 (1987), 76; Nancy Folbre, 'The Unproductive Housewife: Her Evolution in 19th Century Economic Thought,' *Signs: Journal of Women in Culture and Society*, 16 (1991), 468–83; Nancy Folbre and Marjorie Abel, 'Women's Work and Women's Households: Gender Bias in the U.S. Census,' *Social Research*, 56 (1989), 545–70; Margo A. Conk, 'Accuracy, Efficiency and Bias: The Interpretation of Women's Work in the U.S. Census of Occupations, 1890–1940,' *Historical Methods*, 14 no. 2 (1981), 65–72.

17 Toronto *Globe*, 3 Feb. 1883.

18 Haines found that wives contributed 2.3 per cent of family incomes in the United States (our recalculation of his data in Table A3, excluding boarders) and 2.8 per cent in Europe (Haines, 'Industrial Work,' 326). Haines also found that 'others' contributed 1.8 per cent in the United States and 1.5 per cent in Europe (boarders excluded). In Europe, where the share of earnings by the head was smaller than in the United States or Canada, the share of

earnings by the children was also high, according to Haines. In Van den Eeckhout's study of Ghent families, the wife's contribution ranged from 12.3 per cent to 19.8 per cent of family income, depending on the head's occupation ('Family Income,' 91, Table 2). In her study of women workers in Halifax, Sharon Myers concludes: 'It was only under the most severe economic conditions that a married woman with children chose to work outside the home.' Myers, '"Not to be Ranked as Women": Female Industrial Workers in Turn-of-the Century Halifax,' in Veronica Strong-Boag and Anita Clair Fellman, eds., *Rethinking Canada: The Promise of Women's History*, 3rd ed. (Toronto, 1997), 220.

19 The relationship between the age of the household head and the expectation that teenagers would work is explored in Bradbury, *Working Families*; Christine E. Bose, 'Household Resources and U.S. Women's Work,' *American Sociological Review*, 49 (1984), 474–90; M.R. Haines, 'Poverty, Economic Stress and the Family in a Late Nineteenth Century American City: Whites in Philadelphia, 1882,' in T. Hershberg, ed., *Philadelphia: Work, Space, Family and Group Experience in the Nineteenth Century* (New York, 1981), 277–310; Cheryl Elman, 'Turn-of-the-Century Dependence and Interdependence: Roles of Teens in the Family Economy of the Aged,' *Journal of Family History*, 18 (1993), 65–85; and Robert V. Robinson, 'Economic Necessity and the Life Cycle in the Family Economy of Nineteenth Century Indianapolis,' *American Journal of Sociology*, 99 (1993), 49–74.

20 Craig Heron, 'The High School and the Household Economy in Working-Class Hamilton, 1890–1940,' *Historical Studies in Education/Revue d'histoire de l'éducation*, 7 (1995), 217–60, provides a useful analysis of the contributions made by children to Hamilton families. See also Jane Synge, 'The Transition,' 249–70.

21 BCARS, RG 684, box 2, vol. 4, file 2.

22 The situation was even more serious in stage 5, where older wives and husbands could not benefit from the earnings of co-resident children: in stage 5, 20.2 per cent of families had at least one severely underemployed person; and of such families, 89.8 per cent contained a severely underemployed head.

23 *Census of Canada*, Montreal subdistrict 176B, polling subdivision, page 6, lines 6–11.

24 Almost 40 per cent of families having one or more underemployed persons (persons working less than nine months) were in the lowest per-person income quintile (earning less than $102.86 a year per person, where children under ten are counted as half a person). Of all families having two or more severely underemployed persons, 48 per cent were in the lowest per-person income quintile.

25 Selecting families with adults (men and women fifteen years and older, including wives) other than the head, and comparing the work participation of those adults in families with and without underemployed heads, yield the following: families with unemployed heads had an average of 21.8 months of unused work time per year; families with heads who worked nine to eleven months, 15.5 months; and families with heads who worked twelve months, fifteen months. Unused work time is the difference between potential wage-earning months (the number of adults minus the head times 12) and actual months worked by all adults except the head.

26 *Census of Canada*, Montreal district 178A, subdivision 49, page 2, lines 24–33.

27 We recognize that the decision to keep certain family members out of the wage-paid labour force may relate to cultural factors as much as to the availability of a job or the need to do non-waged work in the household. Van den Eeckhout suggests that non-financial considerations encouraged metal workers and artisans to forgo wage earnings on the part of wives: 'Family Income,' 109. See also Claudia Goldin, 'Family Strategies and the Family Economy in the Late Nineteenth Century: The Role of Secondary Workers,' in T. Hershberg, ed., *Work, Space, Family and Group Experience in Nineteenth Century Philadelphia* (Oxford, 1981), 278–9.

28 *Census of Canada*, 1901, Victoria, subdistrict 12, page 2, lines 1–2.

29 See *Victoria City Directory* (1892).

30 The couple was exceptional among working-class families not only in terms of the amount of land owned but also by the apparent relative absence of patriarchal relationships: she was the head of the household, and they jointly owned all of their property.

31 The vacant city lot was assessed in 1901 at $450, and their home and land at $500: Victoria Assessment Roll, 1901.

32 *Census of Canada*, 1901, Victoria, subdistrict 12, page 12, lines 39–40.

33 Ibid., Victoria, subdistrict 12, page 11, line 79.

34 In only 22.4 per cent of families did the number of workers exceed the number of dependants. In 18.5 per cent of cases the number of workers equalled the number of dependants.

35 As families increased in size, the number of dependants rose faster than the number of wage workers. In two-person families the ratio of dependants to workers was 0.9; in three-person families, 1.6; in four-person families, 2.3; in five-person families, 2.8; in six-person families, 3.2; in seven-person families, 3.7; and in eight-person families, 3.7. For all families, the ratio was 2.3.

36 We are much closer to a measure of the importance of unemployment to material standards of living in the Canadian working class. A search for the

combination of variables most strongly associated with family per-person incomes, using the Anova procedure in SPSS-X, yields five variables that, taken together, explain 48 per cent of the variation in per-person incomes. These are city, whether or not the family contained a severely underemployed person, the occupation of the head, the number of workers in the family, and the number of dependants in the family. All five variables yield a significant F ratio. The association between the number of dependants and income levels was also strong: including only monthly earnings and the number of dependants in the regression, with per-person incomes as the dependent variable, yields multiple r square of .66.

7: Living Standards and Survival Strategies

1 See, for instance, Livio Di Matteo and Peter George, 'Canadian Wealth Inequality in the Late Nineteenth Century: A Study of Wentworth County, Ontario, 1872–1902,' *Canadian Historical Review*, 73 (Dec. 1992), 453–83.
2 Toronto *Globe*, 3 Feb. 1883.
3 Children under ten count as half.
4 The figures for the other cities are as follows: for Montreal, families in the poorest quintile had an average of 6.7 unemployed months, whereas those in the highest quintile had 3.6 months; in Victoria, 10.9 months and 3.5 months, respectively; in Winnipeg, 7.4 months and 2.6 months; and in Hamilton, 12.0 months and 5.3 months. For all cities except Halifax the F ratio is significant at .005 or less.
5 David Leadbeater, *Setting Minimum Living Standards in Canada: A Review* (Ottawa, 1992), 5–10.
6 B. Seebohm Rowntree, *Poverty: A Study of Town Life*, 2nd ed. (London, n.d. [1902]), 128, 131.
7 Our estimate of meat consumption is extremely frugal. One labourer, a Mr Gloynes, told a reporter for the Toronto *Globe* that his family 'eat meat two or three times a week; salt meat generally – though I have it once a day when I am working.' (3 Feb. 1883).
8 Or, in other words, 'If the worse comes to the worse we manage to live on that.' *Victoria Colonist*, 16 March 1893.
9 Michael Piva, 'Urban Working-Class Incomes and Real Incomes in 1921: A Comparative Analysis,' *Histoire sociale/Social History*, 16 (1983), 166 n 16.
10 Bettina Bradbury, 'Pigs, Cows and Boarders: Non-Wage Forms of Survival among Montreal Families, 1861–1891,' *Labour/Le Travail*, 14 (fall 1984), 9–46.
11 Moore and Davis Correspondence, Hamilton Public Library, P. Moore to Thomas Beasley, City Clerk, 14 June 1881.

12 Robin S. Harris and Terry G. Harris, eds., *The Eldon House Diaries: Five Women's Views of the 19th Century* (Toronto, 1994), lxiii n 117.

13 Suzanne Morton, *Ideal Surroundings: Domestic Life in a Working-Class Suburb in the 1920s* (Toronto, 1995), 29–31; Larry McCann, '"Living a Double Life": Town and Country in the Industrialization of the Maritimes,' in D. Day, ed., *Geographical Perspectives on the Maritime Provinces* (Halifax, 1988), 93–113.

14 *Census of Canada*, 1901, Victoria, subdistrict 12, page 14, line 37.

15 In his study of real incomes in 1921, Michael Piva found that real annual earnings were relatively high in Montreal and extremely low in Halifax ('Urban Working Class Incomes').

16 Darroch and Soltow focus on Ontario as a whole, and so they emphasize the rural nature of the province. Only 8.5 per cent of their population sample was drawn from the province's five largest cities. Yet the glimpses they provide of city life in 1871 stand in dramatic contrast to life in the province as a whole. Property ownership was more highly stratified: the top 10 per cent owned 79 per cent of all property. In cities, 59 per cent of all heads owned no real property whatever. Though the authors do not present the point clearly enough, age differences seem to have had little effect on property-owning rates among urban household heads. In other words, their analysis does not seem to suggest that inequalities in real estate ownership in cities were significantly mediated by life-cycle effects. Gordon Darroch and Lee Soltow, *Property and Inequality in Victorian Ontario: Structural Patterns and Cultural Communities in the 1871 Census* (Toronto, 1994), 86, 202–3. Darroch has argued elsewhere that life-cycle effects did have a minimal influence on property ownership in Toronto in the late nineteenth century, 'Early Industrialization and Inequality in Toronto, 1861–99,' *Labour/le Travail*, 11 (1983), 31–61.

17 The contingency coefficient for Table 7.4 is .25.

18 Toronto *Globe*, 3 Feb. 1883.

19 For Vancouver, families below the poverty line had an average of 10.0 unemployed months, and families above $70 real income, 4.2 months. The comparable figures for the other cities are: Victoria, 14.5 months and 4.5 months respectively; Winnipeg, 6.4 months and 5.0 months; Hamilton, 11.4 months and 6.8 months; Montreal, 6.3 months and 5.1 months; Halifax, 15.2 months and 18.3 months. Mean unemployed months by three living-standard categories and by city yields a significant F ratio.

20 *Victoria Colonist*, 24 Jan. 1894.

21 Real-income level (the difference between family earnings and estimated living costs) was the dependent variable, and the independent variables were

occupation of head of household grouped into six categories; life cycle (five categories); unemployed months (three categories); average monthly earnings (aggregated into five categories); and city. The model explains 43 per cent of the variance in real incomes. We also ran a logistic regression with below and above the poverty line as the dependent variable. The likelihood ratio assessment of the variables associated with poverty generated by that run is presented here and confirms the analysis in the text.

Likelihood-ratio (LR) assessment of variables associated with poverty, 1901

Variable	−2 log LR	d.f.	Sig.
Average monthly wages	618.2	1	.0000
Family cycle	324.7	5	.0000
Unused months	323.0	2	.0000
City	84.9	5	.0000

22 *Census of Canada*, 1901, district 69, subdistrict g, polling district 7, page 3, line 24; subdistrict g, polling district 7, page 9, line 28.
23 Only one other occupation among heads of households put a majority of families below the real-income poverty line: among families in stage 3 of the family cycle where the head was a primary-sector worker, 56.3 per cent were below the poverty line.
24 Average annual earnings of labourer heads of household, in each stage of the family cycle, were as follows: $316 in stage 1; $342 in stage 2; $361 in stage 3; $341 in stage 4; and $281 in stage 5. Average monthly wages were $31.99 in stage 1; $34.22 in stage 2; $33.59 in stage 3; $33.41 in stage 4; and $29.87 in stage 5.
25 Phyllis Moen and Elaine Wethington, 'The Concept of Family Adaptive Strategies,' *Annual Review of Sociology*, 18 (1992), 235.
26 Only 31.5 per cent of families with children living below the poverty line had children of employable age (i.e., children over fifteen); 47.7 per cent of families with children above the poverty line (above $70 real income) had children of employable age.
27 BCARS, RG 684, box 3, vol. 7, file 4 and file 3.
28 The girl–boy ratio was 0.9 to 1.
29 For an extended discussion of the contributions made by sons and daughters to the family's general welfare, see Bradbury, *Working Families*, 118–51. The interplay between family composition and local economic opportunities requires closer examination than space allows here. Even in cities where there were relatively good possibilities for female employment – Hamilton

and Montreal, for example – families below the poverty line were not as successful in deploying their women workers as were those above the poverty line. In Montreal those below the poverty line used in wage work only 10 per cent of the months available to potential female wage workers; those above the line deployed 18 per cent of the available time. In Hamilton the difference was smaller but still important: 15.8 per cent for those below the poverty line and 19.3 per cent for those above. The reasons for this difference can not be simply explained by the characteristics of the local economy alone. Some of the variation might be explained by the existence of younger children at home and the need for older daughters to look after them. As Hareven has noted in her seminal study, contacts built up by individual families with particular employers and workplaces facilitated more extensive employment within such families and their kin. See Tamara Hareven, *Family Time and Industrial Time: The Relationship between Family and Work in a New England Industrial Community* (Cambridge, Mass., 1982).

30 The best study of this activity is John Bullen, 'Hidden Workers: Child Labour and the Family Economy in Late Nineteenth Century Urban Ontario,' *Labour/Le Travail*, 18 (1986), 163–87.

31 Lorna F. Hurl, 'Restricting Child Factory Labour in Late Nineteenth Century Ontario,' *Labour/Le Travail*, 21 (spring 1988), Table 3, p. 199.

32 BCARS, RG 684, box 2, vol. 4, file 1.

33 Eleven per cent of families above the poverty line with children aged ten to fourteen sent at least one such child into the labour force; only 8.6 per cent of such families below the poverty line did so. The difference is even more pronounced if we look only at families with boys in this age group: 14 per cent of families above the poverty line with boys aged ten to fourteen sent at least one of those boys into the labour force; only 7 per cent of families below the poverty line did so. This pattern of employment of child labour is consistent with the results in chapter 6 (Table 6.6): those families in the lowest income levels were least able to make use of the potential employment of all family members.

34 *Montreal Star*, 8, 22 Jan. 1901.

35 W. Johnston, house painter, Halifax, in *Report of the Royal Commission on the Relations of Capital and Labor* (Ottawa, 1889), vol. 2, 119. Marrion, Victoria, in NA, RG 27, vol. 32, 1901. In 1901, F.H. Holt, of Vancouver, asked the Department of Labour to provide some protection 'as they do in the States,' 'for if things are busy here the place is swamped by hordes of all the floating rabble that can walk into the place.' Ibid.

36 Unfortunately our data do not allow us to distinguish those who took both meals and lodging from those who took lodging alone.

37 Robert V. Robinson, 'Economic Necessity and the Life Cycle in the Family

Economy of Nineteenth Century Indianapolis,' *American Journal of Sociology*
99 (1993), 49–74; Michael B. Katz, Michael J. Doucet, and Mark Stern, *The
Social Organization of Early Industrial Capitalism* (Cambridge, Mass., 1982);
John Modell and Tamara K. Hareven, 'Urbanization and the Malleable
Household: Boarding and Lodging in American Families,' *Journal of Marriage
and the Family*, 35 (1973), 467–79; Bradbury, *Working Families*, 175–81; Richard
Harris, 'The Flexible House: The Housing Backlog and the Persistence of
Lodging, 1891–1951,' *Social Science History*, 18 (1994), 31–53.
38 Robinson,'Economic Necessity,' 63–4; Katz, Doucet, and Stern, *The Social
Organization*, 300.
39 This is especially true as a means of coping with unemployment. Though
poor families were more likely to take in lodgers, there was no relationship
between the presence of lodgers and unemployment in the family even for
those below the poverty line.
40 The percentage of households in each city having at least one lodger is as follows: Vancouver, 22.2; Victoria, 15; Winnipeg, 22.4; Hamilton, 11.6; Montreal, 14.5; and Halifax, 8.4.
41 For families below the poverty line the proportion having one or more lodgers, by stage in the family cycle, was as follows: 27.8 per cent (stage 1); 19.5
per cent (stage 2); 14.4 per cent (stage 3); 13.9 per cent (stage 4); 35.3 per cent
(stage 5); and 71.1 per cent (stage 6).
42 Modell and Hareven, 'Urbanization and the Malleable Household,' 468–9.
43 There is some difference of opinion in the literature on this issue. Bradbury,
in *Working Families*, 175–81, suggests that women in Montreal in the 1880s
could earn as much taking in several boarders as they could working for
wages. But she provides no estimate for the costs of food and cleaning. See
also Bradbury, 'The Home As Workplace,' in Paul Craven, ed., *Labouring
Lives: Work and Workers in Nineteenth Century Ontario* (Toronto, 1995), 452–5.
Peter R. Shergold, *Working Class Life: The 'American Standard' in Comparative
Perspective, 1899–1913* (Pittsburgh, 1982), 84–9, considers costs and concludes
that boarding was not very remunerative.
44 Eric Sager and Peter Baskerville, eds., *1891 Census: Victoria, British Columbia*,
(Victoria, 1991); BCARS, N/D/B77, British Columbia Benevolent Society
(hereafter BS), 1890; *Victoria Street Directory* (1892).
45 Sager and Baskerville, eds., *1891 Census: Victoria; Victoria Street Directory*
(1892).
46 *Census of Canada*, 1901, district 69, subdivision f, polling subdistrict 3, page 9,
line 49; district 33, subdivision a, subdistrict 2, page 4, line 25. Cost estimates
are calculated from the data in Appendix B, below.
47 Families above $70 of real income also used the two strategies, deploying a
wage earner other than the head and taking in a lodger; 35.6 per cent of these

more prosperous working-class families used the two strategies. The difference hints at as-yet-unexplained abilities or opportunities among families above the poverty line to use multiple strategies of survival.

48 Darroch and Soltow, for instance, point out that farmers acquired land 'in a relatively short and early phase of their working lives.' Darroch and Soltow, *Property and Inequality*, 37.

49 Elyce Rotella and George Alter, 'Working Class Debt in the Late Nineteenth Century United States,' *Journal of Family History*, 18 (1993), 111–34.

50 Post office and government savings banks were intended to encourage savings by workers. The increased rate of deposits suggests that some workers were able to take advantage of the opportunity. See David Gagan and Rosemary Gagan, 'Working-Class Standards of Living in Late-Victorian Urban Ontario: A Review of the Miscellaneous Evidence on the Quality of Material Life,' *Journal of the Canadian Historical Association* (Ottawa, 1990), 180–2.

51 Paul Johnson, *Saving and Spending: The Working Class Economy in Britain, 1870–1939* (Oxford, 1985), 87–125, quote from 88.

52 Toronto *Globe*, 3 Feb. 1883. For similar comments, see the testimony of D.S. Cameron, vice-president of the Trades and Labour Council of New Westminster, before the British Columbia Royal Commission on Labour in 1912, BCARS, RG 684, box 1, vol. 3, file 8.

53 Dan Bunbury, 'Safe Haven for the Poor? Depositors and the Government Savings Bank in Halifax, 1832–1867,' *Acadiensis*, 24 (spring 1995), 24–48.

54 Single-person families were grouped into three age categories: 15–39; 40–69; and over 69. For 31 per cent of those aged 15 to 39, living costs exceeded annual earnings.

55 Fifty-two per cent of the occupied sons of labouring heads were in manufacturing.

56 *Census of Canada*, 1901, district 69, subdivision f, polling subdivision 3, page 13, line 7.

57 Donald O. Parsons and Claudia Goldin, 'Parental Altruism and Self-Interest: Child Labor among Late Nineteenth-Century American Families,' *Economic Inquiry*, 27 (1989), 637–59.

58 Van den Eeckhout refers to this as the pursuit of the 'domestic ideal' in 'Family Income of Ghent Working-Class Families ca. 1900,' *Journal of Family History*, 18 (1993), 87–110. For a discussion of servants and social class see Katz, Doucet, and Stern, *The Social Organization of Early Industrial Capitalism*, 85–9. Only 4.3 per cent of families with a working-class head in Hamilton had a domestic servant. In all of our urban centres, only three families in which the head was severely underemployed (working less than nine months) had a domestic servant. In the case of the Kidd family, it would seem that a servant was not required because of the mental or physical incapacity of the wife or

of any other family members. The census asked questions related to such issues, and no one in the Kidd family reported any such afflictions.

59 Our estimated retained earnings (earnings left over after the payment of all family expenses) was $71. This represents 11.5 per cent of total children's earnings and is the maximum amount that the children could have retained for their own use. This figure is remarkably close to that in Parsons and Goldin, 'Parental Altruism,' 652.

60 *Victoria Colonist*, 16 March 1893.

61 Ibid., 17 March 1893.

62 BCARS, RG 684, box 1, vol. 3, file 8.

63 J. Lynnas, ship labourer, Montreal, in *Report*, vol. 3, 363.

64 BCARS, RG 684, box 1, vol. 1, file 1.

65 *Victoria Colonist*, 18 March 1893. Due 'to the intermittent nature of the Stone-cutter's occupation,' the Journeymen's Stonecutter's Association of Toronto believed that 'compensation in the shape of comparatively high wages [is] necessary.' in NA, RG 27, vol. 32.

66 Timothy J. Hatton and Jeffrey G. Williamson, 'Unemployment, Employment Contracts, and Compensating Wage Differentials: Michigan in the 1890s,' *Journal of Economic History*, 51 (1991), 605–32.

67 *Victoria Colonist*, 18 March 1893.

68 Ibid. For a discussion of trends in retail credit, see David Monod, *Store Wars: Shopkeepers and the Culture of Mass Marketing, 1880–1939* (Toronto, 1996), especially chap. 4. The anti-Chinese farce is in *Industrial News*, 9 Jan. 1886. For similar forms of assistance to the casual labour force in Montreal, see Peter DeLottinville, 'Joe Beef of Montreal: Working-Class Culture and the Tavern, 1869–1889,' *Labour/Le Travail*, 8/9 (autumn 1981/spring 1982), 18–20.

69 William Moore to W.J. Aitken, 26 Jan. 1890; Moore to Geo. Hunter, 13 Feb. 1890, Hamilton Public Library, Moore and Davis Letterbook, 1889–90. For other examples of the same situation, see Moore to Mrs. J.A. Hills, 24 July 1891, and Moore to A.D. Perry, 20 Feb. 1892, ibid., 1891–92. On Eaton's see Joy Santink, *Timothy Eaton and the Rise of His Department Store* (Toronto, 1990), 222. On the issue of competition from larger centres, see David G. Burley, *A Particular Condition in Life: Self-Employment and Social Mobility in Mid-Victorian Brantford, Ontario* (Kingston, 1994).

70 For an excellent study of pawnshop activity in England, see Johnson, *Saving and Spending*, 166–88. For the United States, see M. Tebbutt, *Making Ends Meet: Pawnbroking and Working-Class Credit* (New York, 1983). In an article on 'The Unemployed: Methods Employed by Them to Earn a Living,' the Montreal *Herald* reported that sailors pawned their possessions and then 'were only too glad to part with their pawn tickets at an exceedingly low figure.' Montreal *Herald*, 6 Feb. 1897.

71 BCARS, GR 1900, Victoria, vol. 4, 2046 and 2381; GR 2466, Vancouver, vol. 1, 1059.

72 Stormie Stewart, 'The Elderly Poor in Rural Ontario: Inmates of the Wellington County House of Industry, 1877–1907,' *Journal of the Canadian Historical Association* (Ottawa, 1992), 217–33; Diane Purvey, 'Orphanages and Social Change in Vancouver, 1890s to 1930s' (MA thesis, University of Victoria, 1990).

73 James M. Pitsula, 'The Relief of Poverty in Toronto' (PhD thesis, York University, 1979), 41.

74 See, for instance, Robert A.J. McDonald, *Making Vancouver: Class, Status and Social Boundaries, 1863–1913* (Vancouver, 1996), 221–3.

75 Victoria City Archives (hereafter VCA), City Council, Minutes, 1 Feb. 1894.

76 *Victoria Colonist*, 1 Feb. 1894.

77 VCA, City Council, Minutes, 29 Jan., 5 Feb. 1894.

78 *Victoria Colonist*, 11 Feb. 1894.

79 See, for example, VCA, City Council, Minutes, 8 July, 23 Dec. 1891; 6 May 1892; City of Victoria, *Annual Report* (1897). If one adds to the Charitable Aid Fund's expenses the money spent by the city on the Old Men's Home and on the Home for the Aged and Infirm Women, then annual expenditures between 1891 and 1901 varied from 0.1 to 1.8 per cent of the city's total budget.

80 Calculated from Monthly Returns, BS, Minute book, vols. 1 and 2.

81 BS, Minute Book, vol. 2, p. 44.

82 *Victoria Colonist*, 11 Feb. 1894.

83 BS, Cash Book, 50–1.

84 VCA, City Council, Minutes, 19 March 1894. *Victoria Colonist*, 4 Feb. 1894.

85 Sager and Baskerville, eds., *1891 Census: Victoria*; BS, 1891.

86 VCA, PR 126, Friendly Help Society, 22 Feb. 1895. Pitsula, 'The Relief of Poverty,' 45.

87 VCA, Friendly Help Society, 2 March 1895 through 15 Feb. 1896.

88 BS, vol. 2, p. 23; VCA, Friendly Help Society, 15 Feb. 1896.

89 Seventy-three per cent of the 215 men who responded to the Citizen's Relief Committee's call to register for work in February 1894 were single men. *Victoria Colonist*, 11 Feb. 1894.

90 Calculated from monthly returns of the BS. Most of the aid was given during the winter crises: 46 per cent of Benevolent Society expenditures between 1890 and 1895 occurred in December, January, and February. However, poverty did not disappear during the rest of the year: a third of all expenditures took place in the six months from April to September.

91 *Victoria Colonist*, 1 Feb. 1894; Toronto *Globe*, 16 Feb. 1894. This emphasis

parallels that found by Johnson in his study of the British working class in a similar time period (*Saving and Spending*, passim).

92 On the welfare functions of British trade unions, see Johnson, *Saving and Spending*, 75–80.

93 *Second Report of the Bureau of Labor for the Province of Ontario ... 1901* (Toronto, 1902), 28–58.

94 Ibid., 34, 39.

95 Charles Simpkins, labourer, Windsor, in *Report*, vol. 2, 402; cf. John J. Bickley of Cornwall, in ibid., vol. 2, 1085. The tavern could also serve as an informal job-hunting centre: Peter Delottinville, 'Joe Beef of Montreal,' 18.

96 Proceedings of the Fourth Congress of the Canadian Labor Union, 1876, in Leslie E. Wismer, ed., *Proceedings of the Canadian Labor Union Congresses 1873–1877* (Montreal, 1951), 67.

97 'In order to find employment for forty additional men the members of the two cigar-makers' unions voluntarily temporarily limited the working day to six hours.' 'Labor Interests,' Montreal *Herald*, 6 Feb. 1897.

98 The Knights of Labor in Nanaimo, Vancouver, and New Westminster wrote to the Knights in Ontario in December 1886, advising them that 'a large portion of the laboring men in this province at present are unable to obtain employment.' *Industrial News*, 18 Dec. 1886.

99 Walter Licht, *Getting Work: Philadelphia, 1840–1950* (Cambridge, Mass., 1992).

100 Christopher J. Anstead, 'Fraternalism in Victorian Ontario: Secret Societies and Cultural Hegemony' (PhD thesis, University of Western Ontario, 1992), 238; John C.H. Emery, 'The Rise and Fall of Fraternal Methods of Social Insurance: A Case Study of the Independent Order of Oddfellows of British Columbia Sickness Insurance, 1874–1951' (PhD thesis, University of British Columbia, 1993), 47.

101 Anstead, 'Fraternalism,' 138, 386. Not all did, however. The Masons and the Elks, two large fraternal societies, did not provide sick benefits in British Columbia. See Emery, 'The Rise and Fall,' 46.

102 Anstead, 'Fraternalism,' 129.

103 J.S. King, *The Early History of the Sons of England Benevolent Society* (Toronto, 1891), 30.

104 Anstead, 'Fraternalism,' 140.

105 Calculated from *Census of Canada*, vol. 4, Table 1, and Independent Order of Odd Fellows, Grand Lodge of Ontario, *Annual Report* (1902), 88–9.

106 Anstead, 'Fraternalism,' 194; Brian Greenburg, 'Workers and Community: Fraternal Orders in Albany, New York, 1845–1885,' *Maryland Historian* (1977), 35–95; M.A. Clawson, 'Fraternal Orders and Class Formation in the

Nineteenth Century United States,' *Comparative Studies in Society and History*, 27 (1985), 672–95; Johnson, *Saving and Spending*, 55; Christine Gilduff, 'The Ancient Order of United Workmen: The Persistence of Cross Class Organizations in Victoria, B.C.' (unpublished paper, History 341, University of Victoria, 1993); McDonald, *Making Vancouver*, 194–6.

107 Anstead, 'Fraternalism,' 191.
108 Ibid., iii.
109 *Victoria Colonist*, 24 Jan. 1894.
110 Moen and Wethington, 'The Concept of Family Adaptive Strategies,' 243.
111 Terry Copp, *The Anatomy of Poverty: The Condition of the Working Class in Montreal, 1897–1929* (Toronto, 1974); Michael Piva, *The Condition of the Working Class in Toronto, 1900–1921* (Ottawa, 1979).
112 *Victoria Colonist*, 18 March 1893.
113 John Bullen, 'Hidden Workers: Child Labour and the Family Economy in Late Nineteenth Century Urban Ontario,' *Labour/Le Travail*, 18 (1986), 163–88.
114 Eric W. Sager, *Seafaring Labour: The Merchant Marine of Atlantic Canada, 1820–1914* (Montreal, 1989), 230.
115 BCARS, Add. Mss, 1551, Frank Gelsthorpe, Diaries, 28 May 1904.
116 Henry Trachtenberg, 'Peddling, Politics, and Winnipeg's Jews, 1891–1895: The Political Acculturation of an Urban Immigrant Community,' *Histoire sociale/Social History*, 57 (May 1996), 159–86; John Benson, 'Hawking and Peddling in Canada, 1867–1914,' *Histoire sociale/Social History*, 35 (May 1985), 76.
117 *Victoria Colonist*, 21 Jan. 1894.

8: The Working Class, Social Reform, and the State

1 John A. Garraty, *Unemployment in History: Economic Thought and Public Policy* (New York, 1978), 109 n 12.
2 Bryan Palmer, *A Culture in Conflict: Skilled Workers and Industrialism in Hamilton, Ontario, 1860–1914* (Montreal, 1979), 232.
3 Bryan D. Palmer, 'Labour Protest and Organization in Nineteenth-Century Canada, 1820–1890,' *Labour/Le Travail* 20 (fall 1987), 61–83; Douglas Cruikshank and Gregory S. Kealey, 'Strikes in Canada, 1891–1950,' *Labour/Le Travail*, 20 (fall 1987), 85–145; Gregory S. Kealey and Douglas Cruikshank, 'Strikes,' in Donald Kerr and Deryck W. Holdsworth, eds., *Historical Atlas of Canada*, vol. 3 (Toronto, 1990), plate 39.
4 F. Walter, Hamilton, in *Report of the Royal Commission on the Relations of Capital and Labor* (Ottawa, 1889), vol. 2, 796. *Annual Report of the Bureau of Industries ... Ontario, 1889* (hereafter Bureau, *Report*) (Toronto, 1891), 16, notes that 'the annual lay-off in the [Hamilton] stove trade is becoming longer each year.'

5 *Report of the Royal Commission to Inquire into Industrial Disputes in the Cotton Factories of the Province of Quebec* (Ottawa, 1909), 9–10.
6 Eight strikes, according to King, were for higher wages; nine were against a reduction in wages. Ten strikes were over the discharge of employees, 'against being laid off on account of shortage of work,' against 'employment of English persons, strikers being French,' or against employment of apprentices. *Report ... Cotton Factories*, 23–4.
7 John Fraser, quoted in the *Victoria Colonist*, 21 Jan. 1894.
8 Craig Heron and Bryan D. Palmer, 'Through the Prism of the Strike: Industrial Conflict in Southern Ontario, 1901–14,' *Canadian Historical Review*, 58 (Dec. 1977), 425–6.
9 Ibid., 435.
10 *Proceedings of the Trades and Labor Congress of Canada 1886* (hereafter TLC, *Proceedings*, year), 24.
11 Ibid., 30.
12 TLC, *Proceedings*, 1888, 23. Adults and children who came from Britain with the assistance of charities were 'victims of that philanthropic humbug and swindle that is becoming notorious in its efforts to dump London's half-starved poor upon other lands.' 'More Immigrant Scandals,' *Western Clarion*, 6 May 1905.
13 Ibid., 24.
14 TLC, *Proceedings*, 1889, 16, 20. The fear of competition from prisoners and other inmates was often mentioned before the Royal Commission on the Relations of Capital and Labor in the 1880s, as stated in its *Report* (1889). Montreal printers insisted that their jobs were threatened by 'illegal competition' from the Montreal Reformatory School. 'This is the greatest plague we have. It is inconceivable competition'; A. Carmel, Montreal, in *Report* (1889), vol. 3, 451. Convict labour 'has destroyed the broom-making business; you cannot compete with them at all'; Thomas Brick, Hamilton, in *Report* (1889), vol. 2, 819; J. McKenna, Hamilton, in ibid., 905.
15 TLC, *Proceedings*, 1887, 53.
16 Ibid., 29.
17 *Montreal Star*, 12 April 1901.
18 Toronto *Globe*, 3 Feb. 1883.
19 TLC, *Proceedings* 1889, 16, 20. See Ramsay Cook, *The Regenerators: Social Criticism in Late Victorian Canada* (Toronto, 1985), 108ff.
20 W.A. Douglas, Toronto, in *Report* (1889), vol. 2, 20.
21 David R. Roediger and Philip S. Foner, *Our Own Time: A History of American Labor and the Working Day* (London, 1989), vii.
22 Cf. Gary Cross, *A Quest for Time: The Reduction of Work in Britain and France, 1840–1940* (Berkeley, Calif., 1989), 61–2. The Ontario Bureau of Industries reported that the average work week of industrial employees in 1889 was

fifty-nine hours, while the average number of days worked in the year was 270: Bureau, *Report ... 1889* (Toronto, 1891), Part IV, 40.

23 James Floyd, baker, Halifax, *Report* (1889), vol. 5, 183.

24 In the late 1880s the agents reporting to the Ontario Bureau of Industries reported the same commonplace opinion: reducing hours of work would 'increase the number of days employed, or, on the other hand, give employment to a greater number.' Bureau, *Report* (Toronto, 1891), 19–21.

25 William John Vale, Hamilton, in *Report* (1889), vol. 2, 814; see also Arthur Lessel, carpenter, Halifax, in ibid., vol. 5, 39; B. Cameron, moulder, Hamilton, in ibid., vol. 2, 842; J. Floyd, baker, Halifax, in ibid., vol. 5, 183.

26 Benjamin Cameron, moulder, Hamilton, in ibid., vol. 2, 842.

27 TLC, *Proceedings*, 1886, 39.

28 *Palladium of Labor*, 6 Nov. 1886, editorial page. See also 'Slow Murder,' ibid., 24 Nov. 1883.

29 See chapter 2, above. See also Bettina Bradbury, 'The Home As Workplace,' in Paul Craven, ed., *Labouring Lives: Work and Workers in Nineteenth-Century Ontario* (Toronto, 1995), 423–6.

30 Toronto *Globe*, 3 Feb. 1883. See also 'Co-operation,' *Palladium of Labor*, 23 Feb. 1884.

31 *Montreal Star*, 18 April, 20, 21 May 1901.

32 *Labour Gazette*, vol. 9 (1908–9), 993.

33 Ian MacPherson, *Each for All: A History of the Co-operative Movement in English Canada, 1900–1945* (Toronto, 1979), 23.

34 *Labour Gazette* (April 1909), 1124.

35 *Victoria Colonist*, J.N.L. to editor, 18 March 1893.

36 Ibid.

37 P. Martin, painter, Halifax, in *Report* (1889), vol. 5, 121. On the union label as a means of ensuring jobs for 'competent labor,' see 'Why You Should Call for Union Label Goods,' *Industrial Banner* (London, Ont.), May 1897.

38 William Vale, Hamilton, in *Report* (1889), vol. 2, 816.

39 The demand for a bureau of labour statistics was also heard in the 1870s. An editorial on 'Labor Statistics' in the *Ontario Workman*, 24 April 1873, linked the question to unemployment: 'Little or no allowances are made for lost time, occasioned by bad weather, which affects the carpenters, painters and masons very considerably during the year; and the many other causes that operate in throwing out of employment for a time the workmen in the majority of trades.' See also the Fourth Congress of the Canadian Labor Union in 1876, in Leslie E. Wismer, ed., *Proceedings of the Canadian Labor Union 1873–77* (Montreal, 1951), 67–8.

40 Wismer, ed., *Proceedings*, 20.

41 See also Gregory S. Kealey and Bryan D. Palmer, *Dreaming of What Might Be: The Knights of Labor in Ontario, 1880–1900* (Cambridge, Mass., 1982), 316–26.
42 'Equal Pay for Equal Work,' *Palladium of Labor*, 25 Sept. 1886.
43 Ibid.
44 Ibid.
45 *Labor Advocate*, 6 March 1891.
46 'Woman Labor,' *Toiler*, 16 May 1902.
47 On wage dependence and gender, see also Bettina Bradbury, *Working Families: Age, Gender, and Daily Survival in Industrializing Montreal* (Toronto, 1993), especially chaps. 3, 5, and 6.
48 Toronto *Globe*, 3 Feb. 1883. This was probably the same Alfred Taylor who had been a delegate to the Canadian Labor Union congresses in the 1870s.
49 Carroll D. Wright, *The Industrial Evolution of the United States* (Meadville, Pa., 1895), cited in Ester Fano, 'A "Wastage of Men": Technological Progress and Unemployment in the United States,' *Technology and Culture*, 32 (1991), 267.
50 J. Mahoney, cooper, Montreal, in *Report* (1889), vol. 3, 561.
51 Joseph Dickson, Chatham, in *Report* (1889), vol. 2, 473; see also John Crosby, builder, Petrolia, in ibid., 702.
52 Craig Heron, 'Factory Workers,' in Paul Craven, ed., *Labouring Lives: Work and Workers in Nineteenth-Century Ontario* (Toronto, 1995), 505–6. On the reaction of Montreal's cigarmakers to the introduction of labour-saving machinery, see *Montreal Star*, 30 April and 1, 2 May 1901.
53 Toronto *Globe*, 3 Feb. 1883.
54 *Report* (1889), vol. 2, 825–9. William Collins is also quoted in Palmer, *A Culture in Conflict*, 19.
55 Alfred Freeman, in *Palladium of Labor*, 8 Sept. 1883, cited in Ramsay Cook, *The Regenerators: Social Criticism in Late Victorian English Canada* (Toronto, 1985), 106.
56 See the interview with J. Peebles, shoemaker, Hamilton, in *Report* (1889), vol. 2, 864–5.
57 Phillips Thompson, *The Politics of Labor* (New York, 1887), 180.
58 Ibid., 187–8.
59 Ibid., 38.
60 Ibid., 75.
61 Ibid., 188.
62 *Palladium of Labor*, 3 Jan. 1885, cited in Jay Atherton, 'Introduction,' in T. Phillips Thompson, *The Politics of Labor* (Toronto, 1975), xvii.
63 Russell Hann, 'Brainworkers and the Knights of Labor: E.E. Sheppard, Phillips Thompson, and the *Toronto News*, 1883–1887,' in Gregory S. Kealey

and Peter Warrian, eds., *Essays in Canadian Working-Class History* (Toronto, 1976), 49.

64 Thompson, *The Politics of Labor*, 175.

65 Ibid., 188.

66 For other suicides attributed to unemployment, see *Montreal Herald*, 12 Dec. 1896 and 28 Jan. 1897; Hamilton *Daily Spectator*, 16 April 1891; Montreal *Star*, 11 Jan. 1901.

67 Colin McKay, 'Socialism Round the Corner,' *Montreal Herald*, 6 Nov. 1897, reprinted in Ian McKay, ed., *For a Working-Class Culture in Canada: A Selection of Colin McKay's Writings on Sociology and Political Economy, 1897–1939* (St John's, 1996), 47–50. For other socialist analyses of unemployment see 'Startling Figures,' *Industrial Banner* (London, Ont.), May 1897; and A.H. Brentnall, *The Coming Victory; An Inquiry into Political and Social Economy* (Toronto, 1897). The latter pamphlet is no. 10268 in the Canadian Historical Microprint (CHM) series.

68 Colin McKay, 'The Right to Work,' *American Federationist* (April 1903), 258–9; reprinted in Ian McKay, *For a Working-Class Culture*, 50–2.

69 Ibid. In some socialist circles by the early 1900s the argument that job opportunities followed capital investment prompted the rebuttal that surplus labour also followed in the wake of capital. Commenting on the new Grand Trunk Pacific railway, the *Western Clarion* stated: 'Thousands of cheap laborers will now be drawn into the Dominion to be used upon this great enterprise. When it is finished these will be left upon the labor market as an incentive to the workers already there to lead the 'strenuous life.' 'Gulp the Pill,' *Western Clarion*, 18 June 1904.

70 'Modern Wealth Production,' *Western Clarion*, 9 July 1904.

71 'The Victims of the Labor Market,' ibid., 22 April 1905.

72 'The Unemployed Problem,' ibid., 25 March 1905.

73 *Conference on Social Problems* (Toronto, 1893); the pamphlet is in the CHM microprint series, no. 01312. This was a common fear expressed by municipal leaders. See, for example, *Victoria Colonist*, 15, 16 March 1893.

74 Toronto *Globe*, 25 Nov. 1893.

75 *Victoria Colonist*, 16 March 1893.

76 Phillips Thompson, 'Ontario's Capitalist Stew,' *Western Clarion*, 24 March 1906.

77 James M. Pitsula, 'The Treatment of Tramps in Late Nineteenth-Century Ontario,' Canadian Historical Association *Historical Papers* 1980 (Ottawa, 1980), 116–32.

78 'The Unemployed,' *Victoria Colonist*, 4 Jan. 1894.

79 Helen Y.R. Reid, *The Problem of the Unemployed* (Montreal, n.d. [1890s]); CHM series, no. 28879.

80 Mariana Valverde, *The Age of Light, Soap, and Water: Moral Reform in English Canada, 1885–1925* (Toronto, 1991), 49.

81 Herbert Ames, *The City Below the Hill* (Toronto, 1972), 72.

82 Ibid., 73; emphasis added.

83 Dr. Helen MacMurchy, 'Mental Defect as a Cause of Unemployment,' Appendix E in *Report of the Ontario Commission on Unemployment* (hereafter *Report ... on Unemployment*) (Toronto, 1916), 296–7.

84 Valverde, *The Age of Light, Soap, and Water*, 108.

85 *Report ... on Unemployment*, 243.

86 See, for instance, the analysis of Rev. Aubrey Brown, in ibid., 202–4.

87 Udo Sautter, *Three Cheers for the Unemployed: Government and Unemployment before the New Deal* (New York, 1991), 34. Bryce Stewart, first director of the Employment Service, was a follower of Beveridge: James Struthers, *No Fault of Their Own: Unemployment and the Canadian Welfare State 1914–1941* (Toronto, 1983), 19. Beveridge's book *Unemployment: A Problem of Industry* was first published in 1909.

88 *Report ... on Unemployment*, 82.

89 Ibid., 81.

90 The Canadian Manufacturers' Association discussed unemployment insurance at its fortieth annual convention and concluded that the most successful schemes were voluntary ones organized by unions and other associations. *Labour Gazette* (Nov. 1911), 461.

91 Struthers, *No Fault of Their Own*, 8.

92 F.H. Leacy, ed., *Historical Statistics of Canada* (Ottawa, 1983), series A67–9 and D86–106.

93 John Hoolihan, dominion immigration agent, interviewed for the *Report of the Royal Commission Appointed to Inquire into the Immigration of Italian Labourers to Montreal* (Ottawa, 1905), 46. According to the report (p. 28), in April and May 1904, between 200 and 300 'totally destitute' Italian immigrants were living in the streets and parks of Montreal.

94 'The only remedy he saw was the opening up of the lands of the lands of the province, so as to attract the people away from the congested centres of trade, where men jostle with each other in competition for work.' B.H. West, quoted in *Victoria Colonist*, 21 Jan. 1894.

95 Toronto *Globe*, 25 Nov. 1893.

96 'The Unemployed,' *Victoria Colonist*, 4 Jan. 1894.

97 W.A. Douglass, quoted in *Report ... on Unemployment*, 217.

98 Toronto *Globe*, 23 March 1872.

99 Frank Oliver of Edmonton, House of Commons, *Debates*, 22 May 1914, 4158.

100 William Roche, ibid., 22 May 1914, 4158.

101 'The Emigration Fraud,' *Western Clarion*, 13 May 1905.

102 *Report* (1889), vol. 2, 80.

103 *Victoria Colonist*, 18 March 1893.

104 R.H. Coats, memo to Statistical Commission, 1912, in NA, RG 31, box 1420.

105 Canada Department of Labour, *Report for the Fiscal Year Ending March 31, 1915*, 8, cited in Udo Sautter, 'Measuring Unemployment in Canada: Federal Efforts before World War II,' *Histoire sociale/Social History*, 30 (Nov. 1982), 476.

106 *Report of the Board of Inquiry into the Cost of Living* (hereafter *Board of Inquiry*) (Ottawa, 1915), vol. 2, 433.

107 *Report ... on Unemployment*, 211. The same argument appears in the *Board of Inquiry*, vol. 2, 1069.

108 *Victoria Colonist*, 2 Feb. 1894.

109 *Report of the Department of Labour for the Fiscal Year 1907–1908* (Ottawa, 1908), 36–7.

110 Between August 1906 and June 1908 the *Labour Gazette* printed announcements of available jobs in various industries. It is clear that the interest of employers prompted these announcements. See Udo Sautter, 'The Origins of the Employment Service of Canada, 1900–1920,' *Labour/Le Travail*, 6 (autumn 1980), 94 n 19. The assumption that a scarcity of labour existed is most explicit in *Labour Gazette* (Jan. 1910), 819–20.

111 *Board of Inquiry*, vol. 2, 1069.

112 Ibid., vol. 1, 12.

113 Ibid., vol. 2, 1069.

114 Ibid., vol. 1, 12–13.

115 Sautter, 'The Origins of the Employment Service,' 110–12.

9: Conclusion

1 Not included among those without occupations are those living on their own means and housewives.

2 Terry Copp, *The Anatomy of Poverty: The Condition of the Working Class in Montreal* (Toronto, 1974), 140–1.

3 Alexander Keyssar, *Out of Work: The First Century of Unemployment in Massachusetts* (New York, 1981), 51, 70, 302.

4 Ibid., 300.

5 Bettina Bradbury, 'Pigs, Cows and Boarders: Non-Wage Forms of Survival Among Montreal Families, 1861–1891,' *Labour/Le Travail*, 14 (fall 1984), 9–46.

6 Cf. Udo Sautter, *Three Cheers for the Unemployed: Government and Unemployment Before the New Deal* (New York, 1991), chap. 2.

7 *Report of the Board of Inquiry into the Cost of Living* (hereafter *Board of Inquiry*) (Ottawa, 1915), vol. 2, 441.
8 A.C. Pigou, *Unemployment* (1913), cited in John A. Garraty, *Unemployment in History: Economic Thought and Public Policy* (New York, 1978), 142. For one statement of wage-rigidity effects see *Report of the Ontario Commission on Unemployment* (Toronto, 1916), 314.
9 See, for instance, *Board of Inquiry*, 437–43.
10 Thomas Courchene, 'Avenues of Adjustment: The Transfer System and Regional Disparities,' in Michael Walker, ed., *Canadian Confederation at the Crossroads* (Vancouver, 1978); cf. David Alexander, 'New Notions of Happiness: Nationalism, Regionalism and Atlantic Canada,' *Journal of Canadian Studies*, 15 no. 2 (summer 1980), 29–42.
11 Herbert G. Grubel and Josef Bonnici, *Why Is Canada's Unemployment Rate So High?* (Vancouver, 1986).
12 David Frum, *Dead Right* (New York, 1994), cited in Brian Fawcett, 'Dead Wrong,' *Canadian Forum* (Sept. 1995), 36.
13 See, for instance, Jeremy Rifkin, *The End of Work: Technology, Jobs and Your Future* (New York, 1996), 194–7; Julian Barling, *Employment, Stress and Family Functioning* (Chichester, 1990), 189–92. One English study found that unemployment increased the risk of mortality by 20–3 per cent: K.A. Mosher, A.J. Fox, and D.R. Jones, 'Unemployment and Mortality in the OPCS Longitudinal Study,' *Lancet* (1984), 1324–8; Burnett, *Idle Hands*, 284–93.
14 Walter Licht, 'Symposium on *Getting Work*,' *Labor History*, 35 no. 1 (1994), 105.
15 Jack Selody, *The Goal of Price Stability: A Review of the Issues*, Technical Report No. 54, Bank of Canada, 1990, cited in Linda McQuaig, *Shooting the Hippo: Death by Deficit and Other Canadian Myths* (Toronto, 1995), 151.
16 See, however, Diane Bellemaire and Lise Poulin-Simon, *What Is the Real Cost of Unemployment in Canada?* (Ottawa, 1994).
17 Organization for Economic Cooperation and Development (OECD), *The OECD Jobs Study* (Paris, 1994), 29.

Appendix A: The Census as Historical Source

1 A similar method of confirming representativeness is used by Gordon Darroch and Lee Soltow, *Property and Inequality in Victorian Ontario: Structural Patterns and Cultural Communities in the 1871 Census* (Toronto, 1991), 16.
2 See, for instance, David P. Gagan, 'Enumerators' Instructions for the Census of Canada 1852 and 1861,' *Histoire sociale/Social History*, 13–14 (1974), 355–65; George Emery and Jose Igartua, 'David Gagan's "The Critical Years" in

Rural Canada West: A Critique of Methodology and Model,' *Canadian Histor-ical Review*, 62 (1981), 186–96; Gagan, 'Under the Lamppost: A Reply to Emery and Igartua,' ibid., 197–206; Bruce Curtis, 'On the Local Construction of Statistical Knowledge: Making up the 1861 Census of the Canadas,' *Journal of Historical Sociology*, 7 (Dec. 1994), 416–34. For comments on later censuses, see Peter Baskerville and Eric Sager, 'The First National Unemployment Survey: Unemployment and the Canadian Census of 1891,' *Labour/Le Travail*, 23 (spring 1989), 171–8; Eric W. Sager and Peter Baskerville, 'Locating the Unemployed in Urban British Columbia: Evidence From the 1891 Census,' *Journal of Canadian Studies*, 25 no. 3 (fall 1990), 38–54. Peter Baskerville and Eric Sager, 'Finding the Workforce in the 1901 Census of Canada,' *Histoire sociale/Social History*, 56 (Nov. 1995), 521–40. We would like to thank the editors of *Histoire sociale/Social History* for permission to use some of that material in this appendix.

3 See also Edward Higgs, 'Women, Occupations and Work in the Nineteenth Century Censuses,' *History Workshop Journal*, 23 (1987), 76; Nancy Folbre, 'The Unproductive Housewife: Her Evolution in 19th Century Economic Thought,' *Signs: Journal of Women in Culture and Society*, 16 (1991), 468–83; Nancy Folbre and Marjorie Abel, 'Women's Work and Women's House-holds: Gender Bias in the U.S. Census,' *Social Research*, 56 (1989), 545–70; Margo A. Conk, 'Accuracy, Efficiency and Bias: The Interpretation of Women's Work in the U.S. Census of Occupations, 1890–1940,' *Historical Methods*, 14 no. 2 (spring 1981), 65–72.

4 For a parallel argument in the context of the history of crime, see Douglas Hay, 'War, Dearth and Theft in the Eighteenth Century: The Record of the English Courts,' *Past & Present*, 95 (May 1982), 158. See also Catherine Hakim, 'Census Reports as Documentary Evidence: The Census Commen-taries, 1801–1951,' *Social Research*, 28 (1980), 551–80. For a recent appraisal, which suggests that census underenumerations in the United States in the nineteenth century may not have been as dramatic as many have assumed, see Miriam L. King and Diana L. Magnuson, 'Perspectives on Historical U.S. Census Undercounts,' *Social Science History*, 19 (1995), 455–66.

5 Canada, House of Commons, *Debates*, 1901, vol. 3, 3870–908.

6 See Table A7 for the headings as they appeared on the enumerator's sched-ules for the Population Census. For enumerator's instructions, see *Fourth Census of Canada, 1901; Instructions to Officers* (Ottawa, 1901), 16.

7 Department of Agriculture, *The Instructions to Officers Employed in the Taking of the Second Census of Canada, 1881* (Ottawa, 1881), 30; *Instructions to Officers* (1891), 14–15.

8 We aggregate occupations into nine general categories: professional, mana-

gerial/government, clerical, sales, service, primary (mines/forestry/fisher-
ies/agriculture), industrial production, transportation, and general labour.
9 A further question is raised about the three census columns relating to
'months employed': months at trade in factory, months at trade in home, and
months in other occupation than trade in factory or home. How did enumerators decide on how to put a respondent in one or other of these columns?
Were they able to distinguish in any consistent way between a factory, home,
and other kind of worker? At a general level we believe that there is a fair
degree of consistency in the enumerators' decisions. Seventy-five per cent of
those in the factory column appear in our aggregated occupational categories of industrial worker and general labourer. Fifty per cent of those classified as working at home appear in the same two aggregated occupational
categories. Most of the individual-at-home cases in these occupational categories are at least believable 'fits': tradeworkers, such as plumbers, carpenters, dressmakers, and shoemakers, for example. A further 20 per cent of
workers in the at-home column appear in our aggregated occupational
category of service. Most of the occupations in that category were ones that
could be conducted from one's home: 56 per cent were servants or washers.
A discernible level of ambivalence is manifest, however, at this point. It is
hard to understand how servants and washers could be seen to be engaged
as 'employees in factory work.' Many enumerators would seem to have
ignored their instructions to 'refer particularly to employees in factory work'
who worked at home. Instead they listed all people who worked at home,
whether in factory work or other occupations in that column.
   At a general level, the third column, which, as is indicated in our Table A3,
contains 52 per cent of all cases with a known occupation, seems to have
been filled in with reasonable consistency. Only 20 per cent of cases, for
example, fall within an industrial occupational category, whereas 57 per cent
are found in our professional, clerical, sales, and service categories. That 75
per cent of all general labourers (11 per cent of all workers in the 'other than
factory or home' column) were listed in this column is also consistent with
what one would expect.
   When one looks at the distribution of many individual occupations, however, it is often not immediately apparent why a particular individual's occupation was slotted in one or other of the three census columns. Six master
mariners, for example, are found in the factory column, as are nine teachers.
Rather incredibly, twelve 'factory hands' are found in the third column, for
trade other than occupation at home or in factory. None the less we believe
that at a general level the data are valuable. After all two-thirds of all master
mariners did appear in the third column, as did 70 per cent of teachers (a fur-

ther 22 per cent worked at home), and a full 91 per cent of factory hands appeared in the factory column.

10 Some use has been made of these data by D.A. Muise, 'The Industrial Context of Inequality: Female Participation in Nova Scotia's Paid Labour Force, 1871–1921,' *Acadiensis* 20 no. 2 (spring 1991), 3–31. See also 'Wage-Earners by Occupations,' in Census and Statistics Office, *Bulletin I: Wage Earners by Occupation* (Ottawa, 1907). In only forty-two of 14,362 reported cases on earnings did the respondent define the period during which earnings accrued (weekly, monthly, annual, or piece-work).

11 Census and Statistics Office, *Bulletin I*, xxviii.

12 *Fourth Census of Canada, 1901, Instructions to Officers* (Ottawa, 1901), 26–8.

13 *Postal Census of Manufacturers of Canada, 1916* (Ottawa, 1917), xi.

14 *Fourth Census of Canada, 1901, Manufactures* (Ottawa, 1905), lxv and *Postal Census ... 1916*, ix.

15 This probably reflects the movement of women to cities in search of work: thus the provincial average would be less than the city averages.

Index